# ONE POLITICAL ECONOMY, ONE COMPETITIVE STRATEGY?

# One Political Economy, One Competitive Strategy?

*Comparing Pharmaceutical Firms in Germany, Italy, and the UK*

ANDREA M. HERRMANN

OXFORD
UNIVERSITY PRESS

**OXFORD**
**UNIVERSITY PRESS**

Great Clarendon Street, Oxford OX2 6DP

Oxford University Press is a department of the University of Oxford.
It furthers the University's objective of excellence in research, scholarship,
and education by publishing worldwide in

Oxford New York

Auckland Cape Town Dar es Salaam Hong Kong Karachi
Kuala Lumpur Madrid Melbourne Mexico City Nairobi
New Delhi Shanghai Taipei Toronto

With offices in

Argentina Austria Brazil Chile Czech Republic France Greece
Guatemala Hungary Italy Japan Poland Portugal Singapore
South Korea Switzerland Thailand Turkey Ukraine Vietnam

Oxford is a registered trade mark of Oxford University Press
in the UK and in certain other countries

Published in the United States
by Oxford University Press Inc., New York



First published 2008



British Library Cataloguing in Publication Data
Data available

Library of Congress Cataloging in Publication Data
Data available

Typeset by SPI Publisher Services, Pondicherry, India
Printed in the UK on acid-free paper by
the MPG Books Group

ISBN 978–0–19–954343–4

1 3 5 7 9 10 8 6 4 2

*To Elke*

# *Preface*

I vividly remember the moment in which I first envisioned the research project that served as the basis for this book. In spring 2002, I attended the preparatory lecture for the final exam of the 'European Models of Capitalism' course as part of my MSc studies at the London School of Economics (LSE). At the time, Bob Hancké, to whom I am gratefully indebted for his relentless willingness to challenge my ideas in numerous discussions during years to come, recapitulated the key features of his course by illustrating the arguments of the varieties-of-capitalism (VoC) literature in all their functionalist beauty. What struck me was the seemingly perfect institutional equilibrium of coordinated market economies on the one hand, and liberal market economies on the other. Two nationwide homogeneous production regimes, each composed of five complementary institutional subsystems, offered firms within each economy optimal conditions to specialize in the same product-market strategy. The compelling logic underlying this literature made me wonder whether firms have to exploit comparative institutional advantages or whether they can also pursue strategies that are not supported by national institutions. How numerous are deviating firms? Are the latter less successful than their counterparts in pursuing institutionally supported strategies? Most importantly, how can firms compete despite comparative institutional disadvantages?

I would surely not have been able to carry out this research project without the support of many colleagues, friends, and my family, to whom I am more indebted than words of gratitude can ever express. At the European University Institute (EUI) in Florence, where I fully embarked upon this research endeavour during my PhD studies, I was so fortunate to win Colin Crouch as the supervisor of my work. Always empathetic, Colin not only advised me on my research, but also offered invaluable support in all the pivotal moments that were to come, way beyond my period of study in Florence. I am similarly indebted to Rikard Stankiewicz and Wolfgang Streeck who have guided me in my work as co-supervisors ever since the second year of my PhD studies. The astute advice of David Soskice, the fourth member of my thesis jury, allowed me to take an alternative perspective on my findings and to bring loose ends together. I shall not forget how precious his advice has proven to be. I also wish to thank Jaap Dronkers and Martin Rhodes for their feedback, in addition to the many colleagues and friends at the EUI who discussed and commented on my work. My warm thanks to Luigi Burroni, Pepper Culpepper, Anne Daguerre, Arolda Elbasani, Simcha Jong, Christian Kascha, Fabian Lemmes,

George Menz, Jan-Henrik Meyer, Simon Michel-Berger, Christopher Milde, and Antonio Testoni. I also wish to thank everyone of my overall 150 interview partners who enabled me to gain the necessary insights into how pharmaceutical firms operate. Without their patient answers to my nagging questions, I would not have been able to complete this research.

When faced with the challenge of transforming my thesis into a book, I was granted the opportunity to become a postdoctoral research fellow at the Max-Planck-Institut für Gesellschaftsforschung (MPIfG) in Cologne. Having reached the end of this challenge, I cannot imagine a place where I would have found more open-minded colleagues, many of them specialists in my research area, and a more supportive administrative team. My work has greatly benefited from the interaction with my colleagues who showed no sign of fatigue to discuss my ideas in seminars and to comment on parts or the whole of my work. I am gratefully indebted to Patrik Aspers, Jens Beckert, Christian Breunig, Marius Busemeyer, Helen Callaghan, Jan Drahokoupil, Jürgen Feick, Saskia Freye, Achim Goerres, Martin Höpner, Marta Kahancová, Lothar Krempel, Guido Möllering, Sascha Münnich, Geny Piotti, Sigrid Quack, Britta Rehder, Akos Rona-Tas, Armin Schäfer, Martin Schröder, Anna Skarpelis, Alice Szczepanikova, Guido Tiemann, and Raymund Werle. In addition to many of these researchers, Anita Breuer, Annika Hennl, Simon Franzmann, Astrid Prange de Oliveira and her family, Ursula Sharma, and Renate and Bill Weber have made my postdoctoral period at Cologne a joyful experience. I wish to thank them for their support and friendship.

Various institutions have generously provided financial and logistical support without which it would have been impossible to carry out this research project. I am grateful to the DAAD for fully funding three years of my PhD studies at the EUI, and to the EUI for awarding a fourth-year completion grant. Special thanks go to the MPIfG, which not only awarded a postdoctoral research grant, but also offered logistical support which cannot possibly be surpassed by any other research institute in Europe.

One particularly rewarding experience of the past year was the opportunity to spend more than three months visiting Israel. What started as a passionate attempt to animate a personal relationship finally turned into a particularly fruitful professional experience, as I had the opportunity to present my work during seminars and conferences at the University of Haifa, the Hebrew University of Jerusalem, and the Technion – Israel Institute of Technology. The comments I received on these occasions and the discussions with Israeli colleagues and friends were extraordinarily helpful in shaping and sharpening my arguments. I thus wish to thank Zvia and Shlomo Breznitz, Avi Fiegenbaum, Uzi de Haan, Dovev Lavie, David Levi-Faur, Raanan Sulitzeanu-Kenan, and – most importantly – Pieter Vanhuysse for their warm welcome, collegial support, and friendship.

Despite the nomadic academic life I have pursued, some particularly dear friends have not given up keeping track of my ever-changing address. They have given me an opportunity to take valuable moments away from my work, share my concerns at the most impossible hours of the day, and replenish. Without Nicole Bolleyer, Carolin Bunke, Patrick Hartmann, Ulrike Leins, and Carolin Oelschlegel moments of joy would have been less precious, while moments of sorrow more difficult to bear.

Words are insufficient to thank my parents, Elke and Georg Herrmann, as well as my sister Karin for their unconditional support. The mixture of loving encouragement and scepticism with which they followed my professional endeavours strongly motivated me to try and make the most of the privileged conditions under which I was allowed to study. I shall not forget how Elke, Georg, and Karin together with Ina and Julian Herrmann have lent loving support in the darkest moments I faced while working on this book. Yet, no other person has followed my professional and personal ups and downs so compassionately as my mother. To her, this book is dedicated with gratitude.

*Andrea M. Herrmann*
*Köln, March 2008*

# *Acknowledgements*

**Chapter 2** is due to be published in 'Strategic Organization' (Vol 6, Issue no. 4) by Sage Publications London; entitled: 'Contrasting the Resource-based View and Competitiveness Theories: How Pharmaceutical Firms Choose to Compete in Germany, Italy, and the UK'.

**Chapter 5** is due to be published in the 'Socio-Economic Review' (Vol 6, Issue no. 4) by Oxford University Press; entitled: 'Rethinking the link between labour market flexibility and corporate competitiveness: a critique of the institutionalist literature'.

**Chapter 6** is due to be published in 'Competition and Change' (Vol 13, Issue no. 1) by Maney Publishing Leeds/London/Boston, MA.; entitled: 'On the Choice and Success of Competitive Strategies'.

# *Summary Contents*

# Detailed Contents

# *List of Tables and Graph*

# *Graph*

# *List of Abbreviations*

| | |
|---|---|
| BSI | British Standards Institution |
| CEO | Chief Executive Officer |
| CME | Coordinated Market Economy |
| DIN | Deutsches Institut für Normung |
| DQP | Diversified Quality Production |
| DQPs | Diversified Quality Producers (i.e. firms that pursue a DQP strategy) |
| EMEA | European Medicines Agency |
| GMP | Good Manufacturing Practice |
| HR | Human Resources |
| IPO | Initial Public Offering |
| ISO | International Organization for Standardization |
| LCP | Low-Cost Production |
| LCPs | Low-Cost Producers (i.e. firms that pursue an LCP strategy) |
| LME | Liberal Market Economy |
| MSc | Master of Science |
| NCE | New Chemical Entity |
| NIS | National Innovation Systems |
| OE | Organizational Economics |
| PHID | Pharmaceutical Industry Database |
| PRO | Public Research Organization |
| QA | Quality Assurance |
| R&D | Research and Development |
| RBV | Resource-Based View |
| RPI | Radical Product Innovation |
| RPIs | Radical Product Innovators (i.e. firms that pursue an RPI strategy) |
| SCP | Structure-Conduct-Performance |
| SME | Small and Medium Enterprise |
| VIF | Variance Inflation Factor |
| VoC | Varieties of Capitalism |

# PART I

# Specialization in Line with Comparative Institutional Advantages?

# 1

# Introduction

How do firms adapt to the pressures of increasing international competition? Do they exploit the comparative advantage offered by national institutions and specialize in the facilitated competitive strategy? The example of Italy's biotech industry provides a negative answer to this question. When the industry started to take off at the turn of the millennium, its emergence was characterized by a 'process of Darwinian selection' (Vinci 2006). Many of those factors that are widely recognized as conditions sine qua non for the development of biotech firms were absent: Italian venture capital was scarce, the rigid labour market impeded the employment of young scientists with radically new ideas, while the traditional academic system was known for its poorly developed links to firms conducting applied research. Nevertheless, when several international pharmaceutical firms decided to close their R&D facilities in Italy at the end of the 1990s, many scientists employed there decided to try and open their own biotech companies. The newborn firms' founders acquired seed finance from foreign venture capitalists, employed young scientists as *collaboratori a progetto* on a temporary basis, and gradually developed links to universities and hospitals in support of their R&D activities. Given the lack of state support, only the fittest got a chance and succeeded in attracting investment. However, this Darwinian selection process also led to remarkable stability on the part of Italy's biotech firms. While some firms merged or were acquired in the course of the following years, no instance of bankruptcy was known by 2005 (see Chapter 6).

A similar example of firms competing in a suboptimal national environment is provided by those pharmaceutical companies in the UK that improve the administration and side effects of drugs. The process of pharmaceutical development is known for requiring massive long-term investment, as it takes on average more than ten years before a pharmaceutical discovery can be turned into a marketable drug. Yet, the British corporate governance system is renowned for the absence of house banks providing patient capital. Furthermore, product improvements rely on workers with an in-depth understanding of how their firm operates and cooperates with its suppliers. However, a flexible labour market and the related hire-and-fire mentality motivate employees to invest in general rather than specific skills, as the latter are useless whenever new employment has to be sought. So, how do managers succeed in producing improved drugs? The measures taken to this end are similar in most British firms competing on quality. Owned by risk-averse private shareholders, these firms invest massively in the skills of their employees, whom they tie down by offering attractive pension schemes and opportunities for intra-firm career development (see Chapters 3 and 5). Interestingly, though, managers in these firms also point out that such measures are exceptional in Britain.

The present book is about these exceptions. It asks how firms can so numerously deviate and compete through strategies that are not supported by national financial, antitrust, and labour-market institutions. How can firms compete despite comparative institutional disadvantages? The key to this question is that firms are no constrained institution-takers, but run by creative entrepreneurs. Choosing their firms' strategies on the basis of individual technological opportunities, entrepreneurs secure all required input factors not only through national institutions, but also through 'importation' and 'improvisation'. Since three alternative pathways to competitiveness exist, corporate competitiveness is found to arise from entrepreneurial creativity rather than institutional incentives.

To illustrate these arguments, the book begins by estimating the extent of strategy deviation (Chapter 2). Is it only a small number of firms competing in the same economy which dare to be exceptional, or is it the majority? As the pursuit of institutionally unsupported strategies turns out to be the rule rather than the exception, the book further inquires into organizational feasibility (Chapters 3–5). Do firms actually need specific types of finance, component standards, and labour qualifications for each strategy? And, if so, how do they acquire the necessary input factors in different political economies? In this respect, the initial examples are revealing as they show that firms can circumvent national institutions and build alternative production models. But are these functional equivalents sustainable (Chapter 6)? Or, are firms pursuing strategies that are not facilitated by national institutions generally less successful and more susceptible to mergers, acquisitions, and bankruptcy? Addressing questions of strategy success, the book concludes its analyses of how firms compete in different political economies.

This chapter provides a roadmap of the book. Section 1.1 develops the theoretical approaches of four schools of thought which can be summarized as 'the competitiveness literature', since they all address the same question: How does internationalization of trade affect corporate competitiveness? Drawing on these schools of thought and their approaches to the study of competitiveness, Section 1.2 establishes the analytical framework. The gist of the argument is provided in Section 1.3. Here, I also illustrate how my findings contribute to, and are distinct from, similar arguments about production models and institutional foundations of competitiveness. Section 1.4 concludes with an outline of the book's structure.

## 1.1. POLITICAL ECONOMY PERSPECTIVES ON FIRM COMPETITIVENESS IN RESPONSE TO GLOBALIZATION

The way in which firms compete has crucially been influenced by the phenomenon which is so often, and often so imprecisely, referred to that it has become a buzzword: 'globalization'. Contributions to how globalization impacts on corporate competitiveness are numerous and span academic disciplines as diverse as economics, business and management, politics, and innovation studies.[1] In line with major political-economic studies, globalization is understood here as the growing integration of national markets following increasing flows of goods and capital across national borders due to decreasing barriers to trade (e.g. Hall and Soskice 2001*a*: 55; Berger 2005: 9–10; Obstfeld and Taylor 2005).

There is broad agreement that globalization or, more precisely, internationalization of trade is not a recent phenomenon. Attempts to integrate commodity and financial markets are as old as the history of international trade (e.g. Findlay and O'Rourke 2005; Obstfeld and Taylor 2005). It is also largely undisputed that internationalization has accelerated over the past decades due to technological innovations which have translated into falling transportation and communication costs. Economic activity across national borders has never been so easy. As a consequence, firms producing tradable goods have increasingly come under pressure to remain competitive in international markets (see, e.g. Berger 2005).

*How* increasing internationalization changes the competitive behaviour of firms and the shape of national institutions is, however, open to debate. Proponents of the convergence theory argue that the production models and socio-economic institutions of developed economies will look evermore similar. While some suggest that the convergence process is driven by technological innovation imposing a single optimum way of production (Kerr et al. 1973; see also Barro and Sala-i-Martin 1992), others propose that convergence results from the necessity to offer attractive investment locations. Since cross-border activities are, by now, so large that they limit the regulatory capacities

[1] For some of the most recent contributions, see Bhagwati (2004), Berger (2005), Bordo et al. (2005), and Schirm (2006).

of states (Ohmae 1999), 'regime shopping' on the part of footloose capital is said to entail deregulation of national economies (Kurzer 1993). Another version of this argument is that firms, in order to attract investment, will have to adopt the arm's-length model of Anglo-Saxon corporate governance, as investors in a global market are too distant to exert internal monitoring rights (see Rappaport 1986; Cerny 1993, 1994; Underhill 1997). The Thatcherite deregulation of Britain's labour and financial markets at the beginning of the 1980s and the following recovery of the British economy seem to lend empirical support to the convergence theory.

Yet, Thatcher's example has not been followed by most Continental European countries, where labour and financial markets continue to be more regulated, and economic activity is organized differently from the Anglo-Saxon world. Persistent differences in the shape of socio-economic institutions bring proponents of the divergence theory to argue that the same pressure does not necessarily lead to the same outcomes (Maurice et al. 1986; Berger and Dore 1996; Ferner and Hyman 1998; Whitley 1999; Scharpf and Schmidt 2000; Yamamura and Streeck 2003). In its various forms, the divergence argument rests upon the fundamental insight that more than one production regime exists. Consequently, firms can organize interaction with their financiers, suppliers, employers, and customers in different ways. Since different production models are deeply embedded in socio-economic institutions, they cannot simply be transferred from one economy to another (e.g. Albert 1993; Kitschelt et al. 1999; Hall and Soskice 2001*b*; Hancké et al. 2007). Exposed to the same pressure of increasing competition, firms in different institutional environments therefore react with diverse adaptation strategies.

Four strands of literature have proposed particularly straightforward arguments about how firms adapt their product market strategies to increasing competitive pressure. They include neo-liberal trade theory, the market-based view of strategic management, the writings on national innovation systems, and the varieties-of-capitalism literature. While each literature rests on different assumptions about the competitive sources of firms, and how globalization alters their institutional foundations, they agree on one central claim. Firms within the same economy are said to specialize in the same competitive strategy. The following sections seek to illustrate the essential line of reasoning underlying each approach.

### 1.1.1. Classical and Neo-liberal Trade Theory

Classical trade theory considers the endowment of a country with production factors – labour, land, and capital – as its source of comparative advantage

(Ricardo 1821; Heckscher 1919; Ohlin 1933). The more abundant a factor, the less expensive is the production of those goods which intensely rely on that factor. To maximize social welfare following the internationalization of trade, the Heckscher–Ohlin theorem therefore claims that 'each region is best equipped to produce the goods which require large proportions of the factors relatively abundant there' (Ohlin 1933: 12). In other words, firms shall specialize in land-, labour-, or capital-intensive production according to the most available and, hence, least costly input factor. 'It is this difference in the absolute costs of production and prices that (. . .) leads to each region's specializing in the output of those goods that it can produce more cheaply than others' (Ohlin 1924: 89; see also Heckscher 1919: 55–8).

Contrary to Heckscher (1919), Ohlin (1933) does not treat each production factor as a homogeneous unit. Instead, he acknowledges that different types of labour and capital exist, and distinguishes accordingly between 'unskilled', 'skilled', and 'technical labour' (Ohlin 1933: 71–5) as well as between capital 'available for the borrowers during longer or shorter periods' (ibid.: 76). Albeit briefly, Ohlin also illustrates how labour-market institutions, namely trade unions, can influence the provision of different labour groups.

> In fact, by restricting the free choice of occupation, trade unions are often able to influence the supply of labour both in skilled and unskilled trades, and thus to affect the relative wage levels. (. . .) Examples are not difficult to find. Strong trade unions have often been able to raise wages in prosperous industries much above the level for similar work in other industries. (ibid.: 73)

Importantly, though, neither the Heckscher–Ohlin theorem nor its developments, the Stolper–Samuelson (1941) and Ricardo–Viner theorem (see Viner 1937), consider different types of labour and capital in order to understand how their diverse *qualities* influence production decisions. To give an example, it is of no interest that a firm cannot produce sophisticated machinery without 'technical labour'. All that classical, as well as neo-liberal, trade theorists consider is how different types of labour and capital translate into different labour and capital *costs* (e.g. Ohlin 1933: 68–70). In other words, all firms are assumed to compete on costs. The cheaper they can produce a good, optimizing the available production factors, the more competitive they are on international markets. It is thus hardly surprising that the classical trade theorems constitute an important theoretical basis of the convergence argument. In order to provide firms with inexpensive labour and capital, national labour and financial markets need to be liberalized, while regulatory institutions should be abolished (see Cerny 1993; Sinn 2005).

The Heckscher–Ohlin theorem has often been criticized for its partly unrealistic simplicity. The assumption that production factors are immobile, the incapacity to explain intra-industry trade, and the disregard of factors influencing the production decisions of firms other than labour and capital are some examples. Such criticism has led economists to propose modifications to the assumptions on which modern trade theory is based (Bhagwati 2004; Krugman and Obstfeld 2006). Nevertheless, the claim that firms in the same economy specialize in labour- or capital-intensive production strategies, according to the respective factor prices, is still to be found in today's economic analyses (e.g. Sinn 2005; see also Franzese and Mosher 2002).

### 1.1.2. The Market-Based View of Strategic Management

A second school of thought concerned with understanding how firms compete in global economies is the 'market-based view' (MBV) of strategic management studies (Porter 1980, 1985, 1987, 1990; Grant 1998). With Michael Porter as its most important proponent, the MBV approach became the strategic management paradigm of the 1980s. Starting from the observation that an important part of international trade takes place between economies with similar factor endowments, the MBV approach criticizes classical trade theory for its assumption that firms necessarily compete on costs. 'Most theories of trade look solely at cost, treating quality and differentiated products in a footnote' (Porter 1990: 20). '[But, f]irms can and do choose strategies that differ' (ibid.: 19).

Contrary to the suggestions of classical trade theory, firms in MBV models thus have a choice. More precisely, firms choose the competitive strategy they wish to pursue in two stages. First, they decide in which industry they want to compete. This choice is essential as the profitability of industries and, hence, the chances of competitive success are said to differ notably according to the bargaining power of suppliers and buyers, the rivalry among the existing competitors, the barriers to entry, and the ease with which the industry's goods can be substituted (Porter 1990: 34–7; also Baumol et al. 1982; Schmalensee and Willig 1989). Second,

> firms must [then] choose a position within the industry. (. . .) At the heart of positioning is *competitive advantage*. (. . .) There are two basic types of competitive advantage: *lower cost* and *differentiation*. (. . .) Differentiation is the ability to provide unique and superior value to the buyer in terms of product quality, special features, or after-sale service. (Porter 1990: 37, original emphases; see also Porter 1985: chapters 3 and 4)

In other words, firms can compete not only on costs but also on quality.

Unlike classical trade theory, the MBV approach does not consider labour, land, and capital as the only sources of competitiveness. Instead, any item of the value chain that allows firms either to reduce the costs or to improve the quality of their goods is considered a foundation of competitive advantage

(Porter 1990: 40–4). It is, however, noteworthy that this approach, while being more comprehensive, leads to a less parsimonious description of competitive sources, as it brings strategic management scholars to propose long lists of factors which possibly sustain a firm's competitive advantage (e.g. Porter 1985: 81, 123, 343–6).

Porter and his adherents also acknowledge that '[m]any national attributes affect the ease or difficulty of pursuing a particular strategy' (Porter 1990: 67, see also chapter 3; Grant 1998). Even though institutions are not considered separately as 'determinants of national competitive advantage', Porter's numerous country studies show that successful low-cost or high-quality strategies importantly rely on national institutions such as education and training systems, flexible labour markets, the internal monitoring capacities of shareholders, or close inter-firm relations (Porter 1990: part III). 'Differences in national economic structures, values, cultures, institutions, and histories contribute profoundly to competitive success' (ibid.: 19).

While Porter (1987) does not explicitly consider whether internationalization entails convergence or divergence of competitive practices, he discusses the ever-better opportunities for relocating specific value-chain activities to more attractive locations. Despite this faith in 'offshoring', Porter stresses that each firm has a national home base 'where a firm's strategy is set and the core product and process technology (. . .) are created' (Porter 1990: 19; see also Hu 1992). Furthermore, Porter reasons:

> While globalization of competition might appear to make the nation less important, instead it seems to make it more so. With fewer impediments to trade to shelter uncompetitive domestic firms and industries, the home nation takes on growing significance because it is the source of the skills and technology that underpin competitive advantage. (Porter 1990: 19)

In sum, increasing competition makes it evermore important for firms to specialize either in low-cost or high-quality production, depending on the strategy which is better supported by the national home base. This line of reasoning provides a convincing argument for divergence.

### 1.1.3. National Innovation Systems

In line with their strategic management colleagues, theorists on 'national innovation systems' (NIS) criticize classical trade theory for making unrealistic assumptions, such as perfect competition, immobility of production factors, and non-increasing returns to scale. Yet, possibly the most problematic assumption from an NIS perspective is that of identical production technologies (Dalum 1992: 192–5; Fagerberg 1992: 226; see also Andersen 1992: 75).

Since the Heckscher–Ohlin model treats technological capabilities as exogenously given and constant, it is unable to explain why countries differ so notably in their innovative performance. Also the market-based view considers the development of new technologies as exogenous events, even though it acknowledges technological innovation as 'one of the principal drivers of competition' (Porter 1985: 164). Hence, firms can use new technologies to produce either better or cheaper goods. But contrary to NIS studies, the differing technological capabilities of firms are not considered an independent source of competitive advantage (Porter 1985: chapter 5, 1990: 45–7). *The* question of NIS studies – 'why countries differ in regard to technological development' (McKelvey 2002: 117) – is thus neither asked nor answered by either classical trade or MBV theory.

While most NIS scholars define innovation in a broad way (see McKelvey 2002; Meeus and Oerlemans 2005), their empirical analyses usually focus on *technological* innovation (e.g. Freeman 1987; Nelson 1993; Patel and Pavitt 1994*b*; Pavitt and Patel 1999; Casper and Whitley 2004). When trying to account for variation in innovative performance, many answers point to a systematic difference between radical and incremental (technological) innovation (Freeman and Perez 1988; Lundvall 1992*a*: 11–12, 1992*c*: 57–9). The reason is that trade and patent specialization patterns show how firms in some countries perform better in industries, such as automotive engineering, which typically rely on incremental innovation, whereas firms in other economies specialize in radical innovation industries, such as chemicals and, more recently, biotechnology (Dalum 1992; Patel and Pavitt 1994*b*; Casper and Whitley 2004).

Contributors to this literature agree about the foundations of NIS: institutions. And, despite analytical foci on different institutional components, agreement also exists that national education and training systems, financial allocation mechanisms, inter-firm relationships, and public R&D programmes are integral parts of an NIS, explaining its (technological) performance (e.g. Freeman 1987: 4; Lundvall 1992*a*: 13–15; Pavitt and Patel 1999: 100–10). Two particularly noteworthy insights result from the NIS approach. First, non-market-based relationships between economic agents are essential for knowledge creation, which, in turn, forms the basis of innovative performance and, thus, competitive success. Second, the possibilities for establishing non-market-based relationships depend on a country's socio-economic institutions and therefore differ notably from one economy to another.

Over time, the focus of NIS contributions has shifted from more descriptive illustrations of how innovation systems operate to analytical and, sometimes, functionalist explanations of institutional configurations and their innovative outputs. With this shift, the question of how globalization affects NIS has gained momentum. The answer provided by the NIS scholars is unequivocal.

Increasing internationalization entails divergence or, at least, continuing diversity as firms benefit from the peculiar features of their NIS (e.g. Pavitt and Patel 1999).

> The reason is that competitiveness can only be built on heterogeneity: on firms having control over something wanted by others or by firms being able to do something that the competitors cannot do as well, as fast, or as cheap. Little progress would be made in a world of clones. (. . .) National Innovation Systems are, by definition, localized and immobile and thus able to provide firms with valuable capabilities and framework conditions *not available* to competitors located abroad. (. . .) In an age of accelerating globalization, National Innovation Systems thereby play an increasingly crucial role by *preserving heterogeneity* across space. (Lundvall and Maskell 2000: 364, original emphases)

Despite the spread of approaches, NIS theory does not lack its critics. On the one hand, it is precisely the theoretical and analytical variety which causes concern. Hence, the NIS literature is criticized for being 'conceptually diffuse' and 'not theory based', whereby 'the variety of disciplines involved in NSI research' is held accountable for 'the low level of theoretical development and the *ad hoc* character of much NSI research' (Meeus and Oerlemans 2005: 52). On the other hand, and somewhat paradoxically, words of warning are expressed that the systems approach bears 'the risk of getting caught in a functionalist and determinist universe where it is impossible to locate the sources of change. Firms are conceived as puppets on institutional strings' (ibid.: 61; see also Lundvall and Maskell 2000: 363).

### 1.1.4. Varieties of Capitalism

The literature on 'varieties of capitalism' (VoC) meets this criticism in two ways. It ties up several loose ends of NIS studies on the one hand and, thereby, develops into a fully functionalist explanation of how developed capitalist economies operate on the other.[2] Overall, the VoC contributors identify two ideal-typical ways in which economic interaction between firms and their

[2] While it would be a futile effort to try and compile a complete list of contributions to the VoC literature, some landmark pieces need to be mentioned. Fundamental insights into the functioning and performance of capitalist economies were provided by the work of Gerschenkron (1962), Shonfield (1965), Zysman (1983), Dore (1986), Gourevitch (1986), and Lazonick (1991). Early contributions to how differently capitalist economies can be organized (Streeck 1992; Hollingsworth et al. 1994; Herrigel 1996; Hollingsworth and Boyer 1997; Whitley 1999) finally translated in the functionalist VoC model described above (Kitschelt et al. 1999; Hall and Soskice 2001*b*; Hancké et al. 2007).

financiers, employees, and suppliers can be organized. The five institutional subsystems which crucially channel these interaction processes at the national level are: the *corporate governance* system, the *education and training* system, the *industrial relations* system, the system of *inter-company relations*, and the *internal corporate structure* (Hall and Soskice 2001*a*; Amable 2003). These five systems do not only determine the economy's dominant production regime, they also form institutional complementarities, meaning that 'the presence (or efficiency) of one [institution] increases the returns from (or efficiency of) the other' (Hall and Soskice 2001*a*: 17; Hall and Gingerich 2004).

In 'coordinated market economies' (CMEs), firms (have to) compete on product quality, which is fostered by the institutional environment facilitating incremental (technological) innovation. Collective bargaining procedures between the social partners do not only entail comparatively high and homogeneous wages, they also make possible an education and training system that provides employees with specific vocational skills. The latter are at the root of extraordinary labour productivity and high-value-added strategies (Hancké and Herrmann 2007). Since the corporate governance system grants shareholders important control rights, managers cannot take major financial decisions at short notice. Yet, they have access to long-term 'patient' capital because major stakeholders – such as banks, suppliers, employees, or the founding family – also tend to be major shareholders. Finally, permissive antitrust regulation allows suppliers and producers to collaborate in encompassing industry associations in order to elaborate new component standards (Hall and Soskice 2001*a*: 21–7).

The opposite applies to 'liberal market economies' (LMEs). Here, the institutional setting brings firms to compete either on radical innovation or on low costs. Since collective bargaining processes are decentralized, it is difficult to put in place an education and training system where firms collaborate to provide trainees with specific skills. But, wages are flexible. They can therefore be adapted to the low skill levels of those workers who left education after compulsory schooling. And they can serve as an incentive to motivate and reward highly skilled employees for outstanding results. Furthermore, deregulated financial markets give firms easy access to share capital. This, however, needs to be invested in (radical innovation) projects promising high returns in the short run. The reason is that, if their profit expectations are not fulfilled, shareholders rapidly withdraw funds as they have only reduced monitoring possibilities to understand how their investment is used. Since antitrust regulation is suspicious of large-scale firm collaboration, new component standards are developed in small consortia rather than in encompassing industry associations. This helps firms to protect radical innovations from imitation by competitors (ibid.: 27–33).

The question of whether these institutional differences will still persist in the wake of globalization is of central concern to the VoC literature. Like NIS theory, the VoC answer predicts divergence of those national institutions which are at the basis of the respective production regimes. 'Instead of the monolithic movement toward deregulation that many expect from globalization, our analysis predicts a bifurcated response marked by widespread deregulation in liberal market economies and limited movement in coordinated market economies' (ibid.: 58; see also Gourevitch and Hawes 2002). Firms in CMEs are therefore expected to increasingly specialize in high-value-added strategies based on incremental technological innovation, whereas firms in LMEs are said to engage more and more in low-value-added or radical innovation strategies (Hall and Soskice 2001*a*: 36–44; Hancké and Herrmann 2007).

## 1.2. AN ANALYTICAL FRAMEWORK FOR STUDYING COMPETITIVENESS

Taken together, what do these four schools of thought, which I will henceforth refer to collectively as 'the competitiveness literature', teach us about firm behaviour in response to globalization? How do firms cope with increasing competitive pressure? Most importantly, firms within the same economy are found to specialize in the same competitive strategy as they (have to) take advantage of the institutional environment. They increasingly rely on the cheapest production factor, on their 'national home base', their 'national innovation system', or their 'model of capitalism' in order to produce either cheaper, better, or entirely new products.

Thereby, the dominant production regime is determined by the innovative strength of the economy's institutions. Where firms are assumed to use identical production technologies (Heckscher–Ohlin), or where firms have difficulties in accessing technological innovations (see the MBV, NIS, and VoC theories), all they can do is to compete on costs. But as soon as national institutions are found to promote technological development, firms can go beyond low-cost production. Whenever the institutional environment supports incrementally new technologies, firms specialize in the production of high-quality goods. And where the emergence of radically new technologies is facilitated, firms tend to compete on product innovation.

I began this research project with an assessment of strategy specialization patterns. Contrary to most competitiveness studies, I decided not to identify competitive strategies at the macro but at the micro level. Hence, I did not use the technological intensity of a firm's *industry* as proxy for its strategy, since this entails the simplifying assumption that all firms within one industry pursue the same strategy.[3] Instead, I considered the technological intensity of each *individual firm*. More precisely, I considered the technological novelty of a firm's product and its value-chain focus to understand whether it pursues a high-tech, medium-tech, or low-tech strategy. I call the high-tech strategy, where the firm focuses on upstream R&D activities to invent an entirely new good, *radical product innovation* (RPI). With *diversified quality production* (DQP) I refer to the medium-tech strategy which a firm pursues to improve existing goods by focusing on midstream development and production activities. Finally, I call the low-tech strategy *low-cost production* (LCP), as firms imitate existing products and focus on downstream marketing and sales activities in order to sell at lowest possible costs. A more complete discussion of these concepts and their theoretical foundation is provided in Chapter 2.

The study of pharmaceutical firms in Germany, Italy, and the UK seemed particularly appropriate to identify strategy specialization patterns. The analytical focus on pharmaceutical firms is owed to the insight that their competitive strategies can be identified in a straightforward way due to the scientifically established notion of a 'new chemical entity' (see Chapter 2). Furthermore, the pharmaceutical sector has a well-developed high-tech end: the biotechnology industry. This is important as radical technological innovations are rare in general and occur in waves. The latter are more distant in traditional industries, such as metalworking, where it can take years – if not decades – for radically new products to emerge (Utterback 1994; Grant 1998: part IV; Walker 2003: chapter 4). Due to their technology intensity, high-tech industries – and particularly the biopharmaceutical sector – are characterized by more frequent innovation waves. With the decoding of the human genome, new technological opportunities to exploit this knowledge base commercially were opened to such an extent that many firms began to work on the development of new drugs (see Drews 2000). Hence, the share of pharmaceutical firms pursuing an RPI strategy in this industry can be expected to be comparatively large.

These remarks require conceptual clarification of the three company types that make up the pharmaceutical sector: biotech, traditional pharmaceutical,

[3] Examples of studies that use the industry of firms as a measure for their competitive strategy are Porter (1990: chapters 5–9), Nelson (1993), Patel and Pavitt (1994*a*: 83–4), Casper et al. (1999), Pavitt and Patel (1999: 99), Hall and Soskice (2001*a*: 41–4), Amable (2003: 21–3, 200–13), and Casper and Whitley (2004).

and generics firms. I here follow the commonly acknowledged definitions (Drews 2000; Orsenigo et al. 2001; Pammolli et al. 2002; Muffatto and Giardina 2003; Wittner 2003). The broad term of a 'pharmaceutical firm' is generally used for any company which is active in the pharmaceutical industry. Accordingly, a company is identified as a pharmaceutical firm on the basis of the *product* it manufactures, namely a drug that cures or alleviates a disease. The distinction between a biotechnology, a traditional pharmaceutical, and a generics firm is, however, made on the basis of the company's *technological approach*. Thus, 'biotechnology firms' are said to employ the most modern technology as they use processes on the level of the cell and sub-cell to create industrially useful substances. While 'traditional pharmaceutical firms' are aware of, and also resort to, biotechnological opportunities, they tend to use experimental and, hence, less deliberate approaches to drug design. Finally, 'generics firms' are the least technology-intensive, as they do not engage in any research and clinical development activities. Instead, they imitate drugs as soon as their patent protection expires.

The reasons why the study of firms in Germany, Italy, and the UK promises particularly insightful results are threefold (see Chapter 2). To test the specialization hypothesis, it is first necessary to control for factors which influence firms' strategy choices other than those institutions retained as essential by the competitiveness literature. In the pharmaceutical industry, such non-institutional factors include, most importantly, patent legislation, legal price ceilings on pharmaceutical products, and legislative requirements for the quality, safety, and efficacy of medicines. (Thomas III 1994, 2004; Gambardella et al. 2001; Wittner 2003). Essentially, these factors differ notably between the EU, the US, and other developed capitalist economies. However, following the single market project and the foundation of the European Medicines Agency in 1995, which coordinates the evaluation and supervision of health standards with respect to medicinal products across the EU, regulatory requirements are today fairly homogeneous throughout the EU member states (Gambardella et al. 2001; Casper and Matraves 2003: 1868; Wittner 2003; EMEA 2006). To control for their influence on firms' strategy choices, an intra-EU comparison of countries seems appropriate. Second, competitive pressure on firms to take advantage of national institutions and specialize in the supported strategy is particularly high in the EU member states following the single market project.

Finally, within the EU, it is advisable to compare those economies which are most different from each other in their financial, antitrust, and labour-market institutions, thereby offering firms an ideal institutional environment for the pursuit of RPI, DQP, and LCP strategies. These are the UK, Germany, and Italy respectively. Across the competitiveness literature, there is broad agreement that the deregulated environment of the UK facilitates RPI, as economic interaction is flexible. This encourages outstanding employee performance, market races amongst firms to set new standards, and the provision of seed (venture) capital.[4] The regulating institutions in Germany, by contrast, are said to support DQP, as they enable cooperative relations amongst firms and their stakeholders. Accordingly, employees invest in specific skills, suppliers and producers cooperate to establish new standards, and banks offer 'patient' capital.[5] Finally, collective agreements establishing comparatively low minimum wage floors and relationship-based provision of finance of the Italian economy are said to facilitate LCP.[6]

I sampled one of the largest pharmaceutical databases for empirical insights into whether British firms specialize in RPI, German firms in DQP, and their Italian counterparts in LCP. The results might disappoint contributors to the competitiveness literature, as they do not reveal strong specialization effects. Instead, roughly the same share of firms is found to pursue RPI, DQP, and LCP strategies in all three countries (Chapter 2). What is more, firms do not only pursue the same variety of strategies, they are also equally successful in doing so (Chapter 6). Probably more than disappointing, these results are puzzling to proponents of the specialization theory. How is it possible that, in each economy, the majority of firms pursue strategies which are not facilitated by the institutional environment? How do all these deviant firms cope with increasing competitive pressure? Chapters 3–5 seek to answer these questions.

To shed light on the (non-)specialization puzzle, one needs to understand what exactly firms require in order to produce radically or incrementally new goods, or to imitate at low cost. Which input factors are essential for each strategy? The previous review of strategic management contributions (Section 1.1.2.) has shown that the number of causes which may facilitate each strategy is potentially unlimited (see also Porter 1985: 81, 123, 343–6; Pfeffer 1992: 87; Knyphausen-Aufseß 1997: 463–4). Importantly, though, the VoC literature distinguishes the less from the more important input factors by drawing on the idea of 'dynamic capabilities' (see Teece and Pisano 1998 in Hall and Soskice 2001*a*: 6). The literature thereby makes explicit what is implicit in many competitiveness studies. *Financial means*, *labour qualifications*, and *new component standards* are decisive for the success of any strategy because a firm cannot secure them on its own. Instead, they are only provided following the

[4] See in particular Porter (1990: 482–507), Pavitt and Patel (1999), Estevez-Abe et al. (2001), Hall and Soskice (2001*a*: 36–44), Tate (2001), Vitols (2001), Amable (2003), Casper and Matraves (2003), and Casper and Whitley (2004); see also Lindgaard Christensen (1992), Freeman (1992), Walker (1993), and Hollingsworth (2000).

[5] Proponents are in particular Porter (1990: 355–82), Pavitt and Patel (1999), Hollingsworth (2000), Estevez-Abe et al. (2001), Hall and Soskice (2001*a*: 36–44), Tate (2001), Vitols (2001), Amable (2003), Casper and Matraves (2003), Casper and Whitley (2004), and Sinn (2005); see also Lindgaard Christensen (1992), Freeman (1992), and Keck (1993).

[6] See Estevez-Abe et al. (2001: 175–6); see also Porter (1990: 421–53), and Malerba (1993).

successful institutional solution of a coordination problem between a firm and other economic actors (Hall and Soskice 2001*a*: 6–7; see also Andersen 1992: 68–9; Lundvall 1992*a*: 13–15; Patel and Pavitt 1994*a*: 91–2; Hollingsworth 2000: 626–30).

While the provision of *finance* depends on the successful solution of the principal–agent problem between a firm and its financiers (Mayer 1998: 145; Kenyon and Vitols 2004: 11), an *adequately skilled workforce* can only be secured if the free-riding problem related to the training of employees is resolved (Hall and Soskice 2001*a*: 24–6; Le Galès and Voelzkow 2001: 4–5). Similarly, new *component standards* can only be agreed upon if the hold-up problem between competing firms is overcome (see Hall and Soskice 2001*a*: 26–7, 30–1; Tate 2001: 442–4). Depending on how national institutions solve each of these coordination problems, firms are provided with different types of finance, labour qualifications, and component standards. In the analyses of this book, I follow the definition of institutions proposed in most competitiveness studies. This concept is best summarized by Streeck and Thelen (2005*a*: 9–16), who understand institutions as 'formalized rules that may be enforced by calling upon a third party' (Streeck and Thelen 2005*a*: 10).

The competitiveness literature also offers precious insights into the types of each input factor that are required for the respective competitive strategies. To understand how firms compete in a suboptimal institutional environment, the core part of this research therefore dedicates one chapter to each factor and, in each chapter, tests the following hypotheses. First, is it true that RPI, DQP, and LCP strategies respectively require particular financial means (Chapter 3), component standards (Chapter 4), and labour qualifications (Chapter 5)? Since this hypothesis is confirmed in the case of finance and employee skills, Chapters 3 and 5 test a second hypothesis: Is it true that the required financial means and skills are only provided by particular national institutions?

## 1.3. THE ARGUMENT IN BRIEF

My answer to the latter question is 'no', as I show that two institutional alternatives exist which enable firms to pursue strategies that are not facilitated by national institutions: *international labour and financial markets*, and the *possibility of concluding individual contracts*. The first main argument of this book therefore is that firms can compete despite suboptimal national institutions simply *because of* economic internationalization. Globalization does not only give rise to difficulties, it also offers numerous opportunities. Not only does it increase competitive pressure, but it also gives firms ever faster and cheaper access to input factors of other economies. Specific types of capital can therefore be imported and adequately skilled employees can be motivated to emigrate from those countries where their skill types are abundant. I term this first possibility of circumventing national institutions: *importation* via international institutions.

That globalization not only constitutes a threat but also offers opportunities may not strike proponents of the 'relocation argument' as particularly innovative. In essence, their argument comes in two forms. The first and more extreme variant stresses that the increasing need for competitiveness drives firms to relocate entirely to those countries with the most attractive business location (see Hall and Soskice 2001*a*: 54–7). The more moderate variant, often proposed by strategic management scholars, emphasizes the opportunity to achieve superior competitiveness by relocating only those parts of the value chain which are better supported in other economies (see Porter 1986; Ghoshal 1987: 426; Bartlett and Ghoshal 1989; Nohria and Ghoshal 1997; Yip 2002: 362; Berger 2005: chapter 4). For example, the production of basic components is offshored to low-wage, low-skill countries whereas the final assembly is kept in high-skill, high-wage economies (e.g. Berger 2005: chapter 4; Sinn 2005).

While I agree that firms can benefit from economic internationalization, as the latter enables either entire or partial relocation to occur, my perception of globalization as competitiveness enhancing rests upon a different argument. Instead of relocating, firms can gain competitiveness simply from 'staying home' and importing input factors from abroad. I thereby reject the view that increasing competitive pressure necessarily translates into relocation processes. After all, manifold costs and benefits are related to both decisions. As Yip (2002: 364) notes, '[g]lobal sourcing and production have to reconcile several conflicting objectives: cost, productivity, quality, reliability, protection of expertise, and trade barriers. So there is seldom a single sourcing and production configuration that can maximize all of these objectives.' The argument that importation constitutes a viable alternative to relocation is also supported by recent studies of Berger (2005), who finds that, in the same country and the same industry, 'there are companies like Cisco (. . .) that outsource [and offshore] all their manufacturing, and others like Intel (. . .) that do it mostly under their own roof' (ibid.: 252).

This book also identifies a second possible way for firms to circumvent national institutions and secure the required, but not provided, input factors (chiefly, adequately skilled labour): the conclusion of individual contracts. Despite overarching (wage) bargaining procedures, firms can and do opt out of collective agreements in order to employ people with general skills on a temporary basis. Similarly, firms in economies without collective bargaining procedures can build incentives of such kind into employment contracts, that key personnel will be retained and willing to invest in specific skills (see Chapter 4). I term this second institutional alternative for securing input factors without relying on the national framework: *improvisation* on a contractual basis. Thus the second argument of this book is that firms can pursue nationally unsupported strategies because they can build individual networks. They are free to decide whether, with whom, and the specific extent to which they conclude contracts in order to organize business activities.

The argument that firms gain competitiveness due to close links with selected economic actors is central to different strands of studies which can be summarized as 'network literature'. Ever since Marshall's observation that economies of scale are obtained from a division of labour between firms, 'which can often be secured by the concentration of many small businesses of a similar character in particular localities' (Marshall 1920: 266), studies of this phenomenon have gained momentum. Within various academic disciplines, these studies have developed into different literatures: most importantly, on 'industrial districts' and 'local production systems' (socio-economic theory), on 'clusters' (strategic management), and on 'regional innovation systems' (innovation theory). While studies of 'industrial districts' (Piore and Sabel 1984; Pyke et al. 1990; Pyke and Sengenberger 1992; Cossentino et al. 1996), 'local production systems' (Crouch et al. 2001, 2004), and 'clusters' (Porter 1998, 2000) focus on territorially embedded *production* processes, the literature on 'regional innovation systems' (Saxenian 1994; Cooke et al. 1997, 1998) focuses on *innovation* processes.

Despite their different foci, these literatures agree that firms within a geographically limited space jointly succeed in developing new technologies and superior products due to their local proximity – including shared norms and values. Local proximity is crucial for the development of close, trust-based relations between the network members. Close relations, in turn, are at the basis of local economies as they enable firms to specialize in particular innovation or production steps. Strong network links also facilitate the development of a local labour market within which people move regularly from one firm to another, be it out of necessity to find new employment or out of professional aspiration. Finally, close relationships are at the basis of local institutions such as employer associations and consulting agencies, which support network members by providing financial support, facilitating technology transfer, and offering professional or legal advice.

Embeddedness in networks makes firms largely independent of national institutions. Studies of the media sector in Cologne (Baumann and Voelzkow 2004) and the software industry in Pisa (Biagiotti and Burroni 2004) provide recent examples of how firms successfully neutralize national rigidities. However, despite its theoretical and analytical sophistication, the network literature has difficulties to explain how firms can circumvent national institutions *without* being embedded in industrial districts, local production systems, clusters, or regional innovation systems (see also Voelzkow, Elbing, and Martin 2007). As illustrated above, the reason is that the literature perceives geographical proximity as crucial for 'anti-national' models of economic interaction. This, in turn, distinguishes these writings from my argument to which geographical or cultural proximity is of limited importance. My observations of biotech firms based in Central Italy, recruiting temporary contract collaborators from universities all over Italy and entertaining development partnerships with firms throughout Europe, indicate that firms do, indeed, need networks. They need close relations with (potential) business partners. However, I do not find local proximity to be essential for this. Individual firm networks can be developed, and national institutions circumvented, purely on the basis of contracts – irrespective of where business partners are located.

Contributors to the competitiveness literature may disagree with this argument by pointing out that contractual improvisation is costly. This is particularly true for firms in economies with collective bargaining procedures. Here, so the argument goes, firms adhere to collective agreements because defection – i.e. the individual provision of labour skills – is more expensive than adherence (Hall and Soskice 2001*a*). While it seems impossible to measure the actual costs of adherence and defection respectively, three reasons may explain why numerous firms defect in defiance of the literature's expectations. First, contractual improvisation does *not* provide the *same* skill profiles as collective bargaining procedures but *alternative* ones. What do firms gain by following collective agreements if they do not translate into the provision of the required labour qualifications? Second, adherence also has its costs. Even once collective bargaining procedures are established, they need to be maintained. Firms need to make their voices heard during bargaining processes and implement results which often constitute compromises. And compromising in daily business can be extremely costly. Finally, defection can be beneficial. As Streeck (2004: 428, original emphases) argues, '[entrepreneurs] faced with irremovable restrictions on their strategic repertoires (. . .) can and do make use of their defining capacity, their *creativity*, to come to terms with *and even benefit from* them'. While Streeck (1997) illustrates how the necessity to *adapt to* constraints of national institutions can be beneficial, the same can be said for the necessity *to circumvent* national constraints. Whenever individual contracts have to be concluded, this opens up opportunities to explore new, individual, and improved solutions.

The third argument of this book therefore is that competitiveness arises from the flexibility to exploit opportunities and capacities which are individual to each firm. Most importantly, firms need to have the necessary flexibility to seize technological opportunities without being constrained by a specific procedure of input factor provision. As shown in Chapter 6, corporate competitiveness and, accordingly, firms' choices of competitive strategies essentially depend on their technological capabilities to develop inventions into radically new, incrementally new, or imitated products. The acquisition of necessary input factors follows the choice of competitive strategy. Otherwise, all firms would look the same. And '[l]ittle progress would be made in a world of clones' (Lundvall and Maskell 2000: 364).

This argument may seem familiar to strategic management scholars. The claim that firms achieve competitiveness through developing and exploiting individual capabilities is at the core of the 'resource-based view' of the firm (Penrose 1959; Pfeffer and Salancik 1978; Rumelt 1984; Wernerfelt 1984; Barney 1991; Conner 1991; Peteraf 1993). It became the strategic management paradigm of the 1990s, once scholars had realized that the MBV paradigm of the 1980s failed to account for profitability differences of firms within the same industry (Rumelt 1984: 559–60, 1991; Schmalensee 1985). Importantly, proponents of the resource-based view (RBV) stress that 'not all firm resources hold the potential of sustained competitive advantages. To have this potential, a firm resource must have four attributes: (*a*) it must be valuable, in the sense that it exploits opportunities and/or neutralizes threats in a firm's environment, (*b*) it must be rare among a firm's current and potential competition, (*c*) it must be imperfectly imitable, and (*d*) there cannot be strategically equivalent substitutes for this resource' (Barney 1991: 105–6).

Critics of the RBV approach have noted that, despite these conceptual limitations, 'virtually *anything* associated with the firm can be a [competitiveness enhancing] resource' (Priem and Butler 2001: 32, original emphasis): for example, 'brand names, in-house knowledge of technology, employment of skilled personnel, trade contracts, machinery, efficient procedures, capital etc.' (ibid., citing Wernerfelt 1984: 172). In line with this criticism, the analyses of this book do not only lend support to RBV ideas by indicating that firms base their choice of competitive strategies on individual technological opportunities (Chapter 6), they also contrast RBV thoughts by demonstrating that firms which pursue the same strategy employ very similar input factors. In other words, firms can build competitive advantages not only through factor heterogeneity but also when using homogeneous input factors.

By illustrating how firms can secure necessary input factors either through national or international institutions, or by concluding individual contracts, my analyses also complement those strategic management studies – including RBV theory – which focus on individual firm capabilities rather than on the institutions through which such capabilities arise. The highly sophisticated studies of Berger provide a recent example to the extent that it is her 'main argument: (. . .) [that] there are different possible ways for firms to do well under the constraint of the great new pressures to adapt rapidly to international markets' (Berger 2005: 49). But, even though Berger recognizes the importance of institutions for corporate competitiveness, her analyses do not incorporate institutional considerations: 'Though we did not analyze institutions and policies at the national level, we saw their impact everywhere – embedded in the resources that companies have available to develop' (ibid.: 280). Complementing these and similar strategic management studies, this book seeks to propose a coherent theoretical framework on the link between institutions, input factors, and competitive strategies.

This, in turn, brings me to my fourth and last argument. Institutions matter. They constrain firms and dictate a specific form of business interaction. Importantly, though, this does not mean that firms are mere institution-takers. My point is that firms can *choose* through which institutions they want to secure required input factors. *Only then* have firms to 'obey the rules of the game' and comply with the constraints resulting from the chosen institutions. For example, if firms decide to rely on collective agreements for hiring employees with specific skill profiles, they have to pay homogeneous wages and will thus find it hard to motivate outstanding performance through extraordinary bonuses. However, firms are not obliged to adhere to collective agreements. If they decide to opt out and hire people with general qualifications on a contractual basis, they will have difficulties in motivating these employees to participate in specific training programmes. In sum, support from any institution comes with a price. National and international institutions, as well as contracts, do two things at the same time: they enable *and* determine a specific form of business interaction. But, firms can choose by which institutions their business shall be enabled and determined.

A corollary of this reasoning is that firms can compete without having to change existing institutions, as they can rely on institutional alternatives. Incremental institutional change can occur as a side effect (see Campbell 2004; Crouch 2005; Streeck and Thelen 2005*b*), but does not constitute a necessary condition for competitiveness. In other words, firms can, but do not need to, become 'institutional entrepreneurs' (Crouch 2005) or to engage in 'bricolage' (Campbell 2004) so as to achieve international competitiveness. They can, simply, circumvent national institutions through 'importation' and 'improvisation'.

I therefore deem Schumpeter's perception of firms and, more precisely, of entrepreneurs as particularly helpful to understand how they compete in the face of increasing internationalization. While the notion of 'firms' is used throughout this book as an umbrella term for 'managers' and 'entrepreneurs', I follow Schumpeter's view that firms gain competitiveness because they are 'entrepreneurial', not because they are 'managed' (Schumpeter 1934; 1939).

Schumpeter draws a crucial distinction between entrepreneurs and managers (Schumpeter 1934: 74–94, 1939: 103–6, 1947) in that 'the defining characteristic [of the entrepreneur] is simply the doing of new things or the doing of things that are already being done in a new way (innovation). (...) [Thereby,] the "new thing" need not be spectacular or of historic importance. It need not be Bessemer steel or the explosion motor. It can be the Deerfoot sausage' (Schumpeter 1947: 151). Contrary to this, a manager merely 'head[s] the administration of a going concern' (ibid.). Entrepreneurs thus possess the necessary creativity to pursue new business ideas and 'to cope with the resistances and difficulties which action always meets with outside of the ruts of established practice' (ibid.: 152). Managers lack that creative capacity. Following these Schumpeterian distinctions, I argue that firms within the same economy successfully compete through different strategies because they are run by creative entrepreneurs, not by institution-taking managers.

## 1.4. OUTLINE OF THE BOOK

The book is organized as follows. Chapter 2 reveals patterns of strategy specialization. It asks how many pharmaceutical firms compete by pursuing *those* strategies that are facilitated by national financial, antitrust, and labour-market institutions in three ideal-typical economies: Germany, Italy, and the UK. Samples drawn from one of the largest pharmaceutical databases show that deviant firms competing through institutionally unsupported strategies by far outnumber conforming firms. These results do not simply run counter to the expectations of the competitiveness literature, they also constitute the puzzle of this book. How can firms in different economies achieve international competitiveness without taking advantage of national institutions and specializing in the supported strategy?

The link between the institutional provision of key input factors – finance, standards, and labour qualifications – and their impact on competitive strategies is studied for each input factor separately in Chapters 3–5. In examining this link, each chapter combines quantitative assessments and qualitative insights obtained from a total of 150 interviews with managers of pharmaceutical firms in Germany, Italy, and the UK. Chapter 3 focuses on the first factor: financial means. It begins with an outline of the literature's hypotheses on how diverse corporate governance systems provide specific types of finance required for RPI, DQP, and LCP strategies. Balance sheet data show that each strategy does, indeed, rely on particular financial means. The remainder of Chapter 3 thus asks how firms secure the required finance types in those economies where their provision is hindered by national corporate governance institutions. In brief, firms turn to international financial markets and import (seed) finance from abroad. This leads to the summary result that entrepreneurs can circumvent national institutions by relying on *supranational* institutions: open financial markets.

Chapter 4 analyses standardization processes. It starts with a review of the literature's hypotheses on how national antitrust legislation determines firms' standardization approaches, which, in turn, are at the basis of different competitive strategies. In line with Chapter 3, the following analyses reveal that particular standardization processes indeed facilitate RPI, DQP, and LCP strategies. However, contrary to Chapter 2, national institutions are not found to constitute comparative advantages or disadvantages to providing the required standard types. This, in turn, makes it possible to speculate how firms can gain competitiveness independently of national institutions.

Chapter 5 is concerned with analyses of employee skills. In line with Chapters 3 and 4, it is preceded by an outline of existing hypotheses on how different labour-market institutions motivate employees to acquire those qualifications necessary for specific competitive strategies. The subsequent assessments reveal that each strategy actually requires particular skill profiles. Accordingly, the remainder of the chapter analyses how firms acquire the necessary skill types in those economies where their provision is hindered by national institutions. The results reveal two pathways to competitiveness. Akin to the findings of Chapter 3, employers are found to circumvent national labour-market regulation by *relying on supranational institutions*, open labour markets, as they motivate employees to immigrate from abroad. In addition, employers also overcome national rigidities by *improvising on a contractual basis*: be it by (mis)using training subsidies provided by the government or by developing close links to local, national, and international universities.

Since all previous analyses are of a static nature, Chapter 6 attempts to provide dynamic insights through an excursus on the success and choice of competitive strategies. The chapter begins with an assessment of strategy success. Are firms that pursue strategies which are *not* facilitated by national institutions less successful or less sustainable in the long run? Quantitative analyses indicate that the success with which firms pursue different strategies is very similar in diverse institutional environments and, hence, unlikely to be determined by national institutions. And whether firms go bankrupt, merge, are acquired, or continue to pursue the initial strategy does not depend on the provision of input factors by national institutions as well. Instead, strategy sustainability is found to result from the availability of seed finance for new businesses: the easier firms can acquire seed capital, the more susceptible to change are their strategies. Having found that national institutions seem neither to determine nor to punish firms' strategy choices, the second part of Chapter 6 seeks alternative explanations. Comparative analyses of qualitative insights show strategy choices to depend on the willingness of (potential) entrepreneurs to seize technological opportunities so as to develop them into marketable products. Dynamic analyses thus confirm the findings resulting from static assessments: that the influence of national institutions is more limited than suggested by contributors to the competitiveness literature.

Chapter 7 concludes with a summary interpretation of the results obtained. It recapitulates that three institutional pathways to firm competitiveness exist and illustrates how this finding is based on a Schumpeterian perception of firms as entrepreneurs. Furthermore, it relates these results back to various theoretical debates proposed by contributors to the competitiveness literature on the one hand, and by adherents to the resource-based view on the other. Finally, conclusions are drawn about whether globalization leads to convergence or divergence, and about the scope of policymakers to foster competitiveness through institutional reform.

# 2

# Patterns of Strategy Specialization

Do firms within one country specialize in the competitive strategy that is facilitated by national institutions so as to cope with increasing pressures for competitiveness? Chapter 1 has outlined that this claim for specialization is central to the competitiveness literature – including classical and neo-liberal trade theory, the 'market-based view' (MBV) of strategic management studies, the literature on national innovation systems (NIS), and the varieties-of-capitalism (VoC) contributions. Strategic management proponents of the 'resource-based view' (RBV), in contrast, are less straightforward about firm behaviour in the wake of globalization.

To be clear, agreement is broad amongst scholars of competitiveness that firms need a sustainable *competitive advantage* if they want to succeed in their business in the long run. Firms need to pursue a strategy through which they achieve superior performance to their competitors by offering special value to customers (Kogut 1985; Porter 1985; Barney 1991: 102–3; Teece et al. 1997; Walker 2003: 17–18). Customer value can be provided in the form of an entirely new, improved, or low-cost product (Porter 1985; Grant 1998: part III; Hall and Soskice 2001*a*: 36–44; Walker 2003: 20–34; see also Section 2.1).

However, disagreement concerns the question of whether firms should use the *comparative advantage* of their institutional environment as the main source of *competitive advantage*. Should firms choose their competitive strategy in line with national institutions? Ideally not, argue advocates of the RBV. Even though external threats and market opportunities should not be ignored, the actual competitive advantage of a firm can only arise from its internal strengths and weaknesses. Firms need to exploit their idiosyncratic resources and capabilities in order to distinguish themselves from competitors. Only if they use their individual capabilities can firms gain competitive advantage and implement a value-creating strategy not imitated by their rivals (e.g. Rumelt 1984; Wernerfelt 1984; Barney 1991; Conner 1991; Peteraf 1993; Barney and Clark 2007; Newbert 2007).

While convincing in their perception of firms as creative actors, proponents of the RBV approach have been criticized especially in three respects. First, the all-encompassing view of resources as 'all assets, capabilities, organizational processes, firm attributes, information, knowledge, etc. controlled by a firm that enable the firm to conceive of and implement strategies that improve its efficiency and effectiveness' (Barney 1991: 101) leads to a tautological definition of value-creating strategies (Priem and Butler 2001: 25–8). Second, different configurations of resources can generate the same customer value. In other words, the RBV does not identify particular input factors as more important than others to pursue competitive strategies (ibid.: 32–3). Third, due to its focus on internal resources of firms, the RBV tends to neglect the importance of external contexts (Bresser 2004: 1275). Contributors to this approach do therefore not make clear-cut propositions about how firms adapt to the competitive pressures of globalization. Its causal ambiguities and reduced interest in external factors thus make the RBV approach less suitable as an analytical framework for the aim of this research project.

This is different for the competitiveness literature. Its functionalist arguments of how three crucial sets of resources – finance, component standards, and labour qualifications[1] – support different strategies bring the literature to argue that firms choose their strategy in line with national institutions. Using these arguments as analytical framework, this chapter assesses the strategy specialization of pharmaceutical firms in the UK, Germany, and Italy, because these economies are said to offer ideal-typical institutional settings for radical innovation, high quality, and low-cost strategies (see Section 1.2). Since flexible labour and financial markets, as well as liberal antitrust regulation, facilitate radical innovation, British firms are expected to take advantage of, and specialize in, product innovation strategies.[2] Similarly, German firms are said to pursue product improvement strategies as rigid labour, financial, and antitrust institutions sustain the development of high-quality goods.[3] Finally, low-wage and low-cost-of-capital economies, like Italy, presumably facilitate

[1] Section 1.2 illustrates in greater detail that finance, component standards, and labour qualifications are key factors, as firms cannot secure them on their own but only after a coordination problem has been solved with their financiers, suppliers, and employees.

[2] See in particular Porter (1990: 482–507), Pavitt and Patel (1999), Estevez-Abe et al. (2001), Hall and Soskice (2001*a*: 36–44); Tate (2001), Vitols (2001), Amable (2003), Casper and Matraves (2003), and Casper and Whitley (2004); see also Lindgaard Christensen (1992), Freeman (1992), Walker (1993), and Hollingsworth (2000).

[3] Proponents are in particular Porter (1990: 355–82), Pavitt and Patel (1999), Hollingsworth (2000), Estevez-Abe et al. (2001), Hall and Soskice (2001*a*: 36–44), Tate (2001), Vitols (2001), Amable (2003), Casper and Matraves (2003), Casper and Whitley (2004), and Sinn (2005); see also Lindgaard Christensen (1992), Freeman (1992), and Keck (1993).

the specialization in low-price strategies.[4] With increasing internationalization, these specialization effects are expected to become more pronounced (e.g. Hall and Soskice 2001*a*: 36–44; Hancké and Herrmann 2007). To study firm behaviour in the wake of globalization, the competitiveness literature thus offers both a particularly parsimonious and appropriate framework.

When consulting the literature for advice on how to measure strategy specialization, two peculiarities are striking. First, competitiveness scholars hardly provide reference points for assessing specialization patterns *within one economy*. They usually take the 'revealed comparative advantage' as an indicator of strategy specialization, which compares – for a certain industry – the export performance of one economy relative to the export performance of a reference group of countries. If firms in this economy export more than firms of the reference group, the former are said to have specialized in the production of this industry's goods.[5] Standardized measures of patent registrations or citations are used as an alternative measure of relative strategy specialization.[6] But do all the firms, or the absolute majority, or simply a plurality of firms *within one industry of one country* need to pursue the same strategy in order to constitute empirical instances of specialization effects?

These measures entail a second peculiarity. Strategy specialization is systematically assessed through the macro characteristics of firms. That is, firms are attributed a strategy on the basis of the *industry* in which they are active. The finding that specific high-, medium-, or low-tech industries are more developed in one economy than in others is cited as empirical proof of the idea that firms in this economy have specialized in high-, medium-, or low-innovation strategies respectively. But whenever the technology intensity of entire industries is taken as a proxy for competitive strategies, this entails the simplifying assumption that all firms in this industry pursue the same strategy (Rumelt 1984: 559–60; Barney 1991: 100). Yet, is it not more plausible to assume that firms can pursue different strategies?

A noteworthy exception to the identification of relative specialization patterns at the industry level is provided by innovation studies which compare the absolute development of 'market segments' (Casper et al. 1999) or 'subsectors' (Casper and Soskice 2004; Casper and Whitley 2004) within the biotech industry. These studies suggest that biotech firms developing *therapeutics* pursue a radical innovation strategy, as this market segment is characterized

[4] See Estevez-Abe et al. (2001: 175–6); see also Porter (1990: 421–53), and Malerba (1993).

[5] For examples, see Fagerberg (1992), Dalum (1992), Keck (1993: 133–7), and Hancké and Herrmann (2007); see also Porter (1990: 179–541), Amable (2003: 200–9), and Sinn (2005).

[6] See Chesnais (1993: 220–6), Walker (1993: 168–9), Pavitt and Patel (1999), Estevez-Abe et al. (2001: 174–6), and Hall and Soskice (2001*a*: 36–44), and also Amable (2003: 200–9).

by discrete technological innovation. On the other hand, firms in the market segment of *platform technologies* are said to engage in diversified quality strategies, since this segment is particularly susceptible to 'cumulative or incremental patterns of technical change' (Casper and Soskice 2004: 368; see also Casper et al. 1999: 15). Mostly based on studies of the late 1990s, the share of radically innovative therapeutics firms is found to be above average in the UK, whereas the percentage of incrementally innovative platform providers is above average in Germany (Casper et al. 1999: 20–1; Casper and Soskice 2004: 365–6; Casper and Whitley 2004: 98).

However, two difficulties are related to identifying strategies of biotech firms via their industrial sub-sector. First, any young biotech industry is characterized by a comparatively high share of platform technology providers. Since it takes, by now, almost fifteen years to turn a pharmaceutical discovery into a profitable drug (Muffatto and Giardina 2003: 109), many young biotech start-ups which ultimately aim at developing a therapeutic product (have to) commercialize their knowledge by providing platform technologies. But this is usually a temporary means of securing finance, rather than a strategy in itself (Frey 2004). Once providers of platform services have developed their discovery far enough to acquire venture capital, they often turn into dedicated therapeutics firms. With increasing maturity of a country's biotech industry, the share of platform technology firms decreases and specialization patterns disappear – as occurred in Germany as well (Ernst & Young 2005: 65, 2006: 47). Second, 'platform-technology firms create the research tools used in therapeutics' (Casper et al. 1999: 21). In other words, they are service providers, whereas therapeutics firms seek to develop products (Frey 2004). Since the provision of services might follow a different operational logic than manufacturing activities, it seems risky to compare firms of the secondary and tertiary sector. Differences in the organizational structure might be a consequence of special sectoral requirements rather than of particular strategies.

I have therefore decided to identify competitive strategies at the micro level by considering the technology intensity of individual therapeutics firms. In doing so, I also measure how many of these pharmaceutical firms pursue the same strategies across *and* within different economies. Does this micro-level assessment support the strategy-specialization argument? To answer this question, Section 2.1 conceptualizes and operationalizes competitive strategies. This approach is applied in Section 2.2, by sampling one of the largest pharmaceutical databases. To evaluate the results obtained, Section 2.3 discusses whether competitive strategies are mutually exclusive. Building on these insights, the summary assessment of Section 2.4 negates the specialization idea. Section 2.5 summarizes the previous findings and introduces the research puzzle to be solved in Part II of the book: How can firms compete by pursuing a strategy that is not facilitated by national institutions?

## 2.1. HOW TO DISTINGUISH COMPETITIVE STRATEGIES: CONCEPTS AND OPERATIONALIZATION

In line with major analysts of corporate competitiveness (Porter 1980: chapter 1, 1985: chapter 1; Andrews 1987: chapter 2; Grant 1998: chapter 1; Walker 2003: 17–18; see also Hall and Soskice 2001*a*: 14–17), a competitive strategy is understood here as a process that translates into the development of products which offer unique customer value. If pursued successfully, a competitive strategy enables firms to achieve a competitive advantage, i.e. superior performance to their competitors.

The competitiveness literature distinguishes between three, inherently different strategies on the basis of their technology intensity. If a sustainable advantage arises from the development of entirely new products, being the result of a *radical technological innovation*, the developing firm is said to pursue a strategy of 'radical product innovation'.[7] If a firm competes by selling known but improved products as a result of an *incremental technological innovation*, it is found to be engaged in diversified quality production.[8] Finally, if firms sell standardized goods, resulting from the *imitation* of an established technology, they are held to pursue a strategy of low-cost production.[9] In this research project, I follow the differentiation proposed by the literature and distinguish accordingly between *radical product innovation* (henceforth RPI), *diversified quality production* (henceforth DQP) and *low-cost production* (henceforth LCP).

To identify a firm's strategy, I propose to combine two micro-level indicators: the technological novelty of a firm's products and its value chain focus. To this end, the scientifically established notion of a 'new chemical entity' (henceforth NCE) makes pharmaceutical firms particularly appropriate cases to be studied.[10] An NCE constitutes a chemical entity which has not been discovered thus far. It is scientific practice to indicate whether active ingredients or excipients of a pharmaceutical product are NCEs, modifications of already discovered entities, or mere imitations.[11] Accordingly, patent-protected

[7] See Lundvall (1992*a*: 11–12, 1992*c*: 58–9), Estevez-Abe et al. (2001: 149, 174), Casper (2001: 398), and Hall and Soskice (2001*a*: 38–9).

[8] See in particular Streeck (1991), see also Porter (1985: 14), Lundvall (1992*a*: 11–12, 1992*c*: 57–8), Estevez-Abe et al. (2001: 148–9, 174), Casper (2001: 399–400), and Hall and Soskice (2001*a*: 39).

[9] Proponents are Porter (1985: 12–14), Estevez-Abe et al. (2001: 148, 175), and Casper (2001: 398–9); see also Ohlin (1924: 89), Heckscher (1919: 55–8), and Sinn (2005: 18–19).

[10] For an illustration of the different kinds of firms belonging to the pharmaceutical industry, see Section 1.2.

[11] Whilst *active ingredients* are those compounds in a pharmaceutical preparation that exert a pharmacological effect, *excipients* are inactive substances used as carriers for the active ingredients of a medication.

pharmaceuticals can take one of two forms. They may be radically new as they are based on an NCE. Or, they are incrementally new in that they introduce slight changes to already discovered chemical entities, which improves the drugs' efficiency. For example, undesired side effects are limited, or the frequency or quantity with which a drug has to be consumed is reduced. Yet not all pharmaceutical companies engage in research and development (henceforth R&D) activities. As soon as patent protection expires, (generics) firms compete by imitating a product's active ingredients or excipients so as to sell the imitated drug at the lowest-possible prices (see Wittner 2003).

Using this classification, I propose the following differentiation between competitive strategies (see Bottazzi et al. 2001: 1162–7). Pharmaceutical firms inventing drugs based on NCEs pursue an RPI strategy, whereas firms improving already discovered chemical entities compete through DQP. Firms which do not engage in R&D, but focus on imitating innovations made by others, pursue an LCP strategy.

The Pharmaceutical Industry Database (or PHID database), one of the largest pharmaceutical databases worldwide, allows the identification of a firm's competitive strategy via the chemical entities employed in that firm's drugs.[12] Developed by a group of researchers at the University of Siena, the PHID database keeps track of 16,751 pharmaceutical projects carried out by 3,522 firms and public research organizations[13] in seven countries.[14] The latter include Germany, Italy, and the UK, in addition to France, Japan, Switzerland, and the USA.[15] In these countries, any firm that participates, or has participated, in the development of an innovative drug is incorporated in the database. More precisely, a firm is included as soon as it is, or has been, involved in at least one pharmaceutical project which has reached the stage of preclinical development since the 1980s. Even firms whose pharmaceutical projects have not (yet) been granted patent protection are thus recorded. Only (generics) companies which abstain from traditional R&D activities are not considered in the database. Furthermore, and importantly for the aim of this study, pharmaceutical firms are considered only if their projects translate into therapeutic drugs curing or alleviating human diseases. Providers of platform technologies active in the service

[12] An overview of the database's population, the sampling strategy employed, and possible sampling biases is provided in the technical appendix.

[13] Firms and, respectively, public research organizations are identified on the basis of their legal entity, whereby their nationality is determined by the location of their headquarters.

[14] Since this database is constantly updated, these figures refer to November 2004.

[15] To be precise, the PHID database covers sixty-seven countries. However, the number of pharmaceutical projects considered in the other sixty countries is too limited to provide representative results.

sector are not included. The comparison of firms in the manufacturing and service sector is thus avoided (see Casper et al. 1999; Casper and Soskice 2004; Casper and Whitley 2004).

In addition to the novelty of chemical entities, the PHID database contains a second micro-level measure which allows a firm's strategy to be identified: its value-chain focus. The latter can be derived from the database's classification of firms as *developers*, *licensors*, and *licensees*. To understand these terms, it is important to note that the pharmaceutical industry is characterized by a remarkable division of labour (see Gambardella et al. 2001: 36–53). Any drug that is sold on the market must have passed through three major stages. The first is the *research stage* (drug discovery and preclinical development), during which a firm discovers how a chemical entity interacts with other molecules in such a way that a curative effect can be obtained. The second, namely the *development stage*, consists in turning this discovery into a pharmaceutical product. During the phases of 'clinical development I, II, and III', a firm experiments with the form and dosage in which the drug should be administered. Furthermore, undesired side effects are recorded and, if possible, reduced or eliminated. Finally, any relevant information regarding both the drug's features and its production process are documented in the third stage, i.e. the *registration stage*. This documentation is then handed to the responsible national or international authorities in order to obtain a marketing authorization (see Muffatto and Giardina 2003: 112–16; Drews 1999: 117–54).

The Italian researchers administering the PHID database show that these three stages are often not carried out by the same firm. Instead, pharmaceutical companies tend to divide labour, and specialize in upstream, midstream, or downstream activities (see Orsenigo et al. 2001; Bottazzi et al. 2001; Owen-Smith et al. 2002; Pammolli et al. 2002). Interestingly, the division of labour is not only pronounced between innovative pharmaceutical firms on the one hand and generics firms on the other (see Pammolli et al. 2002). It also importantly takes place amongst innovative firms (see Orsenigo et al. 2001; Bottazzi et al. 2001; Owen-Smith et al. 2002).

The latter division of labour is reported in the PHID database by the previously mentioned distinction between *developers*, *licensors*, and *licensees*. A *developer* is a firm with a fully integrated value chain, as it carries out all stages on its own. A drug is thus discovered, developed, and registered by the same firm. A *licensor*, on the other hand, initiates a project which ultimately translates into a new drug. However, focusing on the research stage (i.e. on discovery and preclinical development), the licensor decides at a certain point to out-license its discovery to another firm, which continues the clinical development and registration process. Accordingly, a *licensee* focuses on the stages of (late) clinical development and registration in order to translate the respective

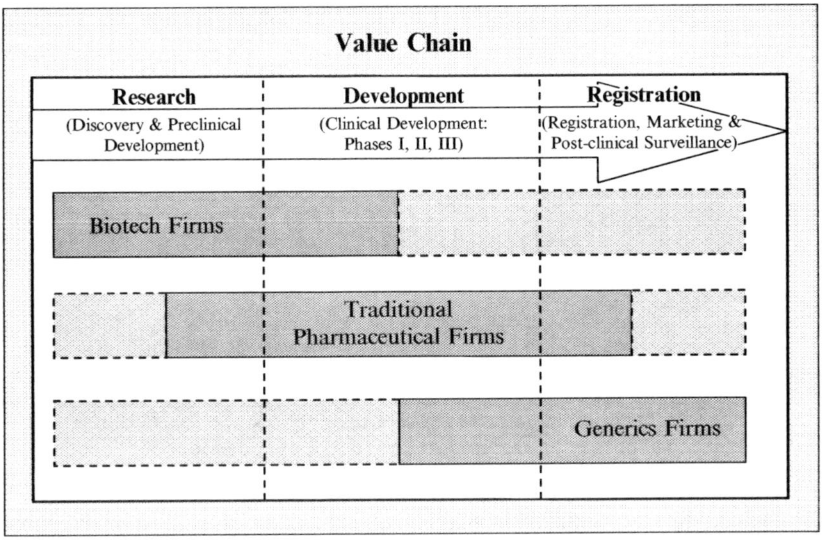


**Graph 2.1.** Labour division in the pharmaceutical industry

***Source:*** Own illustration based on the work of Gambardella et al. (2001), Orsenigo et al. (2001), and Pammolli et al. (2002)

discovery into a marketable drug. Using this distinction, the Italian researchers show that biotech firms tend to be licensors, whereas traditional pharmaceutical firms are often licensees (Orsenigo et al. 2001). Graph 2.1 provides an overview of the division of labour in the pharmaceutical industry.

Combining information on product novelty and value-chain focus makes it possible to identify radical product innovators, diversified quality producers, and low-cost producers as follows.

- A firm pursues an RPI strategy whenever it is the *developer* or *licensor* of a pharmaceutical project which translates into a drug based on an NCE. Since the discovery of the NCE is made by the licensor, the latter is ***radically innovative*** irrespective of whether the licensing agreement is made at the development or the registration stage of a pharmaceutical project.
- Following this logic, a firm pursues a DQP strategy whenever it *develops* or *out-licenses* a project that improves a previously discovered chemical entity. In addition to this, a firm also pursues a DQP strategy if it *in-licenses* a pharmaceutical project based on an NCE *at the stage of clinical development.* At this moment, the previously unknown chemical entity has been discovered so that it is the task of the licensee to improve the entity in order to optimize the drug's effectiveness or dosage. Hence, licensees of

a clinical development agreement, as well as developers or licensors of an improved drug pursue a DQP strategy, as they are not radically but ***incrementally innovative***.

- This leaves us with a third group of firms that conclude *in-licensing* agreements with the purpose of registering and marketing both radically or incrementally new drugs. Interestingly, these firms concur with generics firms in that both abstain from engaging in expensive R&D activities. Instead, their strategy consists in producing and selling drugs at the ***lowest-possible cost***.

## 2.2. DO FIRMS IN GERMANY, ITALY, AND THE UK SPECIALIZE IN THE SAME STRATEGY?

Will this micro-level approach to identifying competitive strategies provide empirical support for the idea that firms use the comparative institutional advantages of their economy and specialize in the facilitated strategy? Do British firms mostly engage in RPI, whereas German companies specialize in DQP, while their Italian counterparts prefer the pursuit of LCP strategies? Tables 2.1–2.3 summarize the results obtained from sampling the PHID database. Given that it takes on average fourteen years to develop a pharmaceutical product (Muffatto and Giardina 2003: 108–9), the sample has been limited to the last twenty years in order to cover a sufficiently long time span, while eliminating outdated results. Accordingly, only those firms were considered which are/have been involved in the advancement of at least one pharmaceutical project since 1985.

The most important finding in answer to the question of strategy specialization is that the obtained strategy patterns of firms are virtually the same for the UK, Germany, and Italy! Since a considerable number of radical product innovators, diversified quality producers, and low-cost producers can be found in the UK, Germany, and Italy alike, strong specialization effects cannot be assessed.

Regarding the sample size, it is noteworthy that the British sample is slightly larger, as comparatively few biotech firms are included in the German, and hardly any in the Italian sample. The reason for this is the difference in age of the British, German, and Italian biotech industries. While this industry began to crystallize in Britain in the 1980s (see Ernst & Young 2003; Thomson Financial 2004), most biotech firms in Germany were founded in the mid to late 1990s (ibid.; see also Hinze et al. 2001: 18–24). Italian biotech firms are even younger, as they were mostly founded around the turn of the millennium

(Chiesa 2004: 10–18; Pozzali 2004; Vinci 2006). Therefore, many of the biotech firms in Germany and Italy that are successful today had not as yet, or only just recently, brought a pharmaceutical project beyond the stage of preclinical development – and were thus not included in the PHID database – when I sampled the latter in November 2004. This explains the smaller size of the German and Italian sample.

Interestingly, though, these age differences do *not* lead to differences in the share of firms pursuing an RPI strategy. Accordingly, Tables 2.1–2.3 illustrate how the division of labour in Britain takes place *between* biotechnology and traditional pharmaceutical firms. In Germany and Italy, by contrast, the lower number of biotech firms means that the division of labour is more pronounced *within* the traditional pharmaceutical industry, namely between (small) research-oriented, and (large) development-oriented firms (see also Gambardella et al. 2001: 45).

A more in-depth interpretation of the results reported in Tables 2.1–2.3 allows us to classify firms with regard to the competitive strategy they pursue. The most clear-cut distinction between competitive strategies can be made between non-innovative low-cost producers on the one hand and innovation-driven pharmaceutical firms on the other. As mentioned above, generics firms are not included in the PHID database and, consequently, in any of the three samples, as they do not engage in R&D activities. Imitating a once patent-protected drug, generics producers are not legally obliged to perform clinical trials as long as they can demonstrate that the imitated drug is bioequivalent to the original pharmaceutical. Avoiding the extremely expensive stages of clinical development is precisely what allows generics firms to produce and market drugs at low prices. The absence of any generics firm from the overall sample thus shows that this category of firms indeed pursues an LCP strategy.

A second group of low-cost producers consists of those firms that specialize in the registration phase of pharmaceutical products. In addition to these ***marketing specialists***, several pharmaceutical firms conclude marketing agreements at the registration stage, even though they are also active in R&D. It is noteworthy that these seemingly ambiguous cases are almost exclusively constituted by large, internationally active firms with an extensive product range. In these cases, the in-licensing of pharmaceutical products does not constitute a competitive strategy in itself, driven by technological considerations. It is rather a commercial tool to grant partner firms access to the home market in order to secure their own international presence. Since these pharmaceutical firms do not pursue a genuine LCP strategy, only the pure marketing specialists are counted as low-cost producers.

Among the pharmaceutical firms which are active in R&D, the distinction between radical product innovators on the one hand and diversified quality

Table 2.1. **Radical product innovators, diversified quality producers, and low-cost producers in the UK**

| Firm type | Firm name | Technology focus | No. of employees | Firm age | Developer NCE | Licensor NCE | Developer non-NCE | Licensor non-NCE | Licensee dev. phase NCE | Licensee dev. phase non-NCE | Licensee reg. phase | Competitive strategy |
|---|---|---|---|---|---|---|---|---|---|---|---|---|
| **Discoverers of NCE** | Cancer Research Technology | TrPh | 67 | 41 | | 1 | | 3 | | | 1 | RPI |
| | Celltech Group | BioT | 724 | 24 | | 1 | | 1 | | | | RPI |
| | Imperial Cancer Research | TrPh | 19 | 102 | | 1 | | 1 | | | | RPI |
| | Pharmagene | BioT | 79 | 7 | | 1 | | 1 | | | | RPI |
| | Protherics | BioT | 219 | 5 | | 2 | | 1 | | | | RPI |
| **Ambiguous cases** | Acambis | BioT | 270 | 12 | | | 1[a] | | | | 1 | RPI |
| | Amarin | BioT | 24 | 15 | | | | 3 | | | 1 | RPI |
| | Antisoma | BioT | 45 | 16 | | | 1[a] | | | | | RPI |
| | CeNeS | BioT | 14 | 7 | | | 7[a] | | | | 1 | RPI |
| | Henderson Morley | BioT | 6 | 8 | | | 1[a] | | | | | RPI |
| | KS Biomedix | BioT | 65 | n.a. | | | 1[a] | | | | 2 | RPI |
| | Onyvax | BioT | 37 | 7 | | | 1[a] | | | | 1 | RPI |
| | PowderJect | BioT | 750 | 11 | | | | 2 | | | 1 | RPI |
| | Scotia | BioT | n.a. | 20 | | | | 4 | | | | RPI |
| | SkyePharma | BioT | 476 | 8 | | | | 4 | | | | RPI |
| | Xenova | BioT | 105 | 17 | | | | 3[b] | | | | RPI |

| | | | | | | | | | | | | |
|---|---|---|---|---|---|---|---|---|---|---|---|---|
| **Diversified quality producers** | Axis Genetics | BioT | n.a. | n.a. | | | 1[a] | | | 2 | | DQP |
| | Britannia | TrPh | 130 | 23 | | | 1 | | | | | DQP |
| | Galen | TrPh | 104 | 36 | | | 1 | | | | | DQP |
| | Nycomed Amersham | TrPh | n.a. | 130 | | | 3 | 5 | | 3 | 3 | DQP |
| | Provalis | BioT | 107 | 7 | | | 1 | | | | | DQP |
| **DQPs and RPIs** | AstraZeneca | TrPh | 11,500 | 91 | 4 | 6 | 16 | 8 | 1 | 12 | 9 | RPI/DQP |
| | GlaxoSmith-Kline | TrPh | 44,679 | 174 | 6 | 20 | 22 | 60 | 3 | 41 | 26 | RPI/DQP |
| | Shire | TrPh | 475 | 18 | | 1 | | 9 | | 5 | 5 | RPI/DQP |
| **Pure diversified quality producers** | Amersham Pharmacia Biotech | TrPh | 4,500 | n.a. | | | | | | 1 | | DQP |
| | Bioglan | BioT | 567 | 72 | | | | | 1 | 1 | | DQP |
| | British Bio-tech | BioT | 250 | 18 | | | | | | 1 | | DQP |
| | Cambridge Antibody Technology | BioT | 290 | 14 | | | | | | 1 | | DQP |
| | Crusade Laboratories | BioT | n.a. | 5 | | | | | | 1 | | DQP |
| | DevCo | TrPh | 8 | 5 | | | | | | 1 | | DQP |
| | Napp | TrPh | 321 | 81 | | | | | | 1 | | DQP |
| | Oxford Glyco Sciences | BioT | 219 | n.a. | | | | | | 1 | | DQP |
| | Smith & Nephew | TrPh | 1,419 | 73 | | | | | | 1 | | DQP |

*(Continued)*

Table 2.1. Continued

| Firm type | Firm name | Technology focus | No. of employees | Firm age | Developer NCE | Licensor NCE | Developer non-NCE | Licensor non-NCE | Licensee dev. phase NCE | Licensee dev. phase non-NCE | Licensee reg. phase | Competitive strategy |
|---|---|---|---|---|---|---|---|---|---|---|---|---|
| **Marketing specialists** | Allergy Therapeutics | TrPh | 180 | 70 | | | | | | | 1 | LCP |
| | Biopharm (UK) | BioT | n.a. | n.a. | | | | | | | 1 | LCP |
| | Cambridge Laboratories | TrPh | 63 | 17 | | | | | | | 1 | LCP |
| | Virogen | BioT | n.a. | n.a. | | | | | | | 1 | LCP |

[a] Project(s) in-licensed at discovery (i.e. research or preclinical development) stage, usually from PROs (universities or research institutes).
[b] Part of projects in-licensed at discovery (i.e. research or preclinical development) stage, usually from PROs (universities or research institutes).

*Source*: PHID database (November 2004).

Table 2.2. Radical product innovators, diversified quality producers, and low-cost producers in Germany

| Firm type | Firm name | Technology focus | No. of employees | Firm age | Developer NCE | Licensor NCE | Developer non-NCE | Licensor non-NCE | Licensee dev. phase NCE | Licensee dev. phase non-NCE | Licensee reg. phase | Competitive strategy |
|---|---|---|---|---|---|---|---|---|---|---|---|---|
| **Discoverers of NCE** | BASF | TrPh | 37,444 | 139 | | 1 | | 1 | | | | RPI |
| | Merz | TrPh | 800 | 96 | | 1 | | 4 | | | | RPI |
| **Ambiguous cases** | Curacyte | BioT | 22 | 5 | | | 1[a] | | | | | RPI |
| | Degussa | TrPh | 6,000 | 5 | | | 1[a] | | | | | DQP |
| | Falk | TrPh | 99 | 44 | | | 1[a] | | | | | DQP |
| | GPC Biotech | BioT | 115 | 7 | | | 1[a] | | | | | RPI |
| | Jerini Bio Tools | BioT | 108 | 10 | | | 1[a] | | | | | RPI |
| | MediGene | BioT | 120 | 10 | | | 1[a] | | | | | RPI |
| | MorphoSys | BioT | 132 | 12 | | | 1[a] | | | | | RPI |
| | Scil Biomedicals | BioT | 100 | 5 | | | 1[a] | | | | 1 | RPI |
| | Wilex Biotechnology | BioT | 22 | 7 | | | 1[a] | | | | | RPI |
| **Diversified quality producers** | Altana | TrPh | 2,800 | 27 | | | | 9 | | 1 | 5 | DQP |
| | Gruenenthal | TrPh | 1,900 | 58 | | | 2 | | | | 5 | DQP |
| | Jenapharm | TrPh | 450 | 54 | | | 2 | | | | | DQP |
| | Madaus | TrPh | 930 | 85 | | | | 5 | 1 | 2 | | DQP |

(Continued)

**Table 2.2. Continued**

| Firm type | Firm name | Technology focus | No. of employees | Firm age | Developer NCE | Licensor NCE | Developer non-NCE | Licensor non-NCE | Licensee dev. phase NCE | Licensee dev. phase non-NCE | Licensee reg. phase | Competitive strategy |
|---|---|---|---|---|---|---|---|---|---|---|---|---|
| | Merck KGaA | TrPh | 1,800 | 336 | | | 2 | 6 | | 4 | | DQP |
| | Merckle | TrPh | 2,000 | 59 | | | 2 | | | | 1 | DQP |
| | Schwarz Pharma | TrPh | 1,200 | 58 | | | 2 | | 1 | 2 | 7 | DQP |
| **DQPs and RPIs** | ASTA Medica | TrPh | 600 | 169 | | 1 | | 1 | 1 | 1 | 3 | RPI/DQP |
| | Bayer | TrPh | 5,181 | 141 | 1 | 3 | 1 | 18 | 1 | 8 | 5 | RPI/DQP |
| | Boehringer Ingelheim | TrPh | 8,000 | 119 | | 7 | 1 | 26 | | 5 | 11 | RPI/DQP |
| | Schering AG | TrPh | 10,042 | 133 | 2 | 2 | 15 | 6 | | 8 | 4 | RPI/DQP |
| **Pure diversified quality producers** | GLE Medicon | TrPh | n.a. | n.a. | | | | | | 1 | | DQP |
| | Medac | BioT | 400 | 34 | | | | | | 2 | | DQP |
| | Paion | BioT | 60 | 4 | | | | | | 1 | | DQP |
| | Revotar | BioT | 22 | 4 | | | | | | 1 | | DQP |
| **Marketing specialists** | Plantorgan | TrPh | 100 | 30 | | | | | | | 1 | LCP |
| | Schwabe | TrPh | 695 | 138 | | | | | | | 1 | LCP |
| | Strathmann | TrPh | 460 | 30 | | | | | | | 1 | LCP |

[a] Project(s) in-licensed at discovery (i.e. research or preclinical development) stage, usually from PROs (universities or research institutes).
[b] Part of projects in-licensed at discovery (i.e. research or preclinical development) stage, usually from PROs (universities or research institutes).

*Source*: PHID database (November 2004).

Table 2.3. Radical product innovators, diversified quality producers, and low-cost producers in Italy

| Firm Type | Firm name | Technology focus | No. of employees | Firm age | Developer NCE | Licensor NCE | Developer non-NCE | Licensor non-NCE | Licensee dev. phase NCE | Licensee dev. phase non-NCE | Licensee reg. phase | Competitive strategy |
|---|---|---|---|---|---|---|---|---|---|---|---|---|
| **Discoverers of NCE** | Abiogen | BioT | 257 | 7 | 1 | 1 | | 7 | | | | RPI |
| | Alfa Wassermann | TrPh | 700 | 56 | | 1 | | 4 | | | 3 | RPI |
| | Ausonia | n.a. | n.a. | n.a. | | 1 | | 3 | | | | RPI |
| | Istituto di Ricerche Sigma Tau | TrPh | 67 | 19 | | 2 | | 5 | | | 5 | RPI |
| | Medioloanum | TrPh | 253 | 32 | | 1 | 1[a] | 4 | | | 1 | RPI |
| | Poli | TrPh | 126 | 25 | 1 | | 3[b] | | | | | RPI |
| | SPA | TrPh | 211 | 57 | | 1 | | 1 | | | | RPI |
| **Ambiguous cases** | Fidia | TrPh | n.a. | 58 | | | 1[a] | | | | | DQP |
| | Italpharmaco | TrPh | 600 | 66 | | | 1[a] | | | | 1 | DQP |
| | Rotta Research | BioT | 188 | 43 | | | | 1 | | | | RPI |
| **Diversified quality producers** | Chiesi | TrPh | 2,600 | 69 | | | 2 | 7 | 2 | 2 | | DQP |
| | Recordati | TrPh | 1,013 | 78 | | | | 8 | 1 | 1 | 4 | DQP |
| | Zambon | TrPh | 836 | 98 | | | 3 | | 1 | 2 | 1 | DQP |

(Continued)

Table 2.3. Continued

| Firm Type | Firm name | Technology focus | No. of employees | Firm age | Developer NCE | Licensor NCE | Developer non-NCE | Licensor non-NCE | Licensee dev. phase NCE | Licensee dev. phase non-NCE | Licensee reg. phase | Competitive strategy |
|---|---|---|---|---|---|---|---|---|---|---|---|---|
| **DQPs and RPIs** | Bracco | TrPh | 1,456 | 77 | 1 | 1 | 1 | 3 | | 1 | 1 | RPI/DQP |
| | Menarini | TrPh | 2,050 | 118 | 1 | | 4 | | 1 | 1 | 5 | RPI/DQP |
| **Pure diversified quality producers** | Bruno | TrPh | n.a. | n.a. | | | | | 1 | 1 | | DQP |
| | Dompe | TrPh | 600 | 64 | | | | | | 1 | 2 | DQP |
| | Eurand | TrPh | 343 | 35 | | | | | | 1 | | DQP |
| | Geymonat | TrPh | 83 | 76 | | | | | 1 | 1 | | DQP |
| **Marketing specialists** | Biotoscana | BioT | n.a. | n.a. | | | | | | | 1 | LCP |
| | Formenti | TrPh | 450 | 50 | | | | | | | 1 | LCP |
| | Guidotti | TrPh | 480 | 90 | | | | | | | 2 | LCP |
| | Lusopharmaco | TrPh | 600 | 53 | | | | | | | 2 | LCP |
| | Mipharm | TrPh | 243 | 6 | | | | | | | 1 | LCP |
| | Neopharmed | TrPh | 332 | n.a. | | | | | | | 1 | LCP |
| | Rottapharm | TrPh | 371 | 43 | | | | | | | 1 | LCP |
| | Segix | TrPh | 74 | 42 | | | | | | | 1 | LCP |

[a] Project(s) in-licensed at discovery (i.e. research or preclinical development) stage, usually from PROs (universities or research institutes).
[b] Part of projects in-licensed at discovery (i.e. research or preclinical development) stage, usually from PROs (universities or research institutes).

*Source*: PHID database (November 2004).

producers on the other, requires particular attention. Whilst one group of ***pure diversified quality producers*** which in-license pharmaceutical projects at the development stage can be unambiguously recognized, the identification of pure radical product innovators is more difficult.

Interestingly, not a single firm exists that merely develops or out-licenses pharmaceutical products based on an NCE. The reason for this resides in the unpredictability of radical pharmaceutical innovation. As in any research project, the chance element involved in pharmaceutical research is high (Muffatto and Giardina 2003: 111). Hence, a pharmaceutical firm *cannot be sure* that it will discover an NCE. It can make all possible efforts, yet it may ultimately end up using its research outcomes for improving an already known chemical entity. The discovery of an NCE is therefore far less frequent than the improvement of a known chemical entity (Bottazzi et al. 2001: 1163). However, a pharmaceutical firm *can decide to focus* on the research stage, i.e. on the discovery and preclinical development of pharmaceutical projects, in that it out-licenses their development and registration. Accordingly, licensors of both NCE and non-NCE projects are more innovative than their licensees. All pharmaceutical firms which have (developed and/or) out-licensed *at least one* pharmaceutical project *based on an NCE* are therefore classified as radical product innovators because they are ***discoverers of NCEs*** with a strong propensity to out-license downstream activities, i.e. clinical development and registration.

This leaves us with a group of ***ambiguous cases***. It is composed of those firms which are either pure licensors of already discovered chemical entities or developers of known chemical entities that were in-licensed at the research stage from public research organizations (henceforth PROs): universities or research institutes. On the one hand, these firms are not particularly innovative as the resulting drugs are based on known chemical entities. On the other hand, they are innovative as the *licensors* focus on the research stage of a pharmaceutical project. Similarly, the *developers* of this group have a research focus, as they collaborate closely with PROs from which they in-licensed pharmaceutical projects before the development stage. Since their classification is not possible purely on the basis of their involvement in the different stages of pharmaceutical projects, I decided to categorize these ambiguous firms on the basis of their technological approach. Accordingly, all biotechnology firms are classified as radical product innovators, because they use modern approaches of molecular biology and genomic sciences which, in turn, enable a more deliberate drug design. Conversely, traditional pharmaceutical firms using experimental approaches to drug design (see Drews 2000) are classified as diversified quality producers.

Another, partly similar group of firms can be identified. It is similar to the group of ambiguous cases in that firms are either developers and/or licensors of already discovered chemical entities. However, unlike the ambiguous cases, these firms do *not* in-license pharmaceutical projects at the research stage but at the *development stage*. This, in turn, suggests that they are incrementally rather than radically innovative. Accordingly, they are classified as ***diversified quality producers***. In addition, all those firms are also categorized as diversified quality producers which are exclusive developers of pharmaceutical products based on known chemical entities.

Finally, a last group of cases consists of those pharmaceutical companies which pursue both an ***RPI and a DQP*** strategy. On the one hand, they are radical product innovators, as they out-license (and develop) pharmaceutical products based on NCEs. On the other hand, these firms pursue a DQP strategy by developing drugs based on previously discovered chemical entities, or by in-licensing pharmaceutical projects at the development stage. These firms are therefore classified as radical product innovators and diversified quality producers alike.

While the identification of a firm's competitive strategy at the micro level is not without its problems, the classification approach thus far clearly illustrates one point. Patterns in the strategies of pharmaceutical firms are strikingly homogeneous in Italy, Germany, and the UK. Yet, the existence of this last group of DQP and RPI strategists raises an important question to be addressed before a final evaluation is possible. Are the three competitive strategies mutually exclusive or can one firm pursue two, or even three, strategies at the same time?

## 2.3. ARE COMPETITIVE STRATEGIES MUTUALLY EXCLUSIVE?

To answer this question, it is important to note how the scope for different strategies varies over time. The path-breaking findings of Abernathy and Utterback (Utterback 1994: 90–101) and further management studies of various industries (Levitt 1965; Klepper and Graddy 1990; Klepper and Simons 1997; Walker 2003: chapter 4) show that firms initiate a product's life cycle by proposing radically new product designs. Once a dominant design has emerged, firms usually start to change their strategy and turn from radical into incremental innovators or imitators. In other words, as time goes by, firms which initially pursued an RPI strategy turn either into diversified quality producers making slight improvements to a once radically new product, or into low-cost producers selling at lowest-possible prices.

Considering the outcome of this transformation process, Porter shows that DQP and LCP are mutually exclusive strategies because 'differentiation [i.e. DQP] is usually costly' (Porter 1985: 119–20) and therefore not compatible with LCP. The reason is that 'a firm must often incur costs to be unique. (...) Providing superior applications engineering support usually requires additional engineers, for example, while a highly skilled sales force typically costs more than a less skilled one' (ibid.: 127–8).

Porter (1990: 48–9) also points out that radical innovations are often made by outsiders to an industry. This supports Utterback's finding that the strongest resistance to radically new technologies often comes from the industry's DQP and LCP strategists which were radically innovative at the last innovation wave. Their behaviour is explained by the significant sunk costs that these firms had to make in order to produce highly sophisticated or particularly cheap goods. Inventing entirely new products would mean competing against their own goods and risking that the latter will sooner or later become obsolete (Utterback 1994: 162–5, 223–6). Studies of traditional industries thus show that RPI, DQP, and LCP are mutually exclusive, as firms maximize their returns on investment if they pursue just one competitive strategy.

This argument also seems to apply to the pharmaceutical industry (see Bottazzi et al. 2001: in particular 1163; Orsenigo et al. 2001). The finding that one clear-cut group of low-cost producers (*marketing specialists*), *(pure) diversified quality producers*, and radical product innovators (*NCE discoverers* being often pure licensors) is contained in the firm sample confirms the idea that LCP, DQP, and RPI are mutually exclusive strategies. But how to explain the occurrence of all the *ambiguous cases* and of those firms that pursue both an *RPI and a DQP* strategy?

Compared to traditional industries, the pharmaceutical industry is peculiar in two respects. First, like all *high-tech* industries, the technology intensity of pharmaceutical R&D allows for a comparatively frequent emergence of radically new products. But contrary to traditional industries, these products – based on NCEs – do not lead to a wholesale transformation of the industry. Their effect rather is to improve the market position of the discovering firm. The technology intensity of the pharmaceutical industry thus makes RPI a particularly attractive strategy, as the risk of making the firm's own products obsolete is low.

The second peculiarity of the pharmaceutical industry is that the development of new products is *extremely expensive* (see, e.g. Muffatto and Giardina 2003: 108–10). Before obtaining a marketing authorization, a pharmaceutical firm must carry out numerous clinical tests to document all features and possible (side) effects of its new product. This means that any radical product innovator which has brought a discovery to the stage of clinical development is faced with the following decision. Does it want to focus on RPI and out-license the development and registration of its discovery, or does it aspire to turn the discovery into marketable drugs on its own?

In the latter case, the firm will find it necessary to start pursuing a DQP strategy, as it can thereby cover the massive costs of clinical development.

The longer a patent shelters a pharmaceutical product from low-cost imitations, the higher the product's returns on investment. Therefore, once a patent expires, pharmaceutical firms often seek to obtain a new patent, or to extend patent protection, by introducing slight improvements to the once radically new drug. Furthermore, a pharmaceutical firm is well advised to in-license pharmaceutical projects in its field of expertise in order to use its development and registration facilities efficiently. Any research-intensive firm that wants to develop and register its pharmaceutical discoveries on its own will thus find it necessary to cover costs by pursuing a DQP strategy in parallel to an RPI strategy. This also opens up the opportunity for the radical product innovator to turn into a pure diversified quality producer.

Following this logic, it can be argued that the group of *ambiguous cases* consists mostly of those firms that have reached the development stage where they must decide whether to pursue a *pure RPI strategy* out-licensing clinical development and registration, *an RPI* ***and*** *a DQP strategy*, or whether to use their expertise to become *(pure) diversified quality producers*. If this lifecycle argument holds true, the *discoverers of NCEs*, the *DQP/RPI firms*, and the *(pure) diversified quality producers* should be older than those firms classified as *ambiguous cases*. To empirically assess this idea, I assigned an ambiguity score of 0 to all NCE discoverers, DQP/RPI firms, and (pure) diversified quality producers, whereas I attributed an ambiguity score of 1 to all ambiguous cases. The result of a bivariate correlation analysis provides empirical support, as it reveals a strong correlation between a firm's age and the pursuit of an unambiguous competitive strategy ($R = -0.405$; $R^2 = 0.164$; $p < 0.001$).

Turning back to those firms which are both RPI and DQP strategists simultaneously, it is interesting to note that this group of firms consists exclusively of the industry's international giants. Interviews with representatives, and webpage analyses, of these RPI/DQP firms revealed that the latter usually embed each strategy in a separate business unit. From an operational point of view, these are independent, because they encompass all departments necessary for discovering, developing, and producing drugs. Accordingly, interviewees repeatedly described the RPI and DQP units as organizationally separate entities, which are only interdependent insofar as they are financed by the same holding company. From a transaction-cost perspective, this interdependence seems to be explained by accounting practices. Given that the development of radically and incrementally new drugs is both risky and extremely expensive, losses of one business unit can be balanced by the profits of the other unit (see also Drews 1999). Despite this financial interdependence, I decided to adopt the view of my interviewees that *one* RPI/DQP firm does not pursue *two* different competitive strategies, but that *two* different business units belonging to one holding company pursue *one* competitive strategy apiece. In sum, the argument that RPI, DQP, and LCP are mutually exclusive strategies, because they all follow a different operational logic, as well as the classification of RPI/DQP firms as two cases, thus seem to be justified from both a theoretical and an empirical perspective.[16]

## 2.4. FINAL ASSESSMENT

Given that strategy patterns have proven to be strikingly homogeneous across countries (Section 2.2) and that the simultaneous pursuit of several strategies does not seem feasible (Section 2.3), firms do not appear to exploit the comparative institutional advantage of their economy by specializing in the facilitated strategy. A final assessment will provide an overview and further insights into this core argument of the competitiveness literature. Do firms in the UK specialize in the pursuit of an RPI strategy, whereas German companies pursue a DQP strategy, whilst their Italian counterparts engage mostly in LCP?

Table 2.4 summarizes the results obtained from sampling the PHID database[17] and negates the idea that the *majority* of firms in one economy specialize in the same strategy. Instead, Table 2.4 shows that firms in Germany, Italy, and the UK pursue RPI, DQP, and LCP strategies to a similar extent. While

**Table 2.4.** Summary results: RPI, DQP, and LCP strategists in the UK, Germany, and Italy

| | **Radical product innovators** | | **Diversified quality producers** | | **Low-cost producers** | | **Total** | |
|---|---|---|---|---|---|---|---|---|
| | **No. firms** | ***% firms*** | **No. firms** | ***% firms*** | **No. firms** | ***% firms*** | **No. firms** | ***% firms*** |
| **UK** | 19 | *47.5* | 17 | *42.5* | 4 | *10.0* | 40 | *39.2* |
| **Germany** | 13 | *39.4* | 17 | *51.5* | 3 | *9.1* | 33 | *32.4* |
| **Italy** | 10 | *34.5* | 11 | *37.9* | 8 | *27.6* | 29 | *28.4* |
| **Total** | 42 | | 45 | | 15 | | 102 | *100.0* |
| **Average** | 14 | *41.2* | 15 | *44.1* | 5 | *14.7* | 34 | |
| **Above average** | | *6.3* | | *7.4* | | *12.9* | | |

*Source*: PHID database.

16 In this respect, it is worth noting that analyses presented in Chapters 3–5 confirm the operational incompatibility of RPI, DQP, and LCP as each strategy requires a very specific and distinct set of input factors.

17 The nine firms which pursue both an RPI and a DQP strategy are counted as two cases each.

47.5 per cent of pharmaceutical firms are *RPI* strategists in the UK, 39.4 per cent of firms pursue this strategy in Germany, and 34.5 per cent of their counterparts do so in Italy. A *DQP* strategy is pursued by 51.5 per cent of German firms, by 37.9 per cent of Italian companies, and by 42.5 per cent of British firms. Finally, the probability that firms engage in *LCP* is 27.6 per cent in Italy, 10.0 per cent in the UK, and 9.1 per cent in Germany. Thus, even though the share of firms engaged in the same strategy varies slightly from one economy to another, it is not drastically different between the countries considered.

Nevertheless, slight specialization patterns can be observed. Table 2.4 accordingly reports the average probability with which firms in Germany, Italy, and the UK pursue RPI, DQP, or LCP strategies. Interestingly, British firms are 6.3 per cent more likely to engage in radical product innovation than the average pharmaceutical firm included in the sample. Similarly, the probability of pursuing a DQP strategy is 7.4 per cent higher for a German firm than for the sample's average company. Finally, Italian firms show a preference for low cost production, as they pursue this strategy 12.9 per cent more often than the average pharmaceutical company. British companies thus seem to prefer RPI, German firms DQP, and Italian firms LCP strategies.

Does this finding suggest that firms in one economy specialize in the institutionally supported strategy as a *plurality*, rather than the majority, pursues this strategic approach? This idea would be supported empirically if the observed specialization patterns were pronounced enough to provide statistically significant results. A crosstab analysis assessing the strength of association between a firm's *country* and its *strategy* offers insights. The results obtained are reported in Table 2.5. At a glance, the table indicates that the modest convergence patterns observed are not statistically significant, which is true for both the Chi-square value (Chi-square = 5.996; 2 cells = 22.2 % with expected count less than 5; $p > 0.10$) and the value of *Gramer's V* (*Gramer's V* = .171; $p > 0.10$). Hence, the identification of competitive strategies through micro-level indicators does not lend empirical support to the idea that a plurality of pharmaceutical firms within the same economy converge on the same strategy.

What are we to think about these results? How are the above micro-level findings compatible with the specialization argument of the competitiveness literature based on macro-level analyses? Ever since the seminal article of Robinson (1950; see also Coleman 1986, 1990), social scientists are warned not to test theories about micro-level relationships on the basis of macro-level data, as the discrepancies between correlations of micro-level indicators and their aggregation at the macro level are substantial. The reason is that, depending on the array rules employed, important information on individual cases is lost when the latter are aggregated at a higher level. This causes correlations of aggregated indicators to deliver stronger results than correlations of the same,

**Table 2.5.** Results of crosstab analysis: 'Country' by 'competitive strategy'[a]

| | | | Competitive Strategy | | | Total |
|---|---|---|---|---|---|---|
| | | | RPI | DQP | LCP | |
| **Country** | **UK** | *Count* | *19.0* | *17.0* | *4.0* | *40.0* |
| | | Expected count | 16.5 | 17.6 | 5.9 | 40.0 |
| | **Germany** | *Count* | *13.0* | *17.0* | *3.0* | *33.0* |
| | | Expected count | 13.6 | 14.6 | 4.9 | 33.0 |
| | **Italy** | *Count* | *10.0* | *11.0* | *8.0* | *29.0* |
| | | Expected count | 11.9 | 12.8 | 4.3 | 29.0 |
| **Total** | | *Count* | *42.0* | *45.0* | *15.0* | *102.0* |
| | | Expected count | 42.0 | 45.0 | 15.0 | 102.0 |

[a] *Chi-Square* = 5.996 (2 cells = 22.2% with expected count less than 5); $p > 0.10$; *Cramer's V* = 0.171; $p > 0.10$.

disaggregated measures. The higher the level of data aggregation, the less representative are macro-level correlations of micro-level effects (Feige and Watts 1972).

A similar argument seems to explain why the above specialization effects are weak compared to the specialization effects revealed by the competitiveness literature.[18] Whenever a firm's strategy is identified through a macro-level indicator, for example its industry, less information on each individual case is preserved than when the firm's strategy is identified through micro-level measures, such as product novelty and value-chain focus. This loss of information seems to explain why strategy specialization is stronger when measured by a macro indicator. Imagine that a firm's industry had been taken as a proxy for its strategy, so that all biotech firms were identified as radical product innovators, all traditional pharmaceutical firms as diversified quality producers, and all generics firms as low-cost producers. Then columns two and three of Tables 2.1–2.3 would reveal a strong specialization of British firms in RPI, of German and Italian firms in DQP, while no firm would specialize in LCP. Yet, such a macro-level assessment of competitive strategies would also entail the simplifying assumption that all firms in one industry pursue the same competitive strategy. All biotech firms engaged in DQP and all traditional pharmaceutical firms pursuing RPI or LCP strategies would be ignored. It is this loss of information on micro-level variety that enables the competitiveness literature to identify convergence trends due to the use of macro-level indicators.

[18] For examples, see Porter (1990: 179–541), Keck (1993), Walker (1993), Pavitt and Patel (1999), Hall and Soskice (2001*a*: 36–44), Amable (2003), and Hancké and Herrmann (2007).

## 2.5. CONCLUSIONS AND OUTLOOK ON FURTHER RESEARCH

The previous assessment of whether firms in different economies specialize in the pursuit of the same competitive strategies has illustrated one crucial point. Whether or not statistically significant specialization patterns are observed depends on the sophistication of the strategy measures employed. The widely diffused approach of competitiveness scholars of identifying competitive strategies through *macro-level* indicators based on the industries of different firms yields strong specialization results. Importantly, though, this approach entails the simplifying assumption that all firms within the same industry pursue the same competitive strategy. The more fine-grained indicator used here, combining the technological novelty of a firm's products and its value-chain focus, has shown however that firms within the same industry can pursue different strategies. And, as soon as this indicator, capturing richer *micro-level* information, is employed, the previously strong specialization results turn out to be decisively more modest and, even, statistically insignificant. In other words, the loss of information that is related to the use of macro-level indicators seems to explain why competitiveness scholars find strong effects of strategy specialization within the same economy. Contrary to this, my analyses indicate that neither the majority nor a statistically significant plurality of pharmaceutical firms pursue the same competitive strategy in Germany, Italy, and the UK alike.

This finding is puzzling. It raises the question of how firms can so numerously compete through strategies that are not supported by national institutions.[19] To be clear, it is less surprising that firms within one economy, and even within one industry, engage in different strategies. In order to gain a competitive advantage, they need to distinguish themselves from their competitors through a strategy that allows them to produce either newer, better, or cheaper products.

However, the puzzle to be solved *how* firms can pursue diverse strategies. Can RBV theory offer the advice that firms, to pursue the same strategy, can employ *different types* of the same input factor, as long as the latter is turned into a valuable, rare, imperfectly imitable, and strategically non-substitutable resource (Barney 1991)? Or is the competitiveness literature nevertheless able

[19] Admittedly, the sample drawn from the PHID database reveals small, albeit statistically insignificant, specialization effects (Section 2.4). Given the limited sample size, one might expect that, with increasing size, specialization patterns become more pronounced and, ultimately, statistically significant. While this would lend empirical support to the specialization argument of the competitiveness literature, the aforementioned puzzle remains the same: How can so many firms deviate and compete through strategies that are not facilitated by national institutions?

to provide answers? Do firms need specific types of one input factor to pursue a given strategy? Find, if so, how can firms secure the required factor types in those economies where they are not provided by national institutions?

Part II will shed light on these questions. By studying those three input factors that are key to any strategy, Chapters 3–5 ask: Do firms require a specific type of finance (Chapter 3), component standards (Chapter 4), and labour qualifications (Chapter 5) for each strategy? Should empirical evidence confirm this argument of the competitiveness literature, the next question to be answered by the respective chapter is: How do firms provide the required factor types in different economies? This question is particularly relevant for those input factor types that are not provided by national institutions. How can firms compete despite comparative institutional disadvantages? Can they draw on functionally equivalent institutions and, if so, on which ones?

Should empirical evidence however support the idea of the RBV approach that firms can use different types of one input factor to pursue the same strategy, the next question to be asked by each chapter is: How have firms succeeded in transforming the respective factor types into valuable, rare, imperfectly imitable, and non-substitutable resources? Does a systematic approach for such transformation procedures exist?

# PART II

# Linking Institutions, Input Factors, and Competitive Strategies

# 3

# Linking Financial Market Institutions, Corporate Finance, and Competitive Strategies

Are competitive strategies influenced by financial market institutions promoting the availability of particular capital types? If so, do firms exploit these comparative institutional advantages? And how do they cope with comparative institutional disadvantages? To begin with, it is hard to imagine how firms could operate without financing their activities. *That* finance constitutes an indispensable input factor for the pursuit of any competitive strategy is indeed uncontested in the competitiveness literature. But does it matter *how* finance is provided? After all, one might be tempted to think that firms, as long as they can cover their expenditure, care little whether their financiers are banks, shareholders, or business angels. This is however erroneous, argues the competitiveness literature. Depending on the terms of financing, different competitive strategies are facilitated. It is thereby unimportant which actors provide finance; what counts are the conditions upon which finance is granted.

The reason for the impact of corporate finance on corporate strategies is that firms cannot acquire capital without solving the related principal–agent problem with their investors. This coordination problem arises as the interests of the firm's managers (agents) can differ substantially from the interests of its financiers (see, e.g. Mayer 1998: 145; Hall and Soskice 2001*a*: 6–7; Kenyon and Vitols 2004: 11). As a rule, investors want to be assured that their money is used in such a way that it yields the highest possible return on investment. But '[m]anagers may indulge in empire-building, which includes investments in large offices, in staff departments or in R&D activities, launching of over-extensive advertising campaigns or acquisitions' (Gelauff 1997: 347). To solve this principal–agent problem, mechanisms need to be found that keep managers in check by aligning their interests with those of external investors. Two such solutions exist. Investors can make sure that their funds are used efficiently either by determining the returns on their investment *ex ante* or by preserving the right to participate in the decision-making on how their funds are used. Whilst the provision of *debt finance* is typically made dependent on the former type of agreement, the provision of *share capital* is made dependent on the latter.

Regarding the provision of share capital, scholars of corporate finance have pointed out that the extent to which shareholders can influence management decisions differs between corporate governance systems. In *insider systems*, as found in Germany for example, shareholders elect a supervisory board, which exerts control over the management board. This supervisory board comprises representatives of both shareholders and employees. It may or may not have the power to appoint managers. More importantly, though, the members of the supervisory board have *inter alia* the right to approve major investment decisions, to control the annual statement of accounts, and to consult the firm's management on major corporate affairs. Thus, shareholders in insider systems not only acquire considerable insight into how a firm is run, they also have notable decision-making power in all major financial issues (Gelauff 1997: 350–1, 357–62; Mayer 1998: 145–9).

In *outsider systems* such as the UK, by contrast, shareholders merely elect the firm's management. They do *not* elect a supervisory board that would, in turn, participate in the decision-making process on major corporate affairs. To monitor whether their funds provide an acceptable return on investment, shareholders are therefore limited to consulting 'outsider' information, like publicly available accounting indicators (e.g. corporate balance sheets or the performance of their shares on the stock market). If these accounting indicators and, hence, the return on investment are disappointing, shareholders may decide to rapidly exit the company by selling their stocks. No other means exists to ensure that managers use the capital provided in a profitable way. Outsider control mechanisms therefore oblige managers to maximize shareholder value and to focus on the short-term performance of their firm's shares (Gelauff 1997: 348–50; Bronk 1998: 5–7; Mayer 1998: 145–9).

Various contributors to the competitiveness literature argue that the diverse mechanisms which credit grantors, insider shareholders, and outsider shareholders use to monitor the return on their investment promote different competitive strategies. While these arguments are most advanced in NIS contributions (Hollingsworth 2000; Casper and Matraves 2003; see also Lindgaard Christensen 1992; Pavitt and Patel 1999: in particular 104–7) and VoC contributions (Hall and Soskice 2001*a*: 36–44; Vitols 2001; Amable 2003; Börsch 2007) to the competitiveness literature, they are also proposed in MBV studies (see Porter 1990) and implicit in Ohlin's (1933: 77) claim that the 'difference between "long" and "short" capital is of a permanent character, and in some cases must be recognised by their being treated as separate factors of production'. Studies of various effects of corporate governance systems have even developed into a separate strand of institutional literature on corporate finance (see, e.g. Gelauff 1997; Bronk 1998; Mayer 1998; Bottazzi and Da Rin 2002; Deeg 2005, 2006). According to these analyses, *debt finance* is particularly conducive to strategies of diversified quality production (DQP) and low-cost production (LCP) alike, while *insider share capital* (i.e. capital provided by shareholders in insider systems)[1] facilitates mostly DQP. *Outsider share capital* (provided by shareholders in outsider systems)[2] is said to promote strategies of radical product innovation (RPI).[3]

Since firms are expected to exploit comparative institutional advantages, the literature proposes that firms specialize: in RPI if they are based in a country with an outsider corporate governance system, in DQP if they are active in an economy with an insider system, and in LCP if their country makes debt finance a particularly attractive option to finance corporate activities – sometimes because no clear-cut corporate governance model exists. In other words, firms in the UK are expected to specialize in RPI, companies in Germany are assumed to prefer DQP, and their counterparts in Italy are said to engage in LCP strategies.[4]

Chapter 2 has cast doubt on this reasoning, as firms in the same economy were found to pursue a similar variety of competitive strategies. How is this possible? Is it that firms can use *different* types of finance to pursue the same strategy, thereby contradicting the aforementioned arguments of the competitiveness literature? After all, these arguments have thus far hardly been systematically tested at the micro level. Hence, a micro-level assessment might show that firms can pursue the same strategy by employing different types of finance

[1] To avoid conceptual confusion, one should be aware that the literature also refers to the *insider system* of corporate governance (Mayer 1998) – associated with important shareholder rights and limited corporate flexibility – as the *stakeholder system* (Mayer 1998; Börsch 2007) or *stakeholder model* (Bronk 1998; Vitols 2001). The type of finance provided is therefore not only called *insider*, but also *long-term*, or *patient share capital/finance* (Bronk 1998; Mayer 1998; Hall and Soskice 2001*a*: 22, see also 29).

[2] For further conceptual clarification, it should be noted that the *outsider system* of corporate governance (Mayer 1998) – associated with limited shareholder rights and high corporate flexibility – is also referred to in the literature as the *shareholder system* (Börsch 2007) or *shareholder model* (Bronk 1998; Vitols 2001). Accordingly, the type of finance provided is not only termed *outsider*, but also *short-term*, or *impatient share capital/finance* (Bronk 1998; see Hall and Soskice 2001*a*: 29).

[3] See in particular Gelauff (1997: 346–56), Bronk (1998), Mayer (1998), Hollingsworth (2000: 626–30), Hall and Soskice (2001*a*: 36–44), Vitols (2001), and Casper and Matraves (2003); see also Lindgaard Christensen (1992), and Amable (2003).

[4] See in particular Bronk (1998: 13–15), Hollingsworth (2000: 626–30), Hall and Soskice (2001*a*: 36–44), Vitols (2001: 350–60), Amable (2003), Casper and Matraves (2003), and Börsch (2007); see also Porter (1990), Gelauff (1997), Mayer (1998), and Deeg (2005).

if the latter constitute a unique resource to the firm – as is suggested by the originators of the RBV theory (see, in particular, Rumelt 1984; Wernerfelt 1984; Barney 1991; Conner 1991; Peteraf 1993). Then, the crucial question would be to understand how firms turn different financial sources into unique corporate resources. Can a systematic process be identified? But, suppose we find that firms need *particular* types of finance for each competitive strategy, as suggested by the competitiveness literature. Then the subsequent question to be answered is: how can firms secure the required financial means in different corporate governance systems? How can they compete despite comparative institutional disadvantages?

To shed light on these issues, the chapter is organized as follows. Section 3.1 develops hypotheses on the importance of particular financial means for competitive strategies. Sections 3.2 and 3.3 test these hypotheses and find support for the argument of the competitiveness literature that RPI, DQP, and LCP strategies require particular types of corporate finance. In its last part, Section 3.3 therefore analyses how firms can compete in those economies where the necessary financial means are scarce. Section 3.4 summarizes the results and concludes with an interpretation that relates the various findings to the arguments of the competitiveness literature on the one hand and the RBV literature on the other.

## 3.1. HYPOTHESES AS TO HOW DIFFERENT TYPES OF FINANCE FACILITATE RPI, DQP, AND LCP STRATEGIES

Why do debt finance, insider share capital, and outsider share capital facilitate different competitive strategies? To begin with the former, *debt finance* is said to promote DQP and LCP, but to hinder RPI strategies (see Gelauff 1997: 346, 353–4; Hollingsworth 2000: 628; Vitols 2001: 352),[5] as it is provided on the condition that creditor and borrower agree on a sum of money, i.e. the amount of interests, which the borrower must pay back in addition to the loan granted. Since the return on investment is fixed from the outset, creditors cannot achieve higher profits than the invested sum itself increased by the amount

[5] It should be noted that the competitiveness literature does not propose explicit arguments on the type of finance that facilitates LCP, because this strategy is often neglected in those two strands which have a specific focus on corporate governance systems: NIS and VoC theories. However, by extrapolating from the literature's reasoning on RPI and DQP strategies to LCP, one can deduce how debt finance, insider share capital, and outsider share capital influence LCP strategies.

of interests. To safely recover their funds, creditors are therefore risk-averse. Instead of investing in RPI projects with an elevated risk of failure, they prefer to invest in DQP or LCP projects which promise secure returns (Gelauff 1997: 346). Whenever firms incur high debts to finance their activities, they are unlikely to pursue an RPI strategy, but are rather engaged in DQP or LCP (see also Gelauff 1997: 353–4).

*Insider share capital*, by contrast, is said to promote DQP because pronounced shareholder control rights motivate actors with a particular interest in a firm to numerously acquire its shares. A firm's founding family, its banks, suppliers, and processors are therefore often major shareholders in insider systems and strongly represented on the supervisory board – together with the employee representatives (Bronk 1998: 11–12; Mayer 1998: 158–9; Casper and Matraves 2003: 1868–70; Kenyon and Vitols 2004: 17–18). This facilitates DQP, but hinders the pursuit of LCP and RPI strategies, for three reasons. First, long-term and trust-based relations develop between a firm and its major stakeholders because the latter, represented on the supervisory board, make sure that managers do not quickly dismiss employees or switch to cheaper suppliers in periods of economic downturn (Bronk 1998: 14). Such job security motivates the workforce to acquire highly-specific qualifications and increases the willingness of suppliers to contribute to the firm's quality management. At the same time, however, long-term relations reduce the firm's leverage on its suppliers to enforce deliveries at the lowest possible prices. Similarly, workers find it hardly necessary to change employment which, in turn, reduces their inventiveness and creativity and, hence, their capacities to come up with radically new ideas (Bronk 1998: 14; Mayer 1998: 159–60; Hall and Soskice 2001*a*: 39–40; Casper and Matraves 2003: 1870–1). Second, since block shareholders often entertain important business relations with 'their' firm, they have a vested interest in its persistence. They are thus risk-averse and prefer market strategies with secure returns to high-risk strategies. Managers are therefore hardly obliged to divest rapidly from unprofitable business units (Gelauff 1997: 353–4; Casper and Matraves 2003: 1871–2). Third, major shareholders are often active in the same or related industries and can thus make an important contribution to the firm's market knowledge. While banks help to evaluate investment projects, suppliers provide valuable information about technological development and niche markets. This, in turn, makes business activities in high-quality segments particularly interesting, while the wholesale shift from existing to radically new production activities becomes less attractive (Bronk 1998: 14–15).

Since reduced monitoring capacities of shareholders in outsider systems oblige managers to focus on the maximization of shareholder value, *outsider share capital* is said to further RPI, but hinder DQP and LCP, for three reasons. First, shareholders prefer high-risk, high-return strategies which, if pursued successfully, maximize shareholder value because 'the costs of bankruptcy in case of total failure of high-risk strategies are divided between shareholders and creditors' (Gelauff 1997: 346). Second, managers – who are highly autonomous in their investment decisions due to the limited monitoring capacities of shareholders – rapidly reallocate resources to those radically innovative projects which promise the highest returns. Outsider share capital can thereby lead to systematic underinvestment in low-risk, low-return strategies:, i.e. DQP and LCP (Gelauff 1997: 348; Casper and Matraves 2003: 1871–2). Finally, outsider shareholder finance also disadvantages DQP and LCP strategies in that it hinders the development of long-term, trust-based relations between a firm, its workforce and suppliers. In order to maintain shareholder value, managers are obliged to dismiss employees and to look for cheaper suppliers as soon as company sales start to decline. In outsider systems, employees are thus discouraged to acquire specific qualifications, while suppliers are reluctant to cooperate closely in a firm's quality management (Gelauff 1997: 352–3; Bronk 1998: 7; Casper and Matraves 2003: 1870–1).

In sum, the following hypotheses on the impact of finance on competitive strategies can be derived from the competitiveness literature:[6]

Hypothesis 1 (H1):
(a) Outsider share capital facilitates RPI, whereas
(b) insider share capital and
(c) debt finance hinder this competitive strategy.

Hypothesis 2 (H2):
(a) Debt finance on the one hand and
(b) insider share capital on the other promote DQP, whereas
(c) outsider share capital hampers this strategy.

Hypothesis 3 (H3):
(a) Debt finance furthers the pursuit of an LCP strategy, whereas
(b) both insider share capital and
(c) outsider share capital hinder this strategy.

To assess the relative importance of particular finance types for competitive strategies, rival explanations need to be tested. While one can hardly contest that *finance* constitutes a necessary input factor for *any strategy*, correlation analyses of the above hypotheses will illustrate whether particular *types* of finance are required for *each of the three strategies*. But even if these analyses reveal strong correlations, it is still unclear whether the respective finance types, or alternative factors, exert a stronger influence on corporate strategies. Only if

[6] See note 3.

particular types of finance have a stronger strategy impact than the strongest rival factor will empirical evidence confirm the claim that these finance types constitute decisive input factors for each strategy.

The strategy studies of the innovation and strategic management literature offer advice on rivalling factors (Levitt 1965; Klepper and Graddy 1990; Utterback 1994; Klepper and Simons 1997; Walker 2003: chapter 4). In addition to input factors resulting from the solution of coordination problems – finance, component standards, and labour qualifications – the strongest determinant of a firm's strategy seems to be its age. As already laid out in Section 2.3, radically new innovations do not often come from incumbent firms, but are rather proposed by small and comparatively young (start-up) companies which are outsiders to the industry (Porter 1990: 48–9; Utterback 1994: 90–101, 160–5). The reason for this is that radical innovation often makes existing products obsolete. Incumbent firms have therefore little interest in pursuing a strategy which accelerates the decline of their own products (Utterback 1994: 160–5, 223–6). Thus, young corporate age seems to facilitate RPI because young firms usually have few or no products that risk becoming obsolete if a radically new innovation is made. The opposite holds true for the pursuit of DQP and LCP strategies. Thus, to assess the relative importance of particular finance types for competitive strategies, the rival hypothesis to be tested is the following.

Hypothesis 4 (H4):
(a) Young corporate age is conducive to the pursuit of an RPI strategy, whereas
(b) advanced corporate age promotes both DQP and
(c) LCP strategies.

## 3.2. HOW IMPORTANT ARE DEBT FINANCE AND SHARE CAPITAL FOR RPI, DQP, AND LCP STRATEGIES?

Sections 3.2 and 3.3 attempt what hardly any of the contributors to the competitiveness literature has done thus far. They systematically assess *at the micro level* whether firms require particular types of finance to pursue RPI, DQP, and LCP strategies respectively. To this end, Section 3.2 analyses whether debt finance and share capital constitute important sources of finance for each of the three strategies. The assessment of whether insider and outsider share capital facilitate RPI and DQP strategies is reserved for Section 3.3, as this question is closely linked to analyses of how corporate governance institutions provide these finance types.

It should be noted that these assessments are based on two sources of information: balance sheet data and in-depth interviews with about twenty financial experts and representatives of corporate finance departments in Germany,

Italy, and the UK. These interviews were crucial for a general understanding of how particular types of finance impact on different strategies. Even though the remainder of this chapter is mostly concerned with discussing quantitative results, namely the importance of particular finance types for different strategies, it has to be stressed that a meaningful structure and interpretation of these analyses has only been possible due to the insights gained from in-depth interviews. The present chapter as well as Chapters 4–6 thus deliberately seek to combine the results of qualitative and quantitative analyses.

Before turning to these analyses, a few words need to be said about the composition of the final sample which will serve as the basis for all further studies: not only of corporate finance but also of standardization processes (Chapter 4), labour qualifications (Chapter 5), and strategy stability (Chapter 6). It should be recalled that the set of pharmaceutical firms,[7] obtained from sampling the PHID database as described in Chapter 2, is limited in two respects. First, it does not include any generics producers, because the PHID database contains only firms that engage in R&D activities. Yet, generics firms are able to pursue LCP strategies precisely because they avoid expensive clinical trials by imitating drugs upon patent expiry. Second, the case sample includes notably less German and Italian than British biotech firms because the British biotech industry began to develop in the 1980s – much earlier than its German and Italian counterparts, where most biotech firms were founded in the mid-1990s and around the turn of the millennium respectively. Therefore, many German and most Italian biotech firms had not brought a pharmaceutical project beyond the stage of preclinical development and were thus not yet registered in the PHID database when the latter was sampled in November 2004 (see Section 2.2).

To obtain more representative results when using the PHID sample as a basis, it was increased in two ways. First, generics firms were added. More precisely, the entire population of British, German, and Italian generics producers were included which in November 2004 could be identified as genuinely national firms having their headquarters in, and concentrating their activities on, the national territory of one country (see Wittner 2003: 51–4, 70–3, 133–4). Hence, six British,[8] nine German,[9] and two Italian[10] generics

[7] As discussed in Section 1.2, a 'pharmaceutical firm' is used as an umbrella term that includes all types of firms which are active in the pharmaceutical industry, namely biotech, traditional pharmaceutical, and generics firms.

[8] Namely *CP Pharmaceuticals*, *Generics (UK)*, *Kent Pharmaceuticals*, *Sussex Pharmaceuticals*, *Tillomed Laboratories*, and *Sterwin Medicines*.

[9] These are: *Aliud Pharma*, *Betapharm Arzneimittel*, *CT Arzneimittel*, *Hexal*, *Lichtenstein Pharmazeutica*, *Merck Dura*, *Ratiopharm*, *Azupharm*, and *Stada Arzneimittel*.

[10] Namely *DOC Generici* and *Dorom*.

producers were added to the data-set and all classified as low-cost producers. Second, to obtain a more homogeneous sample, three German[11] and eight Italian[12] biotech firms were randomly added on the basis of the data provided by Ernst and Young (2002: 15–19)[13] and the 'Italian Biotech Database' of *Venture Valuation* (2006). The competitive strategy of these firms – RPI or DQP respectively – was identified by comparing the classification of Ernst & Young (2002: 15–19) with that of Knut Lange,[14] by consulting the firms' web pages, and by talking to their representatives.[15] With the addition of these 17 generics and 11 biotech firms, the initial sample of 102 pharmaceutical firms was increased to 130. A complete list of these 130 pharmaceutical firms, which serve as empirical basis for the analyses of this chapter, as well as of Chapters 4 and 5, is provided in the technical appendix (see Table A.1 for the British, Table A.2 for the German, and Table A.3 for the Italian firms included).

### 3.2.1. Some Tentative Observations

When studying corporate balance sheets, one finds that – apart from *debt finance* and *share capital* – firms can use three other financial resources. First, there are *retained earnings*. At the end of each accounting period, shareholders must decide what to do with the profits of that period. Consequently, they have two options. They can either distribute or retain profits in the company as a reserve for financing future activities. Of course, shareholders can decide to do both: distribute one part of profits and retain the other as a reserve. Hence, retained earnings constitute that amount of profits (or losses) which shareholders decided to retain over past accounting periods. Second, firms can use *short-term liabilities*, which constitute those liabilities with a duration of less than one year that arise from daily business. Examples are supplier credits, taxes, and social expenditure to be paid, as well as short-term debt, resulting

[11] Namely *DeveloGen*, *Ingenium Pharmaceuticals*, and *Sirenade*.

[12] These are: *Axxam*, *BioXell*, *Newron Pharmaceuticals*, *Nikem Research*, *Novuspharma*, *Primm*, *Shar.dna*, and *Siena Biotech*.

[13] I am grateful to Julia Schüler for forwarding the list of biotech firms which were classified by Ernst & Young as 'TechProduct Companies' and 'Product Companies' respectively.

[14] I wish to thank Knut Lange for fruitful discussions of the British and German biotech industry in general and the classification of biotech firms as RPIs or DQPs in particular.

[15] Based on these insights, *DeveloGen*, *Ingenium Pharmaceuticals*, *Sirenade*, *BioXell*, *Newron Pharmaceuticals*, *Novuspharma*, *Shar.dna*, and *Siena Biotech* were classified as RPIs, whereas *Axxam*, *Nikem Research*, and *Primm* were categorized as DQPs.

for example from the overdraft of current accounts.[16] Finally, firms can finance their activities from so-called *other non-current liabilities*. This term denotes those funds that firms set aside to meet financial obligations which may arise in the future. Pension provisions, provisions for doubtful debts, provisions for outstanding claims, and deferred taxes constitute some of the most prominent examples.

If the hypotheses of the competitiveness literature hold true, analyses should show that – of the five financial resources: share capital, long-term debt, retained earnings, short-term liabilities, and other non-current liabilities – radical product innovators use comparatively high levels of share capital, while low-cost producers rely on high amounts of long-term debt. Diversified quality producers, in turn, should use comparatively high levels of both share capital and long-term debt. Table 3.1 gives an overview of how the average RPI, DQP, and LCP strategist finances its activities. Here, the overall figures (of lines 11 to 13) are also detailed by country, so that the finance structure of RPI, DQP, and LCP strategists is reported separately for the UK (lines 2 to 4), Germany (lines 5 to 7), and Italy (lines 8 to 10). To correct for temporary peaks, each figure was calculated as an average value of the past five years. Overall, data could be obtained for seventy-four pharmaceutical firms. It is accounting practice to refer to the sum of share capital and retained earnings as 'equity capital' (or *Eigenkapital*), while the sum of long-term debt, other non-current liabilities, and short-term liabilities is called 'borrowed capital' (or *Fremdkapital*).

Table 3.1 indicates one trend that is of particular interest for all further analyses. Even though country-specific variations in the *absolute* use of each financial resource can be observed, both RPI and LCP strategists rely on one type of finance *relatively* more than on any other finance type – irrespective of the country in which they are based. While share capital constitutes the most important source of finance for RPI strategists, LCP strategists substantially use short-term liabilities. This suggests that different competitive

[16] It should be noted that, in accounting jargon, the notion of 'debt finance' includes both *short-term debt* (i.e. loans to be repaid within less than one year) and *long-term debt* (i.e. loans to be repaid within more than one year). Yet, it can be assumed that the above hypotheses on the impact of debt finance on competitive strategies only refer to long-term debt. The reason for this assumption is that creditors hardly assess a firm's activities – and, hence, its strategy – in detail before granting short-term loans. When the financial resources of each firm were determined, all short-term debt was therefore counted as short-term liabilities, while only long-term debt was considered as debt finance.

**Table 3.1.** Capital composition of RPI, DQP, and LCP strategists

| Group of firms | Number of cases | Equity capital | | Borrowed capital | | | Total corp. capital (%) |
|---|---|---|---|---|---|---|---|
| | | Ø share capital (%) | Ø retained earnings (%) | Ø long-term debt (%) | Ø other n.-c. liabilities(%) | Ø short-term liabilities (%) | |
| **RPIs UK** | 10 | 254 | −200 | 18 | 2 | 26 | 100 |
| **DQPs UK** | 12 | 44 | 11 | 8 | 6 | 31 | 100 |
| **LCPs UK** | 7 | 1 | 41 | 4 | 4 | 50 | 100 |
| **RPIs Ger.** | 5 | 103 | −38 | 10 | 11 | 14 | 100 |
| **DQPs Ger.** | 8 | 13 | 34 | 8 | 24 | 21 | 100 |
| **LCPs Ger.** | 4 | 6 | 28 | 14 | 13 | 39 | 100 |
| **RPIs Italy** | 8 | 45 | −1 | 18 | 4 | 34 | 100 |
| **DQPs Italy** | 13 | 12 | 29 | 7 | 8 | 44 | 100 |
| **LCPs Italy** | 7 | 5 | 11 | 7 | 14 | 63 | 100 |
| **RPIs total** | **23** | **149** | **−96** | **16** | **5** | **26** | **100** |
| **DQPs total** | **33** | **24** | **23** | **8** | **12** | **33** | **100** |
| **LCPs total** | **18** | **4** | **26** | **7** | **10** | **53** | **100** |
| **Overall** | **74** | **58** | **−13** | **10** | **9** | **36** | **100** |

*Source:* Own calculations based on analyses of seventy-four balance sheets.

strategies are, indeed, facilitated by particular finance types. At first sight, DQP firms seem to constitute an exception to this rule in that it depends on the country whether they finance their activities mostly from share capital, retained earnings, or short-term liabilities. Does this indicate that a DQP strategy can be pursued independently of a particular finance type? Quantitative analyses will provide insights into the statistical significance of the trends indicated in Table 3.1.

### 3.2.2. How Firms Finance RPI, DQP, and LCP Strategies

Do particular types of finance facilitate different strategies? And, if so, are these financial means more important than corporate age, the strongest alternative facilitator of RPI, DQP, and LCP strategies? Three sets of multinomial logistic regression analyses shed light on these questions. The first set (Model 1) regresses *share capital*, *retained earnings*, *long-term debt*, *other non-current liabilities*, and *short-term liabilities*, as well as *corporate age* (as the respective independent variable) ***separately*** on *competitive strategy* (dependent variable)[17] in order to assess the individual explanatory power of each indicator.

The second and third set of analyses (Models 2 and 3) then assess the relative explanatory power of *various finance types* and *corporate age* (independent variables) by regressing them jointly on *competitive strategy* (dependent variable). In doing so, Model 2 carries out the most complete test in that it assesses – in addition to corporate age – the impact of as many finance variables as possible, namely four out of five. Since the five financial resources add up to 100 per cent of a firm's capital, a maximum of four indicators can be introduced into one regression without endangering independent measurement. For one statistical and one theoretical reason, it is most advisable to exclude retained earnings from the analyses. As for the statistical reason, binary correlation analyses show that the firms' use of share capital and retained earnings is highly correlated ($R = -0.970$; $p < 0.001$). This makes sense from an accounting perspective in that the two resources jointly constitute the firms' equity capital. However, the pronounced multicollinearity between share capital and retained earnings also means that the variance inflation factor (VIF) becomes intolerably high as soon as both indicators are jointly included in one regression. This is not the case for the other finance variables, which are notably less correlated amongst each other. From a theoretical perspective, it seems sensible to exclude retained earnings from the analyses because the competitiveness literature does not propose hypotheses about how this financial resource impacts on competitive strategy. The exclusion of other retained earnings does not therefore hinder the assessment of the hypotheses formulated in Section 3.1. Model 2 can thus be written as the following multinomial logistic regression equations:

$$(1)\ \text{Odds}_{\text{RPI/LCP}} = \frac{\text{prob}_{\text{RPI}}}{\text{prob}_{\text{LCP}}}$$

$$= e^{\beta_{10} + \beta_{11}\ \text{share capital} + \beta_{12}\ \text{long-term debt} + \beta_{13}\ \text{other non-current liabilities} + \beta_{14}\ \text{short-term liabilities} + \beta_{15}\ \text{corporate age}}$$

$$(2)\ \text{Odds}_{\text{DQP/LCP}} = \frac{\text{prob}_{\text{DQP}}}{\text{prob}_{\text{LCP}}}$$

$$= e^{\beta_{20} + \beta_{21}\ \text{share capital} + \beta_{22}\ \text{long-term debt} + \beta_{23}\ \text{other non-current liabilities} + \beta_{24}\ \text{short-term liabilities} + \beta_{25}\ \text{corporate age}}$$

[17] Distinguishing between three discrete categories, the strategy variable assigns a value of '1' to any firm that pursues an RPI strategy, a value of '2' to any DQP pursuer, and a value of '3' to any LCP strategist.

The third set of multinomial regression analyses provides insights into the most parsimonious model. It assesses the impact of those independent variables which have emerged from several multinomial regressions as that minimum number of predictors with the highest explanatory power: *share capital*, *long-term debt*, and *corporate age*. Consequently, Model 3 can be written as:

$$(1)\ \text{Odds}_{\text{RPI/L}} = \frac{\text{prob}_{\text{RPI}}}{\text{prob}_{\text{LCP}}} = e^{\beta_{10} + \beta_{11}\,\text{share capital} + \beta_{12}\,\text{long-term debt} + \beta_{13}\,\text{corporate age}}$$

$$(2)\ \text{Odds}_{\text{DQP/LCP}} = \frac{\text{prob}_{\text{DQP}}}{\text{prob}_{\text{LCP}}} = e^{\beta_{20} + \beta_{21}\,\text{share capital} + \beta_{22}\,\text{long-term debt} + \beta_{23}\,\text{corporate age}}$$

It should also be noted that the above analyses were not only run on the basis of the overall sample. They were also carried out separately for the British, German, and Italian samples so as to reveal possible country-specific variations in the extent to which RPI, DQP, and LCP strategists rely on different finance types. While the number of cases per country was sometimes too small to provide statistically significant results, the country-specific analyses in general did not disconfirm the findings based on the overall sample. The same finance types turned out to be particularly conducive to the strategy under investigation, irrespective of the country in which the studied firms were based. Since country-specific variations are negligible, results obtained from the overall sample are reported in Table 3.2.[18]

All three models agree in that share capital comes out as the strongest and most significant predictor of competitive strategy. Thus, empirical evidence supports the hypotheses that share capital facilitates RPI and DQP strategies (hypotheses H1a and H2b), but hampers LCP (hypotheses H3b and H3c). To give an example, Model 3 shows that – all other variables being held constant – an increase in share capital by 1 per cent leads to an increase of the odds of firms pursuing an RPI rather than a DQP strategy by 2.8 per cent (1 – 0.972 = 0.028), while the odds of firms pursuing an RPI rather than an LCP strategy increase by 28.7 per cent. Similarly, the probability of firms engaging in DQP rather than LCP increases by 20 per cent (1 – 0.800 = 0.200) for each additional per cent of share capital used. In other words, the three strategies

[18] It is also interesting to note that multinomial logistic regression analyses with standard errors clustered by country lead to the same results as reported in Table 3.2. This, in turn, supports the finding that country-specific characteristics do not influence the financing approaches of RPI, DQP, and LCP strategists.

**Table 3.2. Importance of finance and corporate age for RPI, DQP, and LCP strategies**
(results of multinomial logistic regression analyses: exponential $B$)

| Independent variables | Model 1: individual impact | | | Model 2: most complete | | | Model 3: most parsimonious | | |
|---|---|---|---|---|---|---|---|---|---|
| | DQP compared to **ref. group: RPI** | LCP compared to **ref. group: DQP** | RPI compared to **ref group: LCP** | DQP compared to **ref. group: RPI** | LCP compared to **ref. group: DQP** | RPI compared to **ref group: LCP** | DQP compared to **ref. group: RPI** | LCP compared to **ref. group: DQP** | RPI compared to **ref group: LCP** |
| **Share capital** | | | | | | | | | |
| Exp ($B$) | .977*** | .808*** | 1.267*** | .967*** | .814*** | 1.271*** | .972*** | .800*** | 1.287*** |
| $R^2_{\text{Nagelkerke}}$ | | .619 | | | | | | | |
| **Retained earnings** | | | | | | | | | |
| Exp ($B$) | 1.037*** | 1.005 | .960*** | | | | | | |
| $R^2_{\text{Nagelkerke}}$ | | .461 | | | | | | | |
| **Long-term debt** | | | | | | | | | |
| Exp ($B$) | .946** | .996 | 1.061** | .865*** | 1.071 | 1.079 | .876*** | 1.050 | 1.087* |
| $R^2_{\text{Nagelkerke}}$ | | .105 | | | | | | | |
| **O. n.-c. liabilities** | | | | | | | | | |
| Exp ($B$) | 1.138** | .984 | .893** | .996 | 1.019 | .985 | | | |
| $R^2_{\text{Nagelkerke}}$ | | .140 | | | | | | | |
| **Short-term liabilities** | | | | | | | | | |
| Exp ($B$) | 1.020 | 1.040*** | .942*** | .974 | 1.023 | 1.004 | | | |
| $R^2_{\text{Nagelkerke}}$ | | .211 | | | | | | | |
| **Corporate age** | | | | | | | | | |
| Exp ($B$) | 1.044*** | .986* | .971** | 1.013 | .978** | 1.009 | 1.011 | .979** | 1.010 |
| $R^2_{\text{Nagelkerke}}$ | | .277 | | | | | | | |
| **$R^2_{\text{Nagelkerke}}$ of entire model** | | | | | .741 | | | .730 | |

Significance levels: * <.10; ** <.05; *** <.01. Constant not reported in table.

differ most notably from each other in their use of share capital, whereby radical product innovators use a high amount, diversified quality producers a medium amount, and low-cost producers a low amount of this finance type.

Long-term debt qualifies as the second most important and significant predictor of competitive strategy in Model 3. However, in contrast to share capital, empirical evidence does not support the hypotheses that debt finance hinders RPI (H1c), but furthers DQP and LCP strategies alike (H2a and H3a). Quite the opposite can be observed, because Model 3 shows that RPI strategists incur significantly more debts than both DQP and LCP pursuers. More precisely, the odds of a firm being an RPI strategist rather than a DQP pursuer increase by 12.4 per cent (1 – 0.876 = 0.124) for each additional per cent of long-term debt used, while the odds of a firm being an RPI strategist rather than an LCP pursuer increase by 8.7 per cent. This finding supports what in-depth interviews with financial experts suggest: creditors do not make their investment decisions dependent upon a firm's strategy (Scholz 2003; Berg 2004). While it cannot be denied that creditors are risk-averse, finance theory also teaches us that creditors decide on the basis of various grounds whether or not to invest in a company. While the corporate strategy may play a role in assessing a firm's creditworthiness, creditors are more interested in available securities which would become their property if the firm went bankrupt (see also Schneck 2007: 565–6, 567–8). In other words, as long as firms possess securities, they will be granted a loan – irrespective of the strategy they pursue. Given that RPI strategists are often young (start-up) companies (see also Model 1), they have comparatively high funding requirements without the possibility of relying on internally generated means of finance. At the same time, the severe scrutiny on the part of creditors seems to constitute a precious source of advice for radically innovative firms, as it helps them to evaluate their business ideas and financial prospects (Scholz 2003; Berg 2004). This may explain why RPI strategists go into debt more substantially than DQP or LCP pursuers.

The analysis of Model 1 on the impact of corporate age provides empirical support for the hypothesis that young age facilitates RPI strategies (hypothesis H4a), whereas mature corporate age is conducive to DQP and LCP strategies (hypotheses H4b and H4c). For each additional year it exists, the odds of a firm pursuing a DQP rather than an RPI strategy increase by 4.4 per cent, whereas the odds of a firm pursuing an LCP rather than an RPI strategy increase by 2.9 per cent (1 – 0.971 = 0.029). Furthermore, the analyses of Model 1 also reveal that young corporate age facilitates not only RPI compared to DQP and LCP strategies, but also LCP compared to DQP. All other variables being equal, each additional year of existence entails that the odds of a firm pursuing a DQP rather than an LCP strategy increase by 1.4 per cent (1 – 0.986 = 0.014).

Interestingly, though, the explanatory power of corporate age decreases notably as soon as finance variables are introduced as additional predictors of competitive strategy in Models 2 and 3. Consequently, both share capital and long-term debt come out in Model 3 as stronger and more significant predictors of a firm's strategy than its age. This can be interpreted to the effect that these finance types constitute necessary and, possibly, more important input factors than corporate age.[19]

It is finally worth noting that internally generated means of finance, namely other non-current liabilities and short-term liabilities, do not come out as significant determinants of competitive strategy in Model 2. The finding that RPI, DQP, and LCP strategists distinguish themselves most notably from each other in the extent to which they use financial means provided by external investors, i.e. share capital and long-term debt (see Models 2 and 3), can be interpreted in favour of the argument that these input factors are decisive for any strategy because they cannot be secured by a firm alone, but only in collaboration with external economic actors (see Section 1.2). The latter do indeed seem able to influence which strategy 'their' firm should pursue. The reason for this will be developed further in Section 3.3.2.

## 3.3. HOW INSIDER AND OUTSIDER SHARE CAPITAL IMPACT ON RPI AND DQP STRATEGIES: COMPETING DESPITE COMPARATIVE INSTITUTIONAL DISADVANTAGES?

While the previous section has provided empirical support for the idea that share capital constitutes an important source of finance for both RPI and DQP strategies, it still remains to be seen whether *different types* of share capital facilitate each strategy. Does outsider share capital further RPI (hypothesis H1a), whereas insider share capital promotes DQP (hypothesis H2b)? It is the aim of Section 3.3 to test the importance of different share types for these two strategies on the one hand (Sections 3.3.1 and 3.3.2) and to show on the other how firms acquire the necessary capital types in different economies (Section 3.3.3).

[19] This interpretation is supported by multinomial regression analyses which are identical to models 2 and 3 with one exception: they use a 'forward stepwise' regression method instead of the commonly preferred 'enter' method. The results of these analyses retain share capital and long-term debt as the only predictors of competitive strategy, which underlines the explanatory power of the two finance indicators.

### 3.3.1. Why Insider and Outsider Share Capital Are Less Important for RPI and DQP Strategies

Insights into how the Italian corporate governance system is organized make it possible to refute hypotheses H1a and H2b without resorting to quantitative analyses, as the following deductive reasoning leads to the conclusion that RPI strategists do not rely mostly on outsider share capital, while DQP pursuers do not predominantly finance their activities from insider share capital. Contrary to most Western economies with one nationwide corporate governance system, three corporate governance systems coexist in Italy. In other words, Italian firms can choose their form of corporate governance. This contrasts with Germany, where all joint-stock companies (taking the form of an *AG* or *GmbH*) are automatically provided with insider share capital, as shareholders enjoy considerable consultation and participation rights (Gelauff 1997: 357–9; Bronk 1998: 11–12; Vitols 2001: 340–5). Also firms in the UK cannot choose their corporate governance system. Here, joint-stock companies (taking the form of a *plc* or an *Ltd*) are necessarily given outsider share capital as shareholders have only limited consultation rights (Bronk 1998: 5–7; Vitols 2001: 340–5).

Italy constitutes an exception to this rule of 'one country, one system of corporate governance' since June 2003. Until then, Italian corporate governance regulation also provided for just one system of corporate control for joint-stock companies. This traditional system – also referred to as *sistema dualistico orizzontale* (Fiori et al. 2004: 60) – is similar to an insider system in that shareholders do not only elect the firm's management, i.e. the board of directors (*consiglio di amministrazione*), but also elect a board of auditors (*collegio sindacale*), which has to ensure that the management complies with the law, the articles of association, and the principles of good administration and management. Furthermore, the board of auditors controls the adequacy of all corporate financial issues (De Vecchi and Roussey 2003: in particular 8). However, unlike the supervisory board of Germany's insider system (*Aufsichtsrat*), the Italian board of auditors (*collegio sindacale*) does not oversee the *efficiency* of managerial decisions. It merely controls the *legitimacy* of the management's actions (Fiori et al. 2004: 56). That said, shareholders of Italian joint-stock companies often enjoy *de facto* important participation rights because they typically hold a large part of shares. As a result, these block shareholders are often members of the firm's board of directors, or entertain very close relationships with the firm's management (Aguilera 1998: 76–82; Deeg 2005; see also Fiori et al. 2004: 56). This is also true for almost all firms of the Italian sample, for which data could be obtained. Hence, the traditional Italian corporate governance system *de lege* and *de facto* grants insider control rights to shareholders (see also Deeg 2005: 541).

In January 2003, the Italian system of corporate governance was reformed by the *decreto legislative* (legislative decree) *6/2003*. The latter put an end to Italy's single corporate governance system, as it added two new systems: an insider control system (also referred to as *sistema dualistico verticale*) and an outsider control system (also termed *sistema monistico*). Interestingly, these two systems are an *explicit* imitation of the German system of insider governance on the one hand, and the Anglo-Saxon system of outsider governance on the other (De Vecchi and Roussey 2003: 4; Fiori et al. 2004: 60). Since then, Italian firms have the choice between three different forms of corporate governance. But, despite this choice, they have remained hesitant – as far as this research project, which ended in 2005, can determine – to change their model of corporate control. The vast majority of Italian firms, and all firms of the Italian sample for which data could be obtained, continued to operate under the traditional system which, as described above, grants insider control rights to shareholders (see Fiori et al. 2004: 61–8; Deeg 2005: 541).

Returning to the hypotheses that insider share capital promotes DQP (H2b), while outsider share capital facilitates RPI (H1a), empirical evidence would support these hypotheses if all German and Italian firms, which massively finance their activities from share capital, pursued a DQP strategy, whereas all British firms that substantially use shareholder funds were engaged in RPI. The balance sheets of individual firms, which are presented at various aggregation levels in Table 3.1, clearly show that this is not the case. Firms which finance their activities most importantly from share capital usually pursue an RPI strategy, irrespective of the country in which they are based. That insider and outsider share capital do *not* facilitate DQP and RPI strategies is also supported by the observation that Italian firms were very hesitant to opt for another corporate governance model after January 2003 (see Fiori et al. 2004: 61–8). Instead of adopting that model which the literature suggests as particularly supportive of the respective strategies, most firms in Italy continued to use the traditional model – irrespective of the strategy they pursued.

### 3.3.2. Why Institutional and Private Share Capital Facilitate RPI and DQP Strategies

While empirical evidence casts doubt on the importance of insider and outsider share capital for different strategies, the shareholder structure of Italian firms suggests an alternative hypothesis as to how particular share types facilitate RPI and DQP strategies. When studying the shareholder structure of radical product innovators and diversified quality producers in Italy, I found that most of these firms are owned by a few block shareholders with substantial insights into how the respective firms are run. Interestingly, though, block shareholders of DQP strategists are often members of the founding family, i.e. private investors. Block shareholders of RPI pursuers, by contrast, tend to be institutional investors: venture capitalists, other firms, or investment funds. It thus seems that institutional share capital facilitates RPI, whereas private shareholder finance promotes DQP. Could this be possible?

To test this new hypothesis, the share capital of all RPI and DQP strategists contained in the sample was divided into their institutional and private components. To this end, all shares held by venture capitalist firms, business angels, companies, banks, and investment funds were counted as *institutional share capital*, while all shares held by the firms' founders, managers, employees, and private investors were counted as *private share capital*.[20] Overall, data for forty cases could be obtained. Table 3.3 provides an overview of the extent to which institutional and private investors hold shares in RPI and, respectively, DQP firms.

Overall, Table 3.3 shows empirical support for the idea that institutional shareholders invest in RPI strategists, whereas private shareholders prefer investing in DQP firms. As indicated by the last two columns of Table 3.3, institutional investors hold 70 per cent of shares in radically innovative firms, but only 41 per cent in incrementally innovative companies. The opposite applies to private investors, who hold 30 per cent of shares in RPI firms, but 59

**Table 3.3.** Ownership structure (institutional and private share capital) of RPI and DQP strategists

| | **UK** (*N* = 12) | | **Germany** (*N* = 17) | | **Italy** (*N* = 11) | | **All 3 countries** (*N* = 40) | |
|---|---|---|---|---|---|---|---|---|
| **Share capital** | **Ø inst.** (%) | **Ø private** (%) | **Ø inst.** (%) | **Ø private** (%) | **Ø inst.** (%) | **Ø private** (%) | **Ø inst.** (%) | **Ø private** (%) |
| **RPI** | 83 | 17 | 61 | 39 | 67 | 33 | **70** | **30** |
| **DQP** | 69 | 31 | 43 | 57 | 15 | 85 | **41** | **59** |
| **Total** | 77 | 23 | 51 | 49 | 39 | 61 | **56** | **44** |

*Source:* Own calculations based on forty interviews.

[20] While business angels are mostly private investors, here they are counted as institutional shareholders. The reason for this is that business angels presumably have the same risk–return preferences as institutional investors, as they have specialist knowledge about investment projects and firms in specific industries.

per cent in DQP pursuers. Even though the overall distribution of institutional and, respectively, private shareholdings varies from one country to another – as British firms hold 77 per cent, German companies 51 per cent, and Italian firms only 39 per cent of institutional share capital – it is striking that radical product innovators in the UK, Germany, and Italy alike rely on higher amounts of institutional share capital than the average firm in each country. Obviously, the reverse argument applies to private shareholdings, which amount to 23 per cent in British, 49 per cent in German, and as much as 61 per cent in Italian firms, whereby diversified quality producers in each economy resort to more private share capital than the average national firm.

Three binary logistic regression analyses provide statistical insights into the importance of institutional and private share capital for RPI and DQP strategies respectively. Since LCP strategists hardly finance their activities from share capital, they are excluded from the following analyses in order not to skew the picture. The first analysis (Model 1) assesses the impact of *institutional share capital* and the second analysis (Model 2) the impact of *corporate age* (the respective independent variable) on *RPI* (dependent variable). The third analysis (Model 3) then tests the relative importance of *institutional share capital* by regressing it together with *age* (independent variables) on *RPI* (dependent variable). Consequently, Model 3 can be written as the following equation:

$$\text{Odds}_{\text{RPI/DQP}} = \frac{\text{prob}_{\text{RPI}}}{\text{prob}_{\text{DQP}}} = e^{\beta_0 + \beta_1 \text{ institutional share capital} + \beta_2 \text{ corporate age}}$$

In line with Section 3.2.2, these analyses were also replicated at the country level. Given that none of them revealed noteworthy country-specific differences, the results obtained on the basis of the overall sample are reported in Table 3.4.[21] Since institutional and private share capital have reversed scores as they add up to 100 per cent of a firm's share capital, the results obtained for RPI strategists also teach us about the importance of private share capital and corporate age for DQP strategists.[22]

The results reported in Table 3.4 confirm, on the one hand, the new hypotheses that institutional share capital facilitates RPI and, respectively,

[21] It should also be noted that multinomial logistic regression analyses with standard errors clustered by country lead to the same results as reported in Table 3.4. This, in turn, supports the finding that country-specific characteristics do not influence the financing approaches of RPI and DQP strategists.

[22] While the values obtained for the impact of private share capital on DQP are the same as those for the impact of institutional share capital on RPI, the scores measuring the importance of corporate age are reversed for DQP and RPI strategies ($\text{Exp.(B)}_{\text{DQP}} = 1 - \text{Exp.(B)}_{\text{RPI}}$).

**Table 3.4.** Importance of institutional share capital and corporate age for RPI (Results of binary logistic regression analyses: exponential *B*)

| Independent variables | Model 1 | Model 2 | Model 3 |
|---|---|---|---|
| Institutional share capital | 1.026** | | 1.029** |
| Corporate age | | .965** | .971** |
| *N* | 40 | 40 | 40 |
| $R^2_{\text{Nagelkerke}}$ | .213 | .367 | .499 |

Significance levels: * <.10; ** <.05; *** <.01. Constant not reported in table.

that private share capital supports DQP strategies. On the other hand, they corroborate the hypotheses that young corporate age is conducive to RPI (hypothesis H4a), while mature age is supportive of DQP (hypothesis H4b). More precisely, Model 3 reveals that, everything else being equal, the odds of firms pursuing an RPI rather than a DQP strategy increase by 2.9 per cent for each additional per cent of institutional share capital used. Likewise, the odds of a firm being an RPI rather than a DQP strategist decrease by 2.9 per cent (1 – 0.971 = 0.029) for each additional year of corporate age. In other words, an increase by one unit of share capital and corporate age has a similarly strong influence on RPI and, by implication, DQP pursuit as the odds increase by 2.9 per cent respectively. These findings can be interpreted to the effect that corporate age and particular types of share capital are important input factors for different strategies. Since the analyses of Section 3.2.2 have shown that the amount of share capital employed by firms exerts a stronger influence on all three strategies than corporate age, because DQP and LCP strategies require a different capital composition but a similar age structure, one might argue that particular share types even constitute the more decisive factor.

Of course, these and the previous analyses should not be considered more than explorative, as they are limited, most importantly, in that the number of observations is fairly narrow. Nevertheless, quantitative analyses corroborate what qualitative interviews have revealed: that institutional share capital facilitates RPI and private share capital assists DQP. The most important reason for this, provided by the financial experts interviewed, is that institutional and private investors differ crucially in their risk–return preferences (Berg 2004; Garda 2005). Accordingly, interviewees pointed out that *private shareholders* tend to be in favour of low-risk, low-return projects, i.e. DQP. This is particularly true for founders, managers, or employees who have a personal interest in the survival of 'their' firm. But it also applies to private investors who acquire shares on the stock exchange without entertaining personal relationships with the respective firms. The reason is that these investors usually lack both in-depth knowledge and time to constantly monitor the development of shareholder value, and to compare the latter with returns from alternative investment projects. It is therefore essential for private investors that the risk of failure of investment projects is reduced, even if this implies limited returns. Consequently, private shareholders (only invest in firms if they can) make sure that the management pursues low-risk, low-return projects. Large amounts of private share capital are therefore conducive to DQP.

The opposite holds true for *institutional shareholders*, such as venture capitalists, banks, and funds, which typically dedicate important resources to learn about the risk-return ratios of numerous investment alternatives. To make the most of their money, institutional investors are willing to accept an increased risk of failure as high-risk projects tend to promise high returns on investment (Vitols 2001: 350–2; see also Bottazzi and Da Rin 2002: 249–50). They therefore invest in radically innovative firms rather than in diversified quality producers. In other words, institutional share capital facilitates RPI because institutional investors (only provide money if they can) make sure that the management pursues high-risk, high-return projects.

That institutional investors only provide funds to firms if the latter pursue a high-risk, high-return strategy is confirmed by anecdotal evidence, which I obtained when interviewing the CEO of a Milanese biotech company in February 2005. For reasons of confidentiality, the latter is here referred to as *Nirema Srl.* Until shortly before that interview, *Nirema* had pursued a low-risk, low-return strategy, as it had carried out contract research for other biopharmaceutical companies. But, akin to many other biotech firms, *Nirema* had become aware that using its knowledge for the development of its own drugs was more profitable than offering research services. Hence, *Nirema* had decided to try and develop a particularly promising discovery into a pharmaceutical product on its own. To finance the shift from DQP to RPI, *Nirema* needed to make important investments. However, the major, and mostly private, shareholders of the firm were at the time unable to cover the financial sums required. Also, returns from the hitherto pursued low-risk strategy had not yielded enough to finance the RPI project in question. *Nirema* had therefore turned to institutional shareholders, venture capitalists, to ask for seed finance. Interestingly, the latter had agreed to provide funds, but only under the condition that the firm embarked fully on the envisaged RPI strategy. As long as *Nirema* continued to concentrate on the pursuit of a low-risk, low-return strategy, the venture capitalists were not interested in providing finance because the returns from this strategy were considered stable but too small (Garda 2005). This experience of *Nirema* illustrates how institutional share capital promotes the pursuit of an RPI strategy.

### 3.3.3. How Institutional Share Capital Is Acquired in Countries with Public Pension and Insurance Systems

All analyses thus far have tested the hypotheses derived from the competitiveness literature: that particular finance types facilitate different competitive strategies. Overall, we have found empirical support for this idea. While large amounts of institutional share capital and debt finance sustain RPI, private share capital promotes DQP. Low-cost production, in turn, is not facilitated by externally provided means of finance, as this strategy tends to be importantly financed from short-term liabilities.

To understand how the institutional environments of different economies support corporate competitiveness, one crucial question results from these findings. Do particular national institutions constitute a comparative advantage for the pursuit of RPI or DQP strategies in that they further the availability of debt finance and private or institutional share capital, respectively? The answer to this question is straightforward for both debt finance and private share capital. Neither the literature nor empirical evidence points to country-specific institutions that would further the provision of these finance types. This is particularly true for the availability of debt finance, because the process of disintermediation – meaning that firms increasingly obtain credits from economic actors other than banks (see, e.g. Schneck 2007: 230) – is an international rather than a national trend. As for private share capital, it is equally hard to imagine how country-specific institutions could promote its availability. Private investors willing to buy shares presumably exist in all economies to the same extent.

Interestingly, this is different for institutional share capital. As Aguilera points out, '[i]nstitutional investors play a minor role in countries where pensions are provided by the state' (Aguilera 1998: 89; see also Bottazzi and Da Rin 2002: 240–1). The reason for this is that the funds, destined for paying (future) pensions, are administered by the state in economies with a public pension system. In private pension systems, however, employees tend to commit parts of their salaries to pension funds and other pension-scheme providers, which then reinvest these sums. Consequently, the number of institutional (re)investors is higher in economies with private pension systems than in countries where pensions are administered by the state. Private pension and insurance systems therefore lead to a more abundant provision of institutional share capital, whereas public pension and insurance systems entail the scare availability of such financial means.

This reasoning supports the argument of the competitiveness literature that country-specific institutions can offer an important comparative advantage.

More precisely, it supports the argument that RPI strategists are privileged in the UK – albeit *not* by the outsider corporate governance system providing outsider share capital, but by the very basic public pension and insurance systems which the government introduced to encourage private arrangements (see Stiglitz and Driffill 2000: 369–71). Similarly, it underlines the literature's suggestion that RPI pursuers in Germany and Italy find it difficult to acquire the necessary type of – institutional rather than outsider – share capital (see in particular Hollingsworth 2000: 626–30; Hall and Soskice 2001*a*: 36–44; Vitols 2001; Amable 2003; Casper and Matraves 2003) due to the public pension and insurance systems. It is furthermore worth noting that the importance of private pension and insurance systems for the provision of institutional share capital is empirically supported by the data presented in Table 3.3. They clearly show that British firms in general, and British RPI strategists in particular, rely on exceptionally large amounts of institutional share capital. At the same time, however, Table 3.3 and the results of Table 3.4 reveal that German and Italian RPI pursuers *also* finance their activities to a significant extent from institutional share capital.

This observation, in turn, constitutes a puzzle to the competitiveness literature. How can RPI strategists in Germany and Italy prosper and acquire institutional shareholder finance, given that public pension and insurance systems lead to the scarce availability of this finance type? In other words, how can RPI pursuers compete in Germany and Italy despite the comparative institutional disadvantages of these economies? The – albeit limited – data available on RPI strategists in Germany and Italy indicate an unambiguous answer: entrepreneurs circumvent national institutions by importing the required financial means from abroad (Pozzali 2004: 122–3; Thomson Financial 2004; Barratti 2005; see also Breschi et al. 2003: 154). Instead of merely relying on funds provided by national institutional investors, radical product innovators in Germany and Italy simply turn to foreign investors. Importantly, though, such importation of finance is only possible due to the existence of international institutions: open financial markets. International institutions thus make it possible to circumvent the rigidities of national institutions.

It was unfortunately not possible to obtain sufficient data on the extent to which the German and Italian RPI strategists *of the PHID sample* are financed by foreign and, respectively, national institutional shareholders. Nevertheless, aggregate statistics on German and Italian *biotech firms* that tend to be RPI strategists provide empirical insights (see Thomson Financial 2004; Ernst & Young 2004: 92, 2005: 110, 2006: 75). While Chapter 2 has demonstrated that a firm's industry is a rather crude proxy for its strategy, because many, but not all, RPI strategists are biotech firms, it must be used here as an alternative – albeit second best – strategy measure due to the lack of more refined data. Interestingly, aggregate statistics on German biotech firms show that the latter are, indeed, financed substantially by foreign venture capitalists. In 2003, 42 per cent of venture capital provided to German biotech companies came from foreign investors. The latter were even more important sponsors for financing rounds of more than €5 million. Here, the share of foreign venture capitalists (65 per cent) by far exceeded the share of German venture capitalists (35 per cent) in 2003 (Ernst & Young 2004: 92). In Italy, the importance of foreign venture capital is even more pronounced. Since Italian venture capital was virtually non-existent in the early years of the new millennium, most venture capitalists who had invested in Italian biotech firms at the time were foreign investors (see Breschi et al. 2003: 154; Pozzali 2004: 122–3; Thomson Financial 2004; Barratti 2005). In other words, an important number of German RPI strategists, and most Italian RPI pursuers, had acquired the necessary institutional share capital from foreign institutional investors.

## 3.4. CONCLUDING INTERPRETATION

What do these findings teach us about whether the comparative advantage of national institutions also offers a source of competitive advantage to RPI, DQP, and LCP strategists? Do firms need particular financial means to pursue the same strategy? And, if so, do firms systematically exploit their country's institutional environment to secure the required finance types? To begin with, the analyses of this chapter have shown that each strategy is facilitated by a particular capital structure. While the pursuit of RPI strategies is sustained by debt finance and institutional share capital, DQP strategies are furthered by private share capital. Low-cost production, in turn, is hardly financed from share capital but from the firms' current business, that is to say, short-term liabilities.

These findings support the argument of the competitiveness literature that externally generated finance exerts a decisive influence on RPI and DQP strategies[23] – even though the causal mechanisms underlying this argument need to be qualified. Rather than DQP and LCP strategists, it is RPI pursuers that benefit from debt finance. The reasons for this are twofold: not only do RPI firms have higher funding requirements than DQP and LCP strategists, but the creditors' severe scrutiny of business ideas and financial prospects before granting a loan also seems to constitute a particularly precious source

[23] See note 3.

of advice for radically innovative firms. In a similar vein, institutional and private share capital, rather than outsider and insider shareholdings, respectively promote RPI and DQP strategies due to differing risk–return preferences of these shareholder types. As private shareholders prefer stable and secure returns over high but risky returns on investment, they seek to influence managers to the effect that the latter pursue DQP projects. The opposite applies to institutional shareholders with a preference for high-return projects.

While these causal chains differ from the reasoning proposed in the competitiveness literature, the latter brings home one essential point. Specific types of one input factor are a source for competitive advantage in that they are at the basis of each strategy. In other words, firms that pursue the same strategy are characterized by a homogeneous factor structure rather than by an idiosyncratic assembly of resources. To be clear, the previous findings do *not* suggest that firms *must* use specific capital types to finance a given strategy. Firms are free to finance each strategy from resources that differ from those employed by their competitors pursuing the same strategy. However, such a quest for resource heterogeneity seems to constitute a competitive disadvantage in that the strategy support, offered by financiers in addition to the respective capital type (like advice, patience, and a particular understanding for the firms' needs), is not exploited. This, in turn, casts doubt on the suggestion of the resource-based view that any type of the same resource can be at the basis of a competitive advantage as long as it can be turned into a valuable, rare, imperfectly imitable, and strategically non-substitutable factor (see, e.g. Rumelt 1984; Wernerfelt 1984; Barney 1991; Conner 1991; Peteraf 1993; Barney and Clark 2007; Newbert 2007). To understand how pharmaceutical firms pursuing the same competitive strategy can build competitive advantages through acquiring *similar* types of financial input factors, the competitiveness literature seems to be particularly instructive.

Based on this insight, the chapter has furthermore asked how firms secure the required types of financial capital in different political economies. Here, empirical evidence has shown that national institutions can offer comparative advantages in that they promote the availability of particular finance types. More precisely, private pension and insurance systems constitute a comparative advantage to RPI strategists as these institutions lead to an abundance of institutional investors. Institutional arrangements that further the availability of debt finance or private investors, thereby offering a comparative advantage to DQP firms, do not however seem to exist.

These findings also support the second argument of the competitiveness literature, namely that national institutions facilitate specific competitive strategies.[24] Yet, this argument too needs to be qualified in that private pension and insurance systems, rather than outsider corporate governance systems, promote the availability of institutional investors and, hence, the necessary capital supply to RPI strategists. In other words, the comparative advantage of private pension and insurance systems can be used as a source of competitive advantage by RPI strategists.

Yet, besides finding empirical support for the idea of comparative institutional advantage, the previous research findings go beyond this argument by showing how firms cope with comparative institutional *disadvantages*. The functionalist perspective of the competitiveness literature suggests that firms are institution-takers. This makes it difficult to understand how they can compete through strategies that are not supported by national institutions. How can RPI strategists acquire institutional share capital in public pension and insurance systems? The answer provided in this chapter is straightforward. RPI firms acquire share capital from foreign institutional investors by relying on international institutions: open financial markets. They simply 'import' finance. The use of national institutions is thus only one way for firms to compete. Importation via international institutions constitutes an alternative pathway to competitiveness.

This casts doubt on the perception of firms as institution-takers. Firms in developed capitalist economies do not seem to be constrained by national institutions to the extent that they would have to exploit their comparative advantages. Quite the contrary: corporate competitiveness arises from the individual creativity of firms to use, or circumvent, national institutions efficiently so as to build individual links with national, or international, investors. This, in turn, indicates support for the idea of the resource-based view that firms must not behave like clones – particularly not if they are exposed to the same environmental constraints. Only individual corporate behaviour leads to competitiveness. Importantly, though, individual behaviour does *not* mean that firms obtain a competitive advantage through idiosyncratic resource composition, but through individual ways of securing specific resource types.

This corporate individualism is also at the basis of Schumpeter's definition of entrepreneurs. As indicated in the introduction, Schumpeter makes a crucial distinction between 'managers', who merely execute orders, and 'entrepreneurs', who relentlessly search for new business opportunities or, at least, for new approaches to established practices (see Schumpeter 1934: 74–94, 1939: 103–6,

[24] See in particular Gelauff (1997: 346–56), Bronk (1998: 13–15), Hollingsworth (2000: 626–30), Hall and Soskice (2001*a*: 36–44), Vitols (2001: 350–60), Amable (2003), Casper and Matraves (2003), and Börsch (2007); see also Porter (1990), Lindgaard Christensen (1992), Mayer (1998), and Pavitt and Patel (1999: in particular 104–7).

1947). It is precisely this relentless search for individual ways of providing the required finance types which forms the basis of corporate competitiveness. In line with Schumpeter, this chapter therefore suggests that competitiveness arises from the entrepreneurial creativity to exploit institutional alternatives, rather than from the sheer use of national institutions.

Do these findings mean that institutions do not matter, or no longer matter, in an international economy? If firms can obtain finance not only via national, but also via international capital markets, can national institutions still influence, let alone discipline, corporate behaviour? The answer possibly unfolds along the following lines. To begin with, not all firms are similar. For DQP and LCP strategists, externally generated finance is comparatively less important. Consequently, the availability of institutional share capital, supported by private pension and insurance provisions, has a reduced impact on their competitive behaviour. This is different for RPI strategists. Depending on whether national pension and insurance systems are private or public, RPI pursuers can either exploit the comparative advantage offered by these institutions, in the former case, or circumvent the scarcity of institutional share capital by turning to foreign investors, in the latter. The local and, possibly, cultural distance between investors and investees therefore seems to influence the severity of business scrutiny on the part of investors and the commitments to be made on the part of investees. In this respect, importation via international institutions seems more demanding which does not, however, imply that RPI strategists in public pension and insurance systems are less successful than their counterparts in private systems (see Chapter 6). In sum, national institutions facilitating the availability of institutional share capital matter, at least to RPI strategists. They indicate which pathway to competitiveness is more opportune and channel the commitments related to this pathway. Yet, they do not matter as a ubiquitous constraint that obliges all firms to compete in a similar manner.

# 4

# Linking Antitrust Legislation, Standards, and Competitive Strategies

Does national antitrust legislation encourage different types of inter-firm collaboration? And, if so, do the latter influence competitive strategies? Chapter 3 has illustrated how the relationship between a firm and its financiers impacts on competitive strategies. This chapter turns to the study of inter-firm collaboration, which, according to the competitiveness literature,[1] crucially affects corporate competitiveness as well.[2] Since 'user–producer relationships are necessary prerequisites for product innovations' (Lundvall 1992*c*: 54; see also Lundvall 1992*a*: 13–14), they are said to influence a firm's innovative capacities (Gelsing 1992: 121–3; Lundvall 1992*c*: 57–9; Hollingsworth 2000: 628; Hall and Soskice 2001*a*: 39–41; Tate 2001: 444–6) and, hence, its product-market strategy (Casper 2001: 404–7; Tate 2001: 444–6; Teubner 2001: 433–5; see also Andersen 1992: 85–90).

Given this agreement on the importance of supplier–producer relations for competitive strategies, it is all the more astonishing that the literature on national innovation systems (NIS) and the market-based view (MBV) of strategic management remain vague about the causal mechanisms that link supplier–producer relations to product-market strategies.[3] While some

[1] See Andersen (1992: 68–9, 82–91), Gelsing (1992), Lundvall (1992*a*: 13–14, 1992*c*), Hollingsworth (2000: 626–30), Hall and Soskice (2001*a*: 6–7, 36–44), and Tate (2001); see also Porter (1990: 71–3, 100–7).

[2] (Neo)classical trade theory constitutes an exception to this claim of the competitiveness literature, as it makes no assertions about inter-firm collaboration. Focusing on land, labour, and capital, trade theory does not consider supplier–producer relations as an individual production factor (see Heckscher 1919; Ohlin 1933).

[3] To give some examples, '"subjective" elements in user-producer relationships' (Lundvall 1992*c*: 58) and 'information-rich seller-buyer relationships' (Andersen 1992: 83) are found to be important for radical innovation (see also Porter 1990: 103; Gelsing 1992: 119; Hollingsworth 2000: 628). Similarly, 'stable user-producer relationships' (Lundvall 1992*c*: 57) are said to develop as

authors point out that supplier–producer relations can facilitate different types of interactive learning (Andersen 1992: 82–3; Lundvall 1992*c*: 57–9) and knowledge accumulation (Andersen 1992: 83–4), causal *connexions* are not specified clearly. And causal *directions* also remain unclear: are supplier–producer relations 'necessary prerequisites for product innovations' (Lundvall 1992*c*: 54), or do the former 'develop' as a result of the latter (Lundvall 1992*c*: 57)?

Due to its functionalist view of national institutions, the 'varieties of capitalism' (VoC) literature is – as the only strand of the competitiveness literature – explicit about how inter-firm relations facilitate competitive strategies (Casper 2001; Hall and Soskice 2001*a*; Tate 2001; Teubner 2001). *Standards* are found to be the causal mechanism that links inter-firm relations to competitive strategies.

> Standards are one of the leading challenges in contemporary capitalism' (Tate 2001: 446) because '[f]irms [can] use standards to reduce internal and external transaction costs; to drive down prices from suppliers; to block or circumvent competitors; to lock in quasi-monopoly profits through control of a proprietary standard (...); and to set baselines for subsequent rounds of innovation. (ibid.: 442)

Despite the importance of standards for a firm's daily business, neither the establishment of, nor compliance with, standards is *de lege* compulsory – unless explicitly specified in a contract. Firms are free to determine and comply with all sorts of standards. However, *de facto* compliance becomes compelling as soon as more than one firm is involved in a production process, because the standards of semi-finished goods supplied by one firm have to fit those of the processing company.

Therefore, contributors to the VoC literature argue, a coordination problem arises whenever suppliers and producers need to agree on the standards for a new product's component, because firms cannot simply determine new standards on their own, but only in collaboration with their suppliers or, respectively, processors (see, in particular, Hall and Soskice 2001*a*: 6–7). Yet, firms tend to have diverging interests in how the new standards should look. Such coordination difficulties are described in the political economy literature as a hold-up problem. The latter arises whenever two or more parties seek to cooperate with the aim of realizing a common goal for the future – in this case with the aim of elaborating a new component standard – because not all

a result of incremental innovation (see also Porter 1990: 103; Hollingsworth 2000: 628). Finally, LCP or 'mass-production' (Andersen 1992: 83) – associated with 'a high degree of standardisation' (Lundvall 1992*c*: 57) and 'information-poor seller-buyer relationships' (Andersen 1992: 82) – is said to enable 'communication between a user and a producer (...) over long distances' (Lundvall 1992*c*: 57; see also Gelsing 1992: 119). Interestingly, though, none of these statements provides an explicit reason for *why* and *how* specific inter-firm relations are required for specific strategies.

aspects of cooperation are contractible. Therefore, certain aspects of the initial contract may have to be revised in the course of the joint project. At that stage, however, one party has often invested more (money) in achieving the common goal and, therefore, faces higher sunk costs than the other. Since the party with lower sunk costs has comparatively less to gain from continuing cooperation, it may seek to extract advantageous concessions in exchange for its agreement to continue the collaboration. In other words, one party holds up the common project for strategic reasons (see Rogerson 1992: 777; Klein 1996; Malcomson 1997: 1916–17).

According to VoC contributors, such situations of deadlock can be prevented or overcome by national institutions which encourage inter-firm collaboration in standard-setting processes (Hall and Soskice 2001*a*: 26–7; Tate 2001: 443–4; Teubner 2001: 433–5). Two ways are identified by which legal systems in general, and antitrust regulation in particular, solve or prevent hold-up. In countries with code-based ('continental') law, hold-up is overcome by the large-scale coordination of firms. In code-based law systems, antitrust legislation is said to be less stringent in that it incorporates 'a producer-oriented tolerance for sectoral (...) cartels' (Tate 2001: 443). Combined with a fault-based approach to product liability, which is based on the recognition of the *bona fides* principle, firms are encouraged to determine new component standards in inclusive industry associations (ibid.; Teubner 2001: 433–5). Such associations are characterized by a large number of members, all paying rather low membership fees. Whenever new component standards are determined, all parties concerned enjoy the same right to participate in the standardization process. Hence, both large and small firms have the same say in the design of new standards (Büthe and Witte 2004: 17–22; see also Tate 2001: 453–4). Consequently, hold-up problems are prevented or solved by majoritarian decision processes and an increased propensity to make compromises (see Büthe and Witte 2004: 12–13). The new component standards resulting from large-scale cooperation are thus of a *coordinated* nature.

The opposite holds true for countries with a common-law tradition, where deadlock is overcome by small-scale competition between firms. In common-law countries, rigorous antitrust legislation and an open, case-based approach towards product liability is said to discourage large-scale cooperation between firms (Tate 2001: 443–4; see also Teubner 2001: 433–5). Instead of coordinating their interests in encompassing associations, firms set new standards in two competitive ways. First, they act on their own by winning a market race. In so doing, firms diffuse their own standard so widely that suppliers and even competitors have to conform to them if they want to market a decent number of products (Hall and Soskice 2001*a*: 31). Second, firms come together in small consortia, where they develop new standards on a contractual basis.

Such consortia differ from encompassing associations in that they admit only a limited number of members, which have to pay high membership fees. Furthermore, consortium members often do not have an equal voice in standard-setting processes. 'Big contributors might receive director seats, special voting privileges, earlier technical access, and greater access to any resulting licences; smaller firms might join, if at all, only as observers with highly restricted rights' (Tate 2001: 466–7). Since consortium associates do not have the same say in the elaboration of new standards, deadlock is overcome by powerful members dictating their interests to less powerful members. The component standards resulting from these standardization procedures are of a *competitive* nature.

Coordinated and competitive standardization processes, in turn, are said to facilitate different competitive strategies. While coordinated standardization facilitates diversified quality production (DQP), competitive standardization supports radical product innovation (RPI). Low-cost production (LCP) is presumably facilitated if firms abstain from engaging in any type of standardization process. In line with their reasoning that firms exploit the comparative advantage of national institutions as a source of competitive advantage (see Chapter 2), the VoC contributors furthermore suggest that firms based in common-law countries (like the UK) have a strong incentive to specialize in RPI, whereas firms in continental-law countries (such as Germany) prefer DQP strategies. Firms in economies where antitrust legislation is only hesitantly enforced by the state (like Italy) can be assumed to specialize in LCP.[4]

Since Chapter 2 has shown that a significant number of firms pursue strategies that are *not* supported by national institutions, this chapter continues research into the question of how firms can compete despite comparative institutional disadvantages. In line with Chapter 3, the present chapter proceeds in two steps. It first assesses at the micro level whether RPI, DQP, and LCP strategies are facilitated by *particular* types of standardization processes. This does not only shed light on the argument of the VoC contributors. It also provides further insight into the suggestion of the resource-based view (RBV) that *any* type of the same resource can form the basis of competitive advantage if it is a valuable, rare, hard-to-imitate, and strategically non-substitutable resource (Barney 1991; see also Rumelt 1984; Wernerfelt 1984; Conner 1991; Peteraf 1993). The results obtained then direct the second step of research. Given that particular types of standardization processes do, indeed, turn out to facilitate RPI, DQP, and LCP strategies, how can firms participate in these processes if they are obstructed by national antitrust legislation?

[4] Hall and Soskice (2001*a*: 26–7, 31, 36–44), and Tate (2001: 443–6); see also Casper (2001: 404–7), and Teubner (2001: 433–5).

To explore the link between institutions, standardization, and competitive strategies, the remaining parts of this chapter are organized as follows. Section 4.1 illustrates the VoC hypotheses on how different standardization processes support RPI, DQP, and LCP strategies. Section 4.2 tests these hypotheses at the micro level and finds support for the claim that each strategy relies on specific standard types. Section 4.3 thus asks how national institutions support the respective standardization procedures, thereby addressing the question of how firms can compete in the face of comparative institutional disadvantages. Section 4.4 summarizes the various findings and elaborates on their implications for the arguments of the VoC and RBV literatures. In line with Chapter 3, it concludes that a Schumpeterian approach, which acknowledges firms to be run by inventive entrepreneurs, is particularly instructive to understand how firms gain competitiveness.

## 4.1. HYPOTHESES AS TO HOW DIFFERENT STANDARDIZATION PROCESSES FACILITATE RPI, DQP, AND LCP STRATEGIES

As indicated in the introduction, contributors to the VoC literature make the most clear-cut suggestions as to how supplier–producer relations in general, and different standardization processes in particular, facilitate RPI, DQP, and LCP strategies. The following hypotheses are therefore essentially based on the arguments of this literature. Thereby, the terms 'standardization' and 'standards' are used as synonyms, even though new standards are commonly understood to result from standardization. But the two terms are treated here as synonymous because, from an analytical perspective, they stand for one particular *type* of inter-firm collaboration rather than representing a process and its outcome.

Various contributors to the VoC literature (Hall and Soskice 2001*a*: 26–7; Tate 2001: 445–6; see also Teubner 2001: 433–5) argue that *coordinated standards*, resulting from cooperation on a large scale, promote the pursuit of *DQP strategies*, because all interested firms can contribute their know-how in order to elaborate high-level standards 'that weed out technically inferior outcomes' (Tate 2001: 446). This, in turn, encourages firms to 'focus on product differentiation and niche production' (Hall and Soskice 2001*a*: 27).

Similarly, VoC scholars argue that *competitive standards*, resulting from market races or the small-scale collaboration of firms, facilitate the pursuit of *RPI strategies* (Hall and Soskice 2001*a*: 30–1; Tate 2001: 445, 468). Since large-scale standardization entails the widespread diffusion of substantial knowledge about product or process features, it can pose a problem for the protection of intellectual property (Tate 2001: 455) which, in turn, is said to be crucial for RPI. Radical product innovators have little to gain from developing a new product if the underlying know-how is then diffused widely during the standardization process without providing any financial compensation (see Casper 2001: 405). Thus, competitive standardization furthers RPI in that the winner of a market race has the exclusive right to grant licences. This not only compensates the (financial) efforts of radical innovators, it also enables the latter to control the extent of knowledge diffusion (see Tate 2001: 468).

But can this dichotomous framework – of coordinated standards facilitating DQP and competitive standards promoting RPI strategies – accommodate hypotheses on LCP? While VoC scholars do not offer explicit propositions as to how different standardization processes facilitate LCP, Tate's (2001) contribution makes it possible to infer that participation in any type of standardization, be it competitive or coordinated, hinders the pursuit of LCP strategies. As illustrated in the introduction to this chapter, standardization is costly. This is particularly true for small-scale standardization processes where consortium members have to pay high membership fees (ibid.: 446–67). But also the large-scale elaboration of coordinated standards requires substantial investments of time and money (Büthe and Witte 2004: 12). This, in turn, militates against the pursuit of price-based LCP strategies. *Abstinence from participation in standardization* is therefore likely to facilitate *LCP strategies*. With regard to the hold-up problem mentioned initially, the idea that low-cost producers abstain from standardization implies that hold-up is simply avoided.

The above reasoning allows us to propose three testable hypotheses on the link between standards and competitive strategies.

Hypothesis 1 (H1):
Competitive standardization, i.e. competitive standards resulting from market races or small-scale collaboration of firms, facilitates RPI.

Hypothesis 2 (H2):
Coordinated standardization, i.e. coordinated standards resulting from large-scale cooperation of firms, supports DQP.

Hypothesis 3 (H3):
Abstinence from standardization processes supports LCP.

In addition to the importance of different standardization types, the strongest alternative explanation for why firms pursue specific strategies needs to be assessed so as to learn about the relative impact of both factors. Should this rival factor turn out to be a better predictor of competitive strategies than the respective standardization types, one can conclude that standards do not constitute necessary input factors, but that they are secondary to firms when pursuing the chosen strategy. As discussed in Chapter 3 (Section 3.1), strategy studies of the innovation and strategic management literature suggest that corporate age constitutes the strongest rival explanation for a firm's competitive strategy (Levitt 1965; Klepper and Graddy 1990; Utterback 1994; Klepper and Simons 1997; Walker 2003: chapter 4). Since radical innovation often makes existing products obsolete, incumbent firms have little interest in pursuing a strategy which accelerates the decline of their own products (Utterback 1994: 160–5, 223–6). Given that newly founded firms usually have hardly any products that risk becoming obsolete if a radically new innovation is made, young corporate age facilitates RPI. The opposite holds true for the pursuit of DQP and LCP strategies. Following this logic, the rival hypothesis to be tested is that:

Hypothesis 4 (H4):
(a) Young corporate age is conducive to the pursuit of an RPI strategy, whereas
(b) advanced corporate age promotes both DQP and
(c) LCP strategies.

## 4.2. HOW IMPORTANT ARE COMPETITIVE AND COORDINATED STANDARDIZATION FOR RPI, DQP, AND LCP STRATEGIES?

To assess the impact of different standardization types on competitive strategies, the above hypotheses need to be operationalized. To this end, contributions to the VoC literature offer helpful insights, even though they typically focus on less-technology-intense sectors, for the most part metalworking industries. For the products of these industries, Tate (2001) refers to *standards* as standards of product components, i.e. the ensemble of technical characteristics of semi-finished goods that make up the final product. Translating this concept to the pharmaceutical industry, a standard can be defined as the characteristics of all those active ingredients and excipients which make up a pharmaceutical product. Since *competitive standards* result from small-scale collaboration between firms, active ingredients or excipients of pharmaceutical products are defined as competitive whenever they are determined by a small number of companies on a contractual basis.

*Coordinated standards*, on the other hand, result from large-scale collaboration between firms in encompassing industry associations. For industrial goods, the large-scale coordination of component standards, as illustrated by VoC contributors, takes place in national and international associations such as the Deutsches Institut für Normung (DIN), the British Standards Institution (BSI), or the International Organization for Standardization (ISO) (see, e.g. Tate 2001). For the pharmaceutical industry, comparable associations that coordinate the standardization of new pharmaceutical ingredients on a large scale exist at both the national and the international level. At the European level, these standardization processes take place within the *European Pharmacopoeia Commission*. In addition, *national pharmacopoeia commissions* exist which determine standards for pharmaceutical ingredients in those areas that are not covered by the European Pharmacopoeia. Like other large-scale associations, it is the task of these commissions to form and coordinate expert committees and working groups within which new monographs are elaborated. A monograph determines the standards for a pharmaceutical ingredient by describing both its characteristics and preparation. All monographs together form the *European* (or respectively *British*, *German*, *Italian*, etc.) *Pharmacopoeia*. Apart from the European and national pharmacopoeia commissions, a few other associations exist which coordinate large-scale standardization, e.g. the German Pharmaceutical Codex (*Deutscher Arzneimittel-Codex*). However, these associations are of minor importance as they only elaborate pharmaceutical standards in those, very few, areas that are not covered by the European Pharmacopoeia or national pharmacopoeia (BfArM 2004).

Whenever a new (pharmacopoeia) monograph is drafted, all interested parties – such as firms, laboratories, and experts – are free to participate in the standardization process. While other procedures exist, interested firms can propose an experienced employee as a member of a newly forming working group. For single-source active substances, it may also occur that the pharmacopoeia commission turns to the firm which developed the substance in question so as to request its collaboration in elaborating a new monograph. Active ingredients and excipients of pharmaceutical products are thus defined as coordinated whenever they are determined by the European Pharmacopoeia or a national pharmacopoeia, or by a comparable large-scale standardization association.

Following the reasoning of the VoC literature, RPI strategists can thus be expected to determine new pharmaceutical standards mostly on their own, or in collaboration with a small number of other firms or research organizations. DQP pursuers, by contrast, should be more inclined to participate in large-scale standardization processes coordinated by the pharmacopoeia commission or comparable associations. LCP strategists presumably abstain from competitive and coordinated standardization alike. Will empirical evidence confirm these hypotheses?

### 4.2.1. Assessing the Strength of Correlations

Seeking to answer the previous question, structured interviews were carried out with Chief Executive Officers (CEOs) and Quality Assurance (QA) managers of those 130 pharmaceutical firms which already served as an empirical basis in Chapter 3.[5] More precisely, this sample consists of the 102 pharmaceutical firms derived in Chapter 2 (Section 2.4) increased by the 28 generics and biotech companies identified in Chapter 3 (Section 3.2).[6] Overall, information on 64 out of these 130 firms could be obtained.

To assess whether particular types of standards facilitate each strategy, CEOs and QA managers were asked whether their firm participates in competitive standardization, i.e. whether the firm develops, or has developed, active ingredients or excipients either on its own or together with a small number of companies or research organizations, so that the ingredients' features are only known to a limited number of actors. Furthermore, interviewees were asked whether employees of their firm are, or have been, members of a working group or an expert committee of the pharmacopoeia commission, or of a comparable standardization association. In addition, interviewees were also asked about the reasons for why their firm has, or has not, engaged in the respective standardization processes. Interviews therefore provided not only quantitative data but also important qualitative insights into how different types of standards impact on competitive strategies.

Table 4.1 gives an overview of the answers obtained. Interestingly, RPI, DQP, and LCP strategists differ notably in their standardization activities, even though the latter do not always correspond to the hypothesized patterns. Overall, low-cost producers display the predicted standardization behaviour most clearly. Although some LCP strategists (16.7 per cent) send employees to participate in working groups of a pharmacopoeia commission or comparable standardization association, the large majority (83.3 per cent) abstain from coordinated standardization. Similarly, not a single low-cost producer for which data could be obtained engages in competitive standardization. Empirical evidence thus indicates support for hypothesis H3 that abstinence from standardization supports LCP.

The standardization behaviour of RPI and DQP strategists, by contrast, is less in line with the above hypotheses. Casting doubt on hypothesis H2, only 43.3 per cent of DQP strategists participate in coordinated standardization – less than one out of two. Is this enough to hypothesize that coordinated standards support DQP? The standardization behaviour of RPI strategists is already more

[5] Remember that a 'pharmaceutical firm' is used as an umbrella term for all firms that are active in the drug industry, including biotechnology, traditional pharmaceutical, and generics firms (see Section 1.2).

[6] A complete list of these 130 pharmaceutical firms is provided in the technical appendix (see Table A.1 for the British, Table A.2 for the German, and Table A.3 for the Italian firms included).

**Table 4.1.** Competitive and coordinated standardization of RPI, DQP, and LCP strategists

| | | RPIs | DQPs | LCPs | Total |
|---|---|---|---|---|---|
| Firms which participate in competitive standardization, alone or with a few other firms or PROs | No. | 19 | 27 | 0 | 46 |
| | % | **100** | **100** | **0** | 80.7 |
| of all firms for which data could be obtained | No. | 19 | 27 | 11 | 57 |
| | % | 100 | 100 | 100 | 100 |
| | | **RPIs** | **DQPs** | **LCPs** | **Total** |
| Firms which participate in coordinated standardization, i.e. send employee(s) to (pharmacopoeia) working-group(s) | No. | 1 | 13 | 2 | 16 |
| | % | **6.3** | **43.3** | **16.7** | 27.6 |
| of all firms for which data could be obtained | No. | 16 | 30 | 12 | 58 |
| | % | 100 | 100 | 100 | 100 |

*Source*: Own calculations based on sixty-four interviews.

in line with hypothesis H1, as almost all of them abstain from coordinated standardization, preferring to elaborate competitive standards. And yet, competitive standardization seems to support not only RPI but also DQP strategies because, akin to all radical product innovators, all diversified quality producers also elaborate new pharmaceutical standards on their own or in collaboration with a few other actors.

This indicates that coordinated and competitive standardization do not constitute mutually exclusive approaches to elaborating new standards, but compatible and even complementary alternatives. RPI, DQP, and LCP strategists do not therefore differ from each other where their involvement in competitive standardization alone is concerned – as both RPI and DQP firms develop competitive standards. Similarly, it is insufficient to consider solely their participation in coordinated standardization, as both RPI and LCP firms abstain from this. Only when we consider jointly whether a firm participates in competitive and coordinated standardization will we find that the three strategies differ notably from each other, as LCP pursuers abstain from both processes, RPI firms engage in competitive but abstain from coordinated standardization, while DQP strategists participate in competitive and – in one out of two instances – also coordinated standardization. To capture these differences in joint standardization approaches, a composite standardization index was created. This measure, very simply, reports the overall standardization activities of firms by assigning a score of

'0' to those firms that elaborate neither competitive nor coordinated standards, a score of '1' to firms that engage either in competitive or in coordinated standardization, and a score of '2' to firms that participate in both processes.[7]

To assess whether particular standardization approaches constitute significant factors for different strategies and, if so, whether they are even more important than corporate age (the strongest rival explanation for why firms pursue specific strategies), three sets of multinomial logistic regression analyses were carried out. In the first two sets (Models 1 and 2), *joint standardization activities* and *corporate age* were regressed separately (as the respective independent variable of each model) on *competitive strategy* (dependent variable),[8] so as to test the individual explanatory power of both variables. Model 3 then assessed the relative importance of *joint standardization* and *age* (independent variables) by regressing them jointly on *competitive strategy* (dependent variable). The multinomial logistic regression analysis carried out in Model 3 can thus be written as the following equations:

$$(1)\ \text{Odds}_{\text{RPI/LCP}} = \frac{\text{prob}_{\text{RPI}}}{\text{prob}_{\text{LCP}}} = e^{\beta_{10} + \beta_{11}\,\text{competitive and coordinated standardization} + \beta_{12}\,\text{corporate age}}$$

$$(2)\ \text{Odds}_{\text{DQP/LCP}} = \frac{\text{prob}_{\text{DQP}}}{\text{prob}_{\text{LCP}}} = e^{\beta_{20} + \beta_{21}\,\text{competitive and coordinated standardization} + \beta_{22}\,\text{corporate age}}$$

To identify possible country-specific variations in the standardization behaviour of RPI, DQP, and LCP strategists, the same multinomial logistic regression analyses were not only carried out on the basis of the overall data-set, but they were also performed separately for the British, German, and Italian samples. While the number of observations per country was sometimes too small to produce statistically significant results, all directional indicators obtained were in line with those of the overall sample. Table 4.2 therefore reports the

[7] While information on both standardization variables was available for fifty-one of those sixty-four firms for which data could be obtained, information was available only for one of the two variables in the remaining thirteen instances. To obtain the largest possible number of observations, these thirteen firms were nevertheless included, whereby it was assumed that they abstain from the unobserved standardization process.

[8] Distinguishing between three discrete categories, the strategy variable assigns a value of '1' to any firm that pursues an RPI strategy, a value of '2' to any DQP pursuer, and a value of '3' to any LCP strategist.

**Table 4.2.** Importance of joint standardization activities and corporate age for RPI, DQP, and LCP strategies
(Results of multinomial logistic regression analyses: exponential *B*)

| **Model** | **1** | | | **2** | | | **3** | | |
|---|---|---|---|---|---|---|---|---|---|
| Comparing **to reference category** | DQP **RPI** | LCP **DQP** | RPI **LCP** | DQP **RPI** | LCP **DQP** | RPI **LCP** | DQP **RPI** | LCP **DQP** | RPI **LCP** |
| **Indep. variables** | | | | | | | | | |
| Joint standard. activities | 1.013** | .959*** | 1.028*** | | | | 1.000 | .954*** | 1.048*** |
| Corporate age | | | | 1.061*** | .993 | .950*** | 1.061*** | 1.020 | .925*** |
| *N* | 64 | | | 64 | | | 64 | | |
| $R^2_{Nagelkerke}$ | .451 | | | .376 | | | .674 | | |

Significance levels: * <.10; ** <.05; *** <.01. Constant not reported in table.

results produced by the analyses of the entire sample, i.e. of those sixty-four firms for which data were available.[9]

Overall, Table 4.2 supports the idea that different standardization approaches facilitate RPI, DQP, and LCP strategies. This is most evident for LCP. Model 1 reveals that a 1 per cent increase in a firm's standardization activities leads to a decrease in the odds of the firm pursuing an LCP rather than a DQP strategy by 4.1 per cent (1 – 0.959 = 0.041), while the odds of it pursuing an LCP rather than an RPI strategy decrease by 2.8 per cent. When controlled for corporate age, the odds of firms engaging in LCP rather than DQP even decrease by 4.6 per cent (1 – 0.954 = 0.046), while the odds of firms engaging in LCP rather than RPI go down by 4.8 per cent (see Model 3) for each additional percentage point of standardization activities. Combined with the insights derived from Table 4.1, this confirms hypothesis H3. Low-cost production is supported by firms abstaining from both competitive and coordinated standardization, as the costs related to these processes are avoided.

The importance of competitive and coordinated standardization for RPI and DQP strategies, however, is less evident. While Model 1 indicates that RPI and DQP firms vary significantly from each other in that a 1 per cent increase in their standardization activities leads to an increase in the odds of firms being DQP rather than RPI strategists by 1.3 per cent, Model 3 shows

[9] Multinomial logistic regression analyses with standard errors clustered by country lead to the same results as reported in Table 4.2. This supports the finding that country-specific characteristics do not influence the standardization behaviour of RPI, DQP, and LCP strategists.

that this variation becomes insignificant as soon as standardization activities are controlled for corporate age. Drawing on the insights gained from Table 4.1, these findings refute hypothesis H1 that competitive standardization facilitates RPI. Given that all observed RPI and DQP strategists engage in competitive standardization, the variation observed in Model 1 is necessarily the result of RPI strategists abstaining from coordinated standardization, whereas 43 per cent of DQP strategists participate in this process (see Table 4.1). However, Model 3 shows that even this variation is insignificant compared to the age differences between RPI and DQP strategists. Model 3 therefore also casts doubt on the modified version of hypothesis H2 that coordinated standardization facilitates DQP *in addition* to competitive standardization.

Contrary to hypotheses H1 and H2, Table 4.2 confirms hypotheses H4 that young corporate age is conducive to RPI (H4a), whereas advanced corporate age promotes DQP (H4b) and LCP strategies (H4c). This is shown not only by Model 2 but also by Model 3, which indicates that for each additional year of corporate age, the odds of firms being DQP rather than RPI strategists increase by 6.1 per cent, while the odds of firms being LCP rather than RPI strategists increase by 7.5 per cent ($1 - 0.925 = 0.075$). Likewise, Models 2 and 3 confirm that the age difference between DQP and LCP pursuers is statistically insignificant.

When considering the overall explanatory power of standardization and corporate age, one can argue that the (non-)elaboration of particular standards is more important for competitive strategies than specific age ranges, as Model 1 (where $R^2 = 0.451$) explains 7.5 per cent more of strategy variation than Model 2 (where $R^2 = 0.376$). One might even deduce from this that the (non-)elaboration of standards constitutes a decisive input factor for different strategies. Importantly, though, the strong explanatory power of standards does not support the idea that particular standardization approaches facilitate RPI, DQP, and LCP strategies. Instead, it suggests that the abstinence from any standardization process promotes imitation-based LCP, while the elaboration of competitive and coordinated standards promotes R&D based strategies: RPI and DQP.

This, in turn, brings us back to the idea that coordinated and competitive standardization do not constitute rival, but complementary, approaches to elaborating new standards. It also raises the question of why all innovative firms engage in competitive standardization and why only one out of two DQP strategists participates in coordinated standardization, from which most RPI and LCP pursuers abstain. In addition to testing the correlational strength between different standard types and competitive strategies, it is thus also worthwhile enquiring about the causes which, according to the VoC scholars, link the two variables.

### 4.2.2. Enquiring About Causal Relationships

When representatives of RPI, DQP, and LCP strategists were asked about the reasons for their firm's standardization approach, they revealed that competitive and coordinated standardization often takes place consecutively. As long as an innovative product has not been brought to market, i.e. obtained a marketing authorization, *competitive standardization* is particularly important. The reason for this is that innovators simply do not gain from diffusing the features of an innovative pharmaceutical ingredient through large-scale standardization as long as they do not know whether the respective ingredient has the necessary curative potential – without intolerable side effects – to obtain regulatory approval. Were they to engage in coordinated standardization before the drug's regulatory approval, innovative firms would merely risk revealing precious information without knowing whether this would yield profits (Grünecke 2004; Steiner 2004; Tom 2005; see also Jenner 2004; Maler 2004).

This explanation supports the VoC reasoning that competitive standardization facilitates innovation as it helps to protect firms' intellectual property (Tate 2001: 445, 468; see also Casper 2001: 405; Hall and Soskice 2001*a*: 30–1). However, contrary to the VoC reasoning, the argument does not only apply to RPI strategists but to all innovative firms, including DQP pursuers. If anything, competitive standardization is possibly more important for DQP than for RPI strategists, as radical inventions can be patent-protected more easily than incremental inventions. Since incremental pharmaceutical improvements are sometimes not inventive enough to obtain patent protection, competitive standardization makes it difficult for imitators to understand how the respective improvements have been achieved. The reason for this is that, unlike patents, the registration files of pharmaceutical products are not publicly accessible and can therefore not be searched by other pharmaceutical firms (Aluse 2005). Consequently, competitive standardization facilitates RPI and DQP strategies as it helps to protect radical and incremental innovation from unwanted imitation.

In line with this reasoning, interviewees of LCP strategists pointed out that the elaboration of competitive standards would mean no more than incurring unnecessary expenditure (Friedner 2005; Collar 2006). Since LCP strategists imitate active ingredients and excipients of successful pharmaceutical products upon patent expiry, they simply do not need to develop new pharmaceutical ingredients. This, in turn, indicates support for the reasoning on which hypothesis H3 is based: LCP strategists abstain from competitive standardization as this notably contributes to cutting costs.

*Coordinated standardization* starts to become important once a radically or incrementally new drug has been approved by the responsible authorities so that the drug's imitation becomes a matter of time. Sooner or later, LCP imitators will find out how to re-engineer the new pharmaceutical ingredients, even though the latter take the form of competitive standards known only to the (small group of) originator(s). At that moment, diffusing the, as yet, hardly known pharmaceutical ingredient through large-scale standardization can entail important regulatory advantages. The requirements on the part of the legislator for purity and quality of pharmaceutical ingredients are extremely strict. Whenever a pharmaceutical company seeks to register a new product, it must demonstrate that all the active ingredients and excipients contained are of adequate quality. To this end, the European and national pharmacopoeia, as well as comparable sources of coordinated standards, serve as important benchmarks. Once a coordinated monograph is elaborated, pharmaceutical firms are free to determine standards that go beyond its quality requirements. But as soon as a monograph exists, a marketing authorization will only be granted if the applicant demonstrates that the respective ingredient fulfils *at least* the monograph's standards. While it is certainly costly to relieve employees of their usual work so as to send them off to pharmacopoeia or comparable working groups, a firm can make sure by doing so that the new monograph is in line with its needs and capacities, e.g. its manufacturing procedures. As a result, regulatory approval of future drugs using the respective pharmaceutical ingredient, as well as reapproval of the original drug, can be obtained faster and more easily (BfArM 2004).

Coming back to the reasoning of the VoC literature, firms do thus not participate in coordinated standardization to elaborate high-level standards 'that weed out technically inferior outcomes' (Tate 2001: 446). When interviewees of firms that participate in coordinated standardization were asked about this motive, they systematically disagreed. Regulatory requirements are generally so demanding that large-scale cooperation can hardly contribute to further improvements. Rather than elaborating standards of higher quality, firms participate in large-scale standardization to establish the features of their pharmaceutical ingredients as a baseline which prevents regulatory claims for different or even higher quality (Steiner 2004; Aluse 2005; Cocker 2005; see also Jenner 2004; Maler 2004).

The regulatory advantages resulting from coordinated standardization motivate not only one out of two DQP strategists, but also one out of six LCP pursuers to elaborate coordinated standards (see Table 4.1). Most LCP pursers, though, seem to find it less expensive to re-engineer pharmaceutical ingredients without seeking to diffuse them through coordinated standardization than to invest in coordinated standardization, even if this facilitates regulatory approval. The reason why only one out of sixteen RPI pursuers engages in coordinated standardization seems to be related to the value-chain focus of radically innovative firms. As illustrated in Chapter 2 (Section 2.1), RPI strategists tend to concentrate on research and early clinical development of new pharmaceutical ingredients. At these stages, it is usually still unpredictable whether the respective inventions can be transformed into marketable drugs.

Since innovative firms do not gain from elaborating coordinated standards at such early stages, almost all RPI pursuers abstain from this process.

## 4.3. COMPETING DESPITE COMPARATIVE INSTITUTIONAL DISADVANTAGES? COMPETITIVE AND COORDINATED STANDARDIZATION IN ECONOMIES WITH DIFFERENT ANTITRUST LEGISLATION

To understand how national institutions impact on different strategies, let us recapitulate that the abstinence from standardization facilitates LCP as it contributes to cutting costs. Competitive standardization, in turn, promotes RPI and DQP in that it helps to protect innovations from imitation, whereas coordinated standardization is particularly important for DQP because it facilitates the (re)approval of pharmaceutical products. As mentioned in the introduction to this chapter, the VoC literature argues that code-based and common-law systems encourage firms to engage in coordinated and competitive standardization respectively. But do these legal systems actually constitute comparative institutional advantages?

To answer this question, it is useful to analyse how firms compete despite comparative institutional disadvantages. How can innovative RPI and DQP strategists in countries with code-based ('continental') law develop competitive standards if permissive antitrust legislation, incorporating 'a producer-oriented tolerance for sectoral (. . .) cartels' (Tate 2001: 443) and a fault-based approach to product liability, encourages firms to determine coordinated standards in inclusive industry associations rather than to elaborate competitive standards in collaboration with a few other firms and public research organizations (PROs) (see Tate 2001: 443–4; Teubner 2001: 433–5; see also Casper 2001)? And how can firms – including, most importantly, DQP pursuers, but also some LCP and RPI strategists – elaborate coordinated standards in countries with a common-law tradition if rigorous antitrust legislation and an open, case-based approach towards product liability discourages large-scale cooperation amongst firms (see Hall and Soskice 2001*a*: 30–1; Tate 2001: 443–4, 446; Teubner 2001: 433–5; see also Casper 2001)?[10]

To begin with, one may find it paradoxical that the VoC literature portrays common law as the more restrictive legal system, even though the latter is said

[10] Since neither the literature nor deductive reasoning provides ideas on how antitrust legislation encourages firms to abstain from standardization, the question of the institutional foundations of LCP is irrelevant.

to encourage small-scale collaboration in the form of competitive standardization. After all, this seems to be a more collusive way of elaborating new standards than coordinated standardization, in which all interested parties have the option to participate. Furthermore, studies indicating that the German *Kartellamt* was for many years particularly restrictive in accepting inter-firm collaboration, and possibly more restrictive than its British counterpart (see Welteke 1976), cast doubt on the tolerance of code-based legal systems. Yet, for the sake of testing the VoC reasoning, its wording shall not be questioned here.

So, how can innovative firms in Germany and Italy elaborate competitive standards, given that permissive antitrust legislation encourages coordinated standardization? When German and Italian representatives of RPI and DQP strategists were asked about the standardization approach of their firm, it was interesting that not a single interviewee perceived the country's legal system in general, and its antitrust legislation in particular, as an obstacle to elaborating new standards with other firms or PROs on a contractual basis. Even more interestingly, this observation holds not only for inter-firm collaboration within the same economy but also across countries, as RPI and DQP strategists cooperate numerously with firms and PROs in other countries. While local proximity was sometimes perceived as an advantage in that it facilitates communication between the cooperating partners, this advantage does not seem to be related to legal traditions. When perceiving the necessity to elaborate new pharmaceutical ingredients in collaboration with a few other innovators, RPI and DQP firms are simply not concerned about national antitrust legislation – at least not in a way that the QA managers interviewed appear to indicate (Grünecke 2004; Aluse 2005; Pellazzo 2005; Rindner 2005).

This, in turn, suggests that the VoC literature has a tendency to portray national institutions as more compelling than they are in the view of firms. The argument that 'German institutions support forms of relational contracting and technology transfer (...) [which] encourage corporate strategies that focus on product differentiation and niche production' (Hall and Soskice 2001*a*: 26–7), combined with the portrait of German and Anglo-Saxon institutions, as well as RPI and DQP strategies, as incompatible opposites rather than compatible alternatives, leads to the impression that innovative firms in Germany find it difficult to elaborate competitive standards. However, the interviews I carried out did not indicate empirical support for this idea. They rather suggest that a code-based legal system does not constitute a comparative institutional *disadvantage* for innovative firms engaging in competitive standardization. By implication, a common-law system does not seem to offer a comparative institutional *advantage* to innovative firms either.

The answer to how firms in the UK elaborate coordinated standards, despite the country's common-law system and its rigorous antitrust legislation, points to the same overestimation of institutional influence on the part of the VoC literature. When British firms were found to elaborate coordinated (pharmacopoeia) monographs as actively as their counterparts in code-based law economies, interviewees were asked about their firm's commitment to coordinated standardization. Again, not a single interviewee indicated support for the idea that British antitrust legislation constitutes an obstacle to coordinated standardization. Instead of contemplating possible consequences of British antitrust legislation, the managers interviewed seemed to be much more concerned about whether they have the necessary human resources to relieve employees of their usual work so as to send them off to pharmacopoeia commissions (Cocker 2005; also Hallerton 2004). After all, coordinated standardization is costly and, thus, rather affordable for bigger firms with a large pool of employees (see Büthe and Witte 2004: 19–20).

A second finding that argues against the importance which the VoC scholars (Casper 2001; Tate 2001; Teubner 2001; Hall and Soskice 2001*a*: 36–44) attach to national antitrust legislation as a determinant of competitive strategy is the internationality of coordinated standardization. As explained in Section 4.2, the development of coordinated pharmaceutical standards nowadays mostly takes place at the supranational level in European pharmacopoeia commissions. Standardization at the national level is far less important than one may assume from reading the VoC literature. Consequently, the same conclusion applies to coordinated standardization as to the elaboration of competitive standards. A common-law system does not seem to constitute a comparative institutional disadvantage for British firms. And, by implication, a code-based law system does not constitute a comparative institutional advantage for German and Italian companies either.

## 4.4. CONCLUDING INTERPRETATION

What do these insights teach us about how firms can use standardization processes as a source of competitive advantage and whether national legal systems offer comparative institutional advantages to this end? Does the pursuit of RPI, DQP, and LCP strategies require particular types of standards? And, if so, does national antitrust legislation foster the availability of the required standard types?

Overall, the distinct standardization behaviour of RPI, DQP, and LCP strategists supports the VoC idea that each strategy requires similar types of input factors. And yet, both the importance of particular standardization approaches for each strategy and the underlying causal mechanisms were found to differ from the VoC suggestions. Most importantly, competitive and coordinated standardization turned out *not* to be mutually exclusive approaches to elaborating standards, as suggested by the dichotomous framework of the

VoC literature. Instead, they constitute compatible and even complementary approaches which are more relevant at different stages in a product's life cycle. As competitive standards help to protect innovations from imitation, they support upstream activities and, thus, not only RPI strategies (see Casper 2001: 405; Hall and Soskice 2001*a*: 30–1; Tate 2001: 444–5, 468) but DQP strategies as well. Coordinated standards, by contrast, facilitate regulatory re(approval) rather than the elaboration of standards of superior quality (Tate 2001: 446), and are therefore a source of competitive advantage to all firms that focus on midstream activities, i.e. primarily to DQP pursuers. Only the standardization behaviour of LCP strategists fully confirms the argument derived from the VoC literature that the abstinence from standardization facilitates LCP as it contributes to cutting costs (see Tate 2001: 466–7; Büthe and Witte 2004: 12).

These findings also shed light on the RBV and its suggestion that firms obtain competitive advantages through resource heterogeneity. In line with Chapter 3, the above analyses cast doubt on this idea, as firms pursuing the same strategy were found to resemble each other in the *homogeneity*, rather than the heterogeneity, of their standardization approaches. Of course, this does *not* suggest that firms are *obliged* to elaborate particular standards in line with the strategies they pursue. DQP firms provide a particularly clear-cut example of this, as roughly 50 per cent participate in coordinated standardization, while the other 50 per cent abstain from this process – possibly because they lack the necessary human resources. Thus, mechanisms compelling DQP strategists to participate in coordinated standardization obviously do not exist. And yet, the abstaining DQP firms seem to be at a competitive disadvantage in that coordinated standards may be elaborated and widely diffused which do not reflect the abstaining firms' production capacities. This, in turn, can significantly slow down (re)approval of pharmaceutical products relying on the respective ingredients. These insights cast doubt on the RBV suggestion that any type of the same input factor can form the basis of a competitive advantage as long as it can be turned into a valuable, rare, imperfectly imitable, and strategically non-substitutable resource (see, e.g. Rumelt 1984; Wernerfelt 1984; Barney 1991; Conner 1991; Peteraf 1993; Barney and Clark 2007; Newbert 2007).

But how can firms then obtain competitive advantages, avoiding mere imitation of each other's behaviour? Chapter 3 has shown that the exploitation of alternative institutional pathways to securing the required input factors offers one possible way of achieving this end. Yet, this possibility seems to be foreclosed in the case of elaborating different standard types. Unlike national pension and insurance systems, the standardization behaviour of firms pursuing the same strategy does not differ from one country to another in line with national antitrust legislation. In other words, firms do not show signs of exploiting (or circumventing) possible comparative institutional advantages (or disadvantages) of their country's legal system. This, in turn, indicates that a competitiveness enhancing link between the shape of national antitrust legislation and the elaboration of pharmaceutical standards does not exist. Contrary to the suggestions of the VoC literature, code-based and common-law systems do not therefore seem to constitute either comparative institutional advantages or disadvantages for the elaboration of pharmaceutical standards.

This finding is particularly interesting as it allows us to develop further ideas about how firms can gain competitive advantages over their competitors. Given that RPI, DQP, and LCP strategists use the same standard types to pursue the chosen strategy and given, furthermore, that they cannot exploit comparative institutional advantages, alternative possibilities need to exist which allow firms to do something better than their competitors. So, how do firms avoid imitating each other? Since the outcome to be reached by a given process is clearly established, it can only be the nature or quality of this process, which allows firms to stand out from each other and gain competitive advantages. To give an example, firms might develop competitive pharmaceutical standards together with extraordinarily knowledgeable partners, or be in a particularly strong position vis-à-vis the other members of the pharmacopoeia commission. This, in turn, would allow them to develop particularly promising competitive standards, or to be exceptionally fast in elaborating coordinated standards. In other words, firms do not seem to gain competitive advantages by employing unique resources, but by securing specific types of resources in a unique way. And yet, it would be a mistake to consider these propositions as more than speculative, since the analyses of this chapter have been unable to consider more than the *type* of standardization processes facilitating particular strategies. Consequently, further research into the *nature* of such factor-providing processes is both needed and promising.

The suggestions as to how firms can achieve competitive advantages through the *nature* rather than the *outcome* of processes providing required input factors corroborates a further finding of Chapter 3. Schumpeter's distinction between 'entrepreneurs' and 'managers' seems to be, again, particularly instructive for understanding how firms compete. As expounded previously, Schumpeter crucially distinguishes between the inventors of new business ideas, 'entrepreneurs', and the uninspired executors of these ideas, 'managers' (see Schumpeter 1934: 74–94, 1939: 103–6, 1947). Applying this distinction to the above insights, we find that it is impossible to understand how firms can build competitive advantages as long as they are perceived as being run by managers who engage in particular standardization processes because this is the thing to do. But once firms are understood as being run by 'entrepreneurs' who relentlessly seek to optimize the nature of the respective standardization process, it might be possible to explain how firms can build competitive advantages through elaborating standards.

# 5

# Linking Labour-Market Institutions, Employee Skills, and Competitive Strategies

How do firms that pursue the same strategy build competitive advantages? Do they seek to build unique resources by employing a highly individual pool of labour skills? Or do they require the same types of skills to pursue strategies of radical product innovation (RPI), diversified quality production (DQP), and low-cost production (LCP) respectively? Can national labour-market institutions offer comparative advantages by facilitating the availability of particular skill types? And, if so, how can firms compete in economies where these institutions constitute comparative disadvantages?

To begin with, it is hard to imagine how firms could operate without a labour force. The view that 'labour' constitutes an indispensable input factor for the pursuit of any competitive strategy is therefore uncontested in the literature. The question, rather, is whether firms that pursue the same strategy are better advised to build competitive advantages by employing a workforce with individual skill profiles, or whether the same skill types are necessary for RPI, DQP, and LCP strategies. According to the resource-based view (RBV) of strategic management, the former is the case (see, e.g. Barney and Clark 2007: chapter 6). Even though contributors to this literature consider the process through which firms build individual skills rather than the skill types themselves, RBV scholars are convinced that firms build competitive advantages by employing valuable, rare, imperfectly imitable, and strategically non-substitutable resources (see, e.g. Rumelt 1984; Wernerfelt 1984; Barney 1991; Conner 1991; Peteraf 1993; see also Acedo et al. 2006; Newbert 2007). Consequently, a unique pool of employee skills seems to be an important source of sustainable competitive advantages, particularly if firms pursue the same strategy.

Contributors to the competitiveness literature, in contrast, suggest that firms pursing the same strategy need employees with similar skill types.[1] While employees with 'general' (Estevez-Abe et al. 2001: 148) or 'multi-tasking' skills (Lindbeck and Snower 2001*a*: 1872–3) are said to be needed for RPI, workers with 'firm-specific' (Estevez-Abe et al. 2001: 148) or 'occupational-specialization' skills (Lindbeck and Snower 2001*a*: 1872) presumably facilitate high-quality production. Low-qualified and, hence, inexpensive labour is claimed to be required for LCP.

The competitiveness literature further argues that in order to build competitive advantages, firms should exploit the comparative advantages offered by national labour-market institutions. These comparative advantages consist in the relative abundance of the aforementioned skill types due to the way in which national labour-market institutions resolve the freeriding problem related to the professional education and training of employees (see Hall and Soskice 2001*a*: 25–6; Culpepper 2001; Le Galès and Voelzkow 2001: 4–5). More precisely, this collective-action problem consists in the unwillingness of *employers* to invest in sophisticated training programmes if they fear that competitors will freeride their educational efforts by poaching trained employees without investing in training programmes themselves. In a similar vein, *employees* are not interested in acquiring highly specific skills if the risk of being dismissed at short notice is high, because firm-specific skills are, by definition, of little use within the context of another firm. In sum, as long as no mechanism exists that insures employers against the risk of poaching and employees against the risk of dismissal at short notice, they are both reluctant to invest in highly specific skills.

Depending on how national labour-market institutions resolve this freeriding problem, employees thus acquire different types of skills, the competitiveness literature argues further.[2] In *rigid labour-market economies* like Germany, freeriding is overcome in that long-term employment assures both employers and employees that their investment in sophisticated training programmes will pay off. Long job tenures result from wage-bargaining centralization, powerful works councils, long notice periods, and a pronounced use of competition clauses. In centralized bargaining systems, wage levels are homogeneous, as employees with equivalent skills are paid equivalent wages. Homogeneous wage levels, in turn, on the one hand assure employers that highly skilled work-

[1] For particularly prominent proponents, see Porter (1990: 73–6), Estevez-Abe et al. (2001: 146, 174–6), Hall and Soskice (2001*a*: 36–44), Lindbeck and Snower (2001*a*); see also Ohlin (1933: 12, 68–75), Porter (1985: 127), King and Wood (1999: 376), Franzese and Mosher (2002: 181), and Sinn (2005: 18–19, 93).

[2] See Estevez-Abe et al. (2001: 145, 149–55), Hall and Soskice (2001*a*: 24–7, 29–30), Lindbeck and Snower (2001*a*), see also Ohlin (1933: 72–3), Porter (1990: 73–6), and Sinn (2005).

ers, once trained, are unlikely to leave their company, as financial incentives are limited. On the other hand, they also assure employees 'that they are receiving the highest feasible rates of pay in return for the deep commitments they are making' to invest in specific skills (Hall and Soskice 2001*a*: 25). In a similar vein, works councils with authority over lay-offs, as well as long notice periods and competition clauses, tie employees to the firm. Since such rigid labour-market institutions make frequent changes of employment disadvantageous, employers are willing to offer sophisticated training, which, in turn, provides their workforce with *high* and *specific skills*.[3]

In *flexible labour-market economies* like the UK, by contrast, freeriding is prevented by institutions that deter employers and employees from investing in sophisticated training. Typically, a flexible labour market is characterized by wage-bargaining decentralization, weak works councils, short notice periods, and a limited use of competition clauses. These labour-market institutions have the opposite effect of the aforementioned long-term-oriented institutions: they lead to short job tenures as they facilitate hiring and firing at will. Since employers in flexible labour markets are not insured against the risk of poaching, they are unlikely to provide elaborate training programmes. Accordingly, the costs of further education (secondary vocational and tertiary) are passed on to potential employees (see Hall and Soskice 2001*a*: 29–30). But whenever employees decide to engage in further education, they are better off if they do not acquire specific, but rather general skills, because the latter are useful for all firms that need a certain business function and, consequently, are adequately rewarded. This makes it easier to find new employment in case of dismissal. Employees who decide to continue education and training in flexible labour markets therefore tend to gain *high* and *general skills*.[4]

Finally, in economies where collective agreements establish comparatively *low wage floors*, such as Italy, both employers and employees seem to be best advised to exploit this comparative cost advantage. Employers are thus unlikely to offer education and training programmes, while employees, once they have finished compulsory schooling, possibly decide to start working rather than to invest in further education. Accordingly, employees in low-wage economies can be assumed to have *low skill levels* (see King and Wood 1999: 376; Amable 2003: in particular 102–14, 197–213).

The relative abundance of employees with high and specific, high and general, and low skills is perceived as an important, comparative institutional

[3] For proponents of this line of reasoning, see Estevez-Abe et al. (2001: 145, 149–55), Hall and Soskice (2001*a*: 24–7), and Lindbeck and Snower (2001*a*).

[4] For proponents of this reasoning, see Estevez-Abe et al. (2001: 145, 149–55), Hall and Soskice (2001*a*: 29–30), and Lindbeck and Snower (2001*a*).

advantage of rigid, flexible, and low-wage economies respectively. Since firms are expected to exploit these advantages, it is a central claim of the competitiveness literature that companies specialize in RPI if they are based in countries with flexible labour-market institutions, in DQP if they are active in economies with rigid labour markets, and in LCP if they are located in low-wage economies.[5] In other words, firms in the UK are expected to specialize in RPI, companies in Germany are assumed to prefer DQP, and their counterparts in Italy are said to engage in LCP strategies.

Yet, Chapter 2 has cast doubt on this argument. To understand whether firms gain competitive advantages by hiring employees with an individual skill profile, as stipulated by RBV scholars, or whether they exploit comparative institutional advantages in order to hire employees with similar skill profiles, as suggested by contributors to the competitiveness literature, the remainder of this chapter proceeds as follows. Section 5.1 develops the hypotheses of the latter literature as to why particular skill types facilitate RPI, DQP, and LCP strategies respectively. Section 5.2 assesses these hypotheses at the firm level and finds support for the claim of the competitiveness literature. Section 5.3 therefore asks how pharmaceutical firms secure the required skills in different labour-market economies. In doing so, the most important contribution of this section consists in illustrating how firms circumvent the comparative disadvantages of national labour-market institutions. Section 5.4 summarizes the various findings and links them back to several theoretical debates.

## 5.1. HYPOTHESES AS TO HOW DIFFERENT TYPES OF EMPLOYEE SKILLS FACILITATE RPI, DQP, AND LCP STRATEGIES

To develop hypotheses as to why different skill types facilitate RPI, DQP, and LCP strategies, it is first necessary to clarify the concepts of *specific* and *general skill profiles* on the one hand, and *high* and *low skill levels* on the other. To begin with the latter dyad, contributors to the competitiveness literature (e.g. Soskice 1999: 108; Estevez-Abe et al. 2001: 176; Hall and Soskice 2001*a*: 25–6) offer useful advice as they repeatedly point out that the German vocational training system provides workers with high skill levels. In line with this conception, *low skill levels* are understood here as the completion of compulsory

[5] For proponents of this argument, see Heckscher (1919: 54–7), Ohlin (1933: 12, 68–75), Estevez-Abe et al. (2001), Hall and Soskice (2001*a*: 36–44), Sinn (2005: 56–9, 93); see also Porter (1990: 67–8, 73–6), Lindbeck and Snower (2001*a*), and Franzese and Mosher (2002).

schooling only, while *high skill levels* are defined as both secondary vocational and tertiary education.

As for the conceptualization of different skill profiles, Becker makes an insightful distinction by suggesting that specific skills are useful only within the context of one firm (Becker 1975: 26–7). Employees acquire these skills by working for the same firm for a prolonged period of time and by receiving specific training, which 'increases the future marginal productivity of workers [only] in the firm providing it' (Becker 1975: 19). General skills, in contrast, are defined as those skills that employees can use within the context of all firms in which a certain business function is required (Becker 1975: 19–20). Hence, employees acquire these skills by frequently changing employment and by receiving 'general training [which] increases the marginal productivity of trainees by exactly the same amount in the firms providing the training as in other firms' (Becker 1975: 26).

While this distinction is highly consistent at a theoretical level, it is in practice hard to find employees that hold either completely specific or completely general skills. Furthermore, Estevez-Abe et al. (2001: 148) point out that, in addition to specific or general skills, employees can hold a third skill profile, namely industry-specific skills. Following the above reasoning of Becker, these skills are useful in all firms of the same industry. They are typically acquired through apprenticeship and vocational schools and, therefore, increase the marginal productivity of trainees in all firms which are active in the industry of the firm providing training, while they do not increase the trainees' productivity in firms outside this industry.

Seeking to balance these theoretical and practical concerns, *specific skills* are understood here as narrowly employable skills, typically a mixture of firm- and industry-specific skills, which are not transferable across industries as they are acquired through apprenticeship and vocational training programmes. General skills, in contrast, are defined as widely employable skills that are transferable across industries as they are acquired through further education programmes other than apprenticeship or vocational training.

How do these skill profiles facilitate RPI, DQP, and LCP strategies? To begin with DQP, various contributors to the competitiveness literature suggest that this strategy requires employees with high-level and specific skills (Estevez-Abe et al. 2001: 174–5; Hall and Soskice 2001*a*: 25–6, 39; see also Lindbeck and Snower 2001*a*; Sinn 2005: 18–19, 93). On the one hand, workers need high skill levels in order to use and maintain sophisticated machines and perform complex (assembly) tasks. Specific skills, on the other hand, are necessary because the in-depth knowledge of the company, its market, suppliers, and customers enables employees to continuously improve products and production processes, and to adopt products to specific customer needs. Furthermore, employees with an in-depth understanding of how their firm operates are able to work autonomously and to take on responsibility. They know, for example, how to rectify mistakes that occur during the production process, which, in turn, contributes to maintaining a high level of product quality.

High-level and general skills, in contrast, are said to be necessary for RPI strategies (Estevez-Abe et al. 2001: 174–5; Hall and Soskice 2001*a*: 40–1; see also Lindbeck and Snower 2001*a*). To come up with entirely new ideas, employees need to be highly skilled and understand how certain technologies or industrial processes work. General skills are additionally required because employees can adapt more easily to a constantly changing environment, which, in turn, is characteristic of the pursuit of an RPI strategy.

Finally, the pursuit of an LCP strategy is said to rely on low-skilled employees with basic compulsory education because such employees are comparatively inexpensive.[6] Even though employees with low-level skills often cannot rectify mistakes that occur during the production process without precise instructions from their superiors, this does not harm the pursuit of LCP strategies, as product quality is less important than product costs.

This reasoning makes it possible to derive three sets of testable hypotheses on the importance of different skill types for competitive strategies:

Hypothesis 1 (H1):
(a) High-level and
(b) general skills facilitate the pursuit of RPI strategies, whereas

Hypothesis 2 (H2):
(a) High-level and
(b) specific skills form the basis of DQP.

Hypothesis 3 (H3):
(a) While employees with low-level skills are essential for LCP strategies,
(b) this strategy requires neither specific nor general skill profiles.

To understand *how* important these skill types are for RPI, DQP, and LCP strategies, it is necessary to assess not only their absolute but also their relative explanatory power, because it is not uncommon that an initially strong explanation turns out to be insignificant as soon as a rival hypothesis is tested. Chapters 3 and 4 have already pointed out that the strongest rival explanation for why firms pursue different strategies seems to be their age. As demonstrated by strategic management scholars in general (Levitt 1965; Klepper and Graddy 1990; Utterback 1994; Klepper and Simons 1997; Walker 2003: chapter 4), and Utterback

[6] For proponents of this argument, see Estevez-Abe et al. (2001: 175–6), Hall and Soskice (2001*a*: 44); see also Ohlin (1933: 12, 69), King and Wood (1999: 376), and Sinn (2005: 31–3).

(1994) in particular, radically new innovations rarely come from incumbent firms. Instead, they are frequently proposed by small and comparatively young (start-up) companies which are outsiders to the industry. The reason for this is that radical innovation often makes existing products obsolete. Incumbent firms have therefore little interest in pursuing a strategy which accelerates the decline of their own products (Utterback 1994: 90–101, 160–5, 223–6). Thus, young corporate age seems to facilitate RPI because young companies usually have few or no products that risk becoming obsolete if a radically new innovation is made. The opposite holds true for the pursuit of DQP and LCP strategies. Thus, to assess the relative importance of particular finance types for competitive strategies, the rival hypothesis to be tested is the following.

Hypothesis (H4):
(a) Young corporate age is conducive to the pursuit of an RPI strategy, whereas
(b) advanced corporate age promotes both DQP and
(c) LCP strategies.

## 5.2. HOW IMPORTANT ARE DIFFERENT SKILL TYPES FOR RPI, DQP, AND LCP STRATEGIES?

In line with Chapters 3 and 4, Section 5.2 attempts what hardly any of the contributors to the competitiveness literature has done thus far. It assesses the above hypotheses *at the micro level* to understand whether firms require particular skill types to pursue RPI, DQP, and LCP strategies respectively.[7] In doing so, Section 5.2.1 employs a measure that reflects both skill levels and profiles at the same time, while Section 5.2.2 uses an indicator that captures only particular skill profiles, so as to test their respective importance for each of the three strategies.

The data on which these analyses are based were gathered by carrying out structured interviews with Human Resources (HR) managers of those 130 pharmaceutical firms which have already served as an empirical basis in Chapters 3 and 4.[8] More precisely, this sample consists of the 102 pharmaceutical firms derived in Chapter 2 (Section 2.4) increased by the 28 generics and biotech companies identified in Chapter 3 (Section 3.2).[9]

[7] For the most systematic assessment of these hypotheses at the macro level, see Estevez-Abe et al. (2001).

[8] It is perhaps worth recalling at this point that a 'pharmaceutical firm' is used as an umbrella term for all firms that are active in the drug industry, including biotechnology, traditional pharmaceutical, and generics firms (see Section 1.2).

[9] A complete list of these 130 pharmaceutical firms is provided in the technical appendix (see Table A.1 for the British, Table A.2 for the German, and Table A.3 for the Italian firms included).

Overall, interviews with HR managers in 69 of these 130 firms could be carried out. Importantly, these interviews provided not only quantitative but also qualitative insights, which, in turn, were crucial for structuring and interpreting the following analyses. They also form the basis of Section 5.3 and its illustrations of how firms exploit comparative institutional advantages or, conversely, cope with the disadvantages of national labour-market institutions. Akin to the two previous chapters, this chapter too deliberately seeks to combine qualitative and quantitative analyses.

It should also be noted that Section 5.2 reports the quantitative results obtained from analysing the *overall* data-set of sixty-nine pharmaceutical firms. Importantly, though, these results have all been cross-checked by *country-level* analyses. While the number of firms observed per county was sometimes too small to provide statistically significant results, country-level analyses confirmed the overall findings. One and, more importantly, the same skill type systematically turned out to be more important than the others for pursuing the competitive strategy under investigation, irrespective of the country in which the observed firms were based. Since country-specific analyses are in line with the findings based on the overall sample, only the latter are reported in the following sections.

### 5.2.1. Why Skill Levels Are Less Important for Different Strategies

To assess the hypotheses of Section 5.1, the above conceptualizations suggest that the educational attainment of employees, i.e. the highest degree of education they have completed, constitutes an ideal proxy for their skill types, as this indicator captures skill levels and profiles at the same time. As for the skill levels, employees who have completed compulsory schooling can be said to be low skilled, whereas employees with a secondary vocational or tertiary education are highly skilled. As for the skill profiles, employees with a tertiary education can be said to has general skills, while employees with a secondary education hold specific skills. The part of the workforce with a basic compulsory education, presumably, has neither general nor specific skills.

If the above hypotheses hold true, we should thus find that a significant share of employees in RPI firms holds a degree at the level of tertiary education, whereas the workforce of DQP pursuers mostly hold degrees at the level of secondary vocational education, whilst people employed in LCP firms often have not completed more than compulsory schooling. To gather information about the skill levels of their firm's workforce, HR managers were asked to specify the percentage of employees who have completed compulsory schooling, who hold a degree at the level of secondary vocational education, and at the level of tertiary education respectively.[10] Table 5.1 provides an overview of the answers obtained, detailing them by competitive strategy and country.

Two particularly noteworthy observations can be made on the basis of Table 5.1. First, country-specific variations can be observed in the *absolute* extent to which RPI, DQP, and LCP pursuers employ particular skill types. As interviews with several HR managers indicated, these variations seem to result from differences in how vocational training programmes are designed in Germany, Italy, and the UK (Jon 2004, 2005; Nokich 2004; Garda 2005; Sigillia 2005). Importantly, British, German, and Italian education systems alike offer vocational training courses which provide the enrolled trainees with nationally recognized qualifications required for skilled trade professions.

**Table 5.1.** Skill levels of workforces employed by RPI, DQP, and LCP strategists

| Group of firms | Number of cases | Employees with basic compulsory education (%) | Employees with secondary vocational education (%) | Employees with tertiary education (%) | Total |
|---|---|---|---|---|---|
| RPIs UK | 7 | 12.2 | 14.7 | 73.1 | 100 |
| DQPs UK | 8 | 29.2 | 17.8 | 53.0 | 100 |
| LCPs UK | 4 | 43.7 | 25.8 | 30.5 | 100 |
| RPIs Germany | 6 | 4.5 | 23.7 | 71.8 | 100 |
| DQPs Germany | 11 | 4.5 | 59.4 | 36.1 | 100 |
| LCPs Germany | 9 | 5.6 | 62.1 | 32.3 | 100 |
| RPIs Italy | 7 | 11.9 | 31.6 | 56.5 | 100 |
| DQPs Italy | 10 | 13.2 | 37.0 | 49.8 | 100 |
| LCPs Italy | 4 | 6.3 | 40.0 | 53.7 | 100 |
| **RPIs overall** | **20** | **9.8** | **23.3** | **66.9** | **100** |
| **DQPs overall** | **29** | **14.3** | **40.2** | **45.5** | **100** |
| **LCPs overall** | **17** | **14.7** | **48.4** | **36.9** | **100** |
| **Total** | **66** | **13.0** | **37.2** | **49.8** | **100** |

*Source:* Own calculations based on sixty-six interviews with HR officers in British, German, and Italian pharmaceutical firms.

[10] During interviews with HR managers, these levels of educational attainment were defined as follows:

- *Employees with basic compulsory education* have left education after the minimum number of schooling years required by law. Also, those employees who have completed *secondary, but non-vocational education* were counted as employees with basic compulsory education as they acquire neither advanced general nor specific skills.
- *Employees with secondary vocational education* have completed education with a certificate in vocational training.
- *Employees with tertiary education* have completed education with a university degree or comparable higher education.

The vocational training to be completed in order to obtain such qualifications is particularly well developed and established in Germany. Here, the dual system (*Duales System*) foresees at least two years of professional education provided by vocational colleges (*Berufsschulen*) in collaboration with firms (OECD 1995: 276–8; Gries et al. 2005: 17–19). While countrywide-recognized 'National Vocational Qualifications' (NVQs) can also be obtained in the UK, the training programmes leading to these awards are less well established, however (EIRO 2004*b*; EMIRE 2007).[11] Unlike in Germany, training is not necessarily provided by specialized vocational colleges, but can also be provided by general education colleges and institutes of higher education which, moreover, are often private and thus not free of charge (EIRO 2002; Gries et al. 2005: 32–4). Most importantly, though, the collaboration between the providers of vocational education and firms is not institutionalized, so that British trainees tend to receive less specific preparation for their professional career. Akin to the UK, vocational schools in Italy do not systematically collaborate with firms when providing professional education. However, the educational course to be pursued in order to obtain a training qualification is well established as it is provided by specialized colleges (*istituti tecnici* and *istituti professionali*) which are usually public and, hence, free of charge (OECD 1995: 286–8; Gries et al. 2005: 41–3). Due to Italy's centralized bargaining system, these *istituti* can also offer comparatively sophisticated training courses (see Hancké and Herrmann 2007). These differences in the British, German, and Italian education systems seem to explain why the absolute availability of employees with secondary vocational skills and, hence, the employed workforce holding these skills varies from one country to another.

The second, particularly revealing observation to be made on the basis of Table 5.1 is that, despite country-specific variations in the *absolute* skill types employed, certain types seem to be *relatively* more important for one strategy than for the two others. More concretely, DQP and LCP strategists in all three countries seem to pursue similar employment policies as they rely on particularly high shares of workers not only with secondary vocational training but also with a tertiary education, whereas RPI pursuers mostly employ people with a tertiary education. People with a basic compulsory education constitute the smallest group of employees in most firms, irrespective of the strategy they

[11] The pharmaceutical sector provides an example in that NVQs have been well established and widely used in the *pharmaceutical* industry. However, they have not yet been adapted for the *biopharmaceutical* industry, where they have thus only been poorly used. The reason is that the description of biopharmaceutical qualifications have tended to be research-based and fairly academic. It is only recently that the sector has become more developed, with the result that DQP strategists have recognized the need for vocational qualifications, especially for laboratory chemists, process operators, and engineers (Jon 2007).

**Table 5.2.** Importance of educational attainment for RPI, DQP, and LCP strategies (results of multinomial logistic regression analyses: exponential *B*)

| **Model** | 1 | | | 2 | | | 3 | | |
|---|---|---|---|---|---|---|---|---|---|
| Comparing to **reference category** | DQP **RPI** | LCP **DQP** | RPI **LCP** | DQP **RPI** | LCP **DQP** | RPI **LCP** | DQP **RPI** | LCP **DQP** | RPI **LCP** |
| **Independent variables** | | | | | | | | | |
| Tertiary education | .968* | .970* | 1.065*** | | | | | | |
| Secondary vocational edu. | | | | 1.023 | 1.029* | .949** | | | |
| Basic compulsory education | | | | | | | 1.018 | .999 | .983 |
| Corporate age | 1.017 | .992 | .991 | 1.023* | .990 | .987 | 1.029*** | .996 | .976** |
| *N* | | 66 | | | 66 | | | 66 | |
| $R^2_{\text{Nagelkerke}}$ | | .332 | | | .289 | | | .198 | |

Significance levels: * <.10; ** <.05; *** <.01. Constant not reported in table.

pursue or the country they are based in. It almost seems as if RPI, DQP, and LCP pursuers try to avoid employing people with this education level. While these observations seem to confirm hypotheses H1a and H1b, they cast doubt not only on hypotheses H2a and H2b but, even more importantly, on hypotheses H3a and H3b.

To test the statistical robustness of these observations, six sets of multinomial logistic regression analyses were carried out. While the first three sets assessed the absolute impact of *minimum*, *secondary*, and *tertiary education* (as the model's respective independent variable) on *competitive strategy* (as the model's dependent variable), the second sets tested the relative importance of these three education types by regressing *each type* together with *corporate age* (independent variables) on *competitive strategy* (dependent variable). Interestingly, the directional indicators, the strengths of association, and the scores of statistical significance obtained from the first three sets of analyses hardly changed when corporate age was added as a control variable in the second three sets. Table 5.2 therefore reports only the results obtained from the second sets of multinomial regression analyses, i.e. those regressions testing the relative explanatory power of tertiary (Model 1), secondary (Model 2), and basic compulsory (Model 3) education together with corporate age. Written as the following equations, Model 1 gives an example of the calculations performed:

$$(1)\ \text{Odds}_{\text{RPI/LCP}} = \frac{\text{prob}_{\text{RPI}}}{\text{prob}_{\text{LCP}}} = e^{\beta_{10} + \beta_{11}\,\text{educational attainment} + \beta_{12}\,\text{corporate age}}$$

$$(2)\ \text{Odds}_{\text{DQP/LCP}} = \frac{\text{prob}_{\text{DQP}}}{\text{prob}_{\text{LCP}}} = e^{\beta_{20} + \beta_{21}\ \text{educational attainment} + \beta_{22}\ \text{corporate age}}$$

The results reported in Table 5.2 confirm the observations made on the basis of Table 5.1. In line with hypotheses H1a and H1b, Model 1 shows that RPI strategists employ significantly more people with a tertiary education than both DQP and LCP pursuers. When controlled for corporate age, a 1 per cent increase in the tertiary education of a firm's workforce leads to an increase in the odds of the firm being an RPI rather than a DQP strategist by 3.2 per cent (1 – 0.968 = 0.032), while the odds of the firm pursuing an RPI rather than an LCP strategy increase by 6.5 per cent. This supports the claims of hypotheses H1a and H1b that a workforce with high and general skills is required for RPI. However, Model 2 casts doubt on hypotheses H2a and H2b, which state that high-level and specific skills are necessary for DQP, because LCP pursuers employ more workers with secondary vocational training than DQP strategists. Controlled for a firm's age, a 1 per cent increase in the secondary education of its workforce increases the likelihood of this firm being an LCP rather than a DQP strategist by 2.9 per cent. If they have any effect at all, employees with high-level and specific skills thus seem to facilitate LCP rather than DQP. Finally, Model 3 illustrates that – when controlled for corporate age – neither RPI, nor DQP, nor LCP strategists employ workers with a minimum education to a statistically significant extent. This calls hypotheses H3a and H3b into question as empirical evidence does not support the idea that LCP strategists require a low-skilled workforce.

How are we to understand these results? Interviews with HR managers suggest the following interpretation. Firms that specialize in research and development activities typically require a high number of scientists who, usually, hold university degrees. This explains why RPI strategists that focus on early value-chain activities substantially rely on employees with a tertiary education. Contrary to RPI pursuers, DQP firms do not focus on research and development (R&D) activities, however, but rather carry out downstream activities such as production, marketing, and sales. Accordingly, DQP strategists employ relatively fewer scientists, managers, and department heads with a tertiary education, as they also need production and sales employees with a secondary and, occasionally, minimum education.

The reason why – most notably, German and Italian – LCP strategists with a focus on production, marketing, and sales activities do *not* employ more 'inexpensive' workers with a basic compulsory education is not, however, related to the value-chain focus of low-cost producers. Instead, two alternative explanations seem to account for this seeming paradox. The first is a regulatory aspect, namely the strict requirements for purity of pharmaceutical products imposed by the European legislator. The latter only grants product approval if the applying pharmaceutical firm respects the EU Guide to Good Manufacturing Practice (GMP). With regard to employee skills, the GMP guide stipulates that '[t]he manufacturer should have an adequate number of personnel with the necessary qualifications and practical experience' (EudraLex 2003: chapter 2). More concretely, this means that pharmaceutical companies are only allowed to employ people below a certain age limit if the latter have completed at least secondary education. This is a part of the explanation for why the sales force and even production workers of LCP strategists are rather highly skilled.

However, the second and – in the eyes of the HR managers interviewed – possibly more important explanation is that highly skilled workers are highly productive! When HR managers of German and Italian LCP strategists were asked whether a workforce with high education would not constitute an undesirable cost burden, their answers indicated the opposite. Skilled and 'expensive' employees were usually perceived as more beneficial because they are able to work autonomously, so that they are more productive than employees with low skill levels who require constant supervision (Asoni 2005; Coin 2005; Freel 2005; Winer 2005; Cottidiani 2006). Interestingly, this idea was also confirmed by HR managers from British LCP firms. Instead of perceiving a low-skilled workforce as an inexpensive benefit for the pursuit of an LCP strategy, HR managers repeatedly deplored the shortage of workers with a secondary vocational education in the UK (see also EIRO 2004*b*). Accordingly, British HR managers agreed that they were willing to pay higher wages for employees with higher skill levels, as the latter are usually more productive (Jon 2004, 2005; Perrisson 2006; Wellam 2006). This contributes to the explanation of why not only LCP strategists, but also RPI and DQP pursuers, show a preference for *not* employing people with only a basic compulsory education.

The finding that a balance exists between workers' level of education and their productivity is unsurprising to the extent that a firm's cost competitiveness is usually measured by its unit labour costs, i.e. the ratio between the wage or salary of employees and their unit output (OECD 2007). In other words, cost competitiveness is not determined by absolute wage levels, but by wage levels relative to workers' performance. Hence, firms – including low-cost producers – can well afford to pay employees high wages if the latter are appropriately productive. And employees are appropriately productive if they are adequately skilled. A balance thus seems to exist between the educational level of employees and their productivity on the one hand and their wage levels on the other. The higher the education level, the more productive the employees are and the higher the wages are they can duly claim.

This balance indicates that skill *levels* do not have a significant impact on the pursuit of different strategies. Consequently, hypotheses H1a, H2a, and H3a on the importance of high and low skill profiles for RPI, DQP, and LCP strategies can be discarded. Given, however, that RPI pursuers rely so notably on employees with university education, while workers with secondary vocational training seem to be especially important for DQP strategists, it could be possible that particular skill *profiles* are required for these strategies. The importance of general and, correspondingly, specific profiles may however not have emerged fully from the above analyses, because 'educational attainment' constitutes a proxy for skill levels and profiles alike. To assess hypotheses H1b, H2b, and H3b, it is thus necessary to use a proxy that only reflects the skill profiles of employees.

### 5.2.2. Why Skill Profiles Facilitate RPI and DQP Strategies

How to measure specific and general skills at the micro level in a meaningful way?[12]

To this end, it was necessary to compose a new indicator on the basis of the interviews conducted, which combines those factors that the competitiveness literature considers crucial for employees in order to acquire specific skills: employment tenure (Estevez-Abe et al. 2001: 145, 150–1; Hall and Soskice 2001*a*: 27, 41; Lindbeck and Snower 2001*b*: 183), vocational training (Hall and Soskice 2001*a*: 25, 30), and on-the-job training (see Lindbeck and Snower 2001*a*). Since these factors were added up to form one 'skill specificity indicator', the 'skill generality index' was derived from the specificity index by assigning it the reversed scores. To avoid repetition, I will only describe below how the specificity indicator was composed.

Overall, up to 5 points were assigned to each interviewed firm on the basis of the three aforementioned criteria. Hence, up to 2 points were credited according to the firm's *average job tenure*. Whenever job tenure was lower than 4 years, 0 points were awarded, assuming that employees do not work long enough for the same firm to develop specific skills. One point was assigned for job tenure between 4 and 7.9 years. And 2 points were allocated for average tenure of more than 8 years, because such long-term employment presumably

[12] Contrary to *micro-level* assessments of skill profiles (see, for example, Iversen and Soskice 2001: 881–3), studies that measure skill profiles on the basis of *macro-level* data are more frequent, yet less fine-grained and, hence, less insightful for the purpose of our analyses (see, for example, Patel and Pavitt 1994a: 90; Estevez-Abe *et al.* 2001: 170).

allows employees to gain an in-depth understanding of how their firm operates.[13] Second, the extent to which companies *employ former trainees* was considered. In doing so, no points were allocated to firms which do not offer (vocational) training to young people during their education. Similarly, no points were allocated to firms that offer (vocational) training without aiming to employ trainees at the end of their educational programme. In these cases, firms can be assumed to use trainees as a source of inexpensive labour rather than take the opportunity to educate future employees in specific skills. Consequently, 1 point was credited to firms whenever they employed former trainees at the end of their (vocational) education period. The third criterion considered was the *annual on-the-job training* provided by a firm. Whenever less than 50 per cent of a firm's employees received on-the-job training, or whenever more than 50 per cent participated in on-the-job training courses that equipped them mostly with *general* skills, 0 points were assigned; 1 point was attributed if at least 50 per cent of a firm's employees received on-the-job training for acquiring mostly *industry-specific* skills. Finally, 2 points were allocated to those firms where at least 50 per cent of the workforce participated in on-the-job training courses that provide mostly *specific* skills.

Table 5.3 provides an overview of the extent to which RPI, DQP, and LCP strategists rely on employees with specific and general skills, respectively. Interestingly, and contrary to Table 5.1, Table 5.3 does not report noteworthy country-specific variations. Firms pursuing the same strategy seem to employ the same mixture of skill profiles, irrespective of the country in which they are based. Furthermore, the results of Table 5.3 indicate support for hypotheses H1b, H2b, and H3b in that RPI strategists importantly rely on employees with general skills, whereas DQP pursuers employ workforces with specific skills. Low-cost producers, in turn, are situated in-between, as they recruit employees who have neither general nor specific skills.

To assess the statistical robustness of these observations, three sets of multinomial logistic regression analyses were carried out. In doing so, the '0 to 5 scale' in which skill profiles were originally measured was expanded to a '0 to 100 scale' in order to improve the interpretability of the results obtained.[14] Since the specificity index assumes the reversed scores of the generality index,

[13] The reason for having chosen 4 and 8 years as thresholds is that the first and second promotions usually take place within these time spans, and an employee's decision to switch companies is often significantly influenced by a firm's attitude towards promotion. However, interviews also revealed that the longer employees work for a firm, the less likely they are to leave it. For this reason, further thresholds (e.g. 12 years) were not introduced.

[14] This was done by multiplying all original values by a factor of 20.

**Table 5.3.** Skill profiles employed by RPI, DQP, and LCP strategists[a]

| **Group of firms** | **Number of cases** | **Skill specificity** (the higher the score, the more specific are the skills) | **Skill generality** (the higher the score, the more general are the skills) | **Total** (maximum score obtainable) |
|---|---|---|---|---|
| RPIs UK | 7 | 1.4 | 3.6 | 5 |
| DQPs UK | 8 | 3.4 | 1.6 | 5 |
| LCPs UK | 4 | 2.0 | 3.0 | 5 |
| RPIs Germany | 7 | 1.7 | 3.3 | 5 |
| DQPs Germany | 12 | 3.7 | 1.3 | 5 |
| LCPs Germany | 9 | 3.1 | 1.9 | 5 |
| RPIs Italy | 7 | 1.7 | 3.3 | 5 |
| DQPs Italy | 10 | 3.7 | 1.3 | 5 |
| LCPs Italy | 4 | 2.3 | 2.7 | 5 |
| **RPIs overall** | **21** | **1.6** | **3.4** | **5** |
| **DQPs overall** | **30** | **3.6** | **1.4** | **5** |
| **LCPs overall** | **17** | **2.6** | **2.4** | **5** |
| **Total** | **68** | **2.7** | **2.3** | **5** |

[a] The specificity and generality index rank skill profiles of employees on a scale from 0 to 5.

*Source:* Own calculations based on sixty-eight interviews with HR managers in British, German, and Italian pharmaceutical firms.

the results obtained are the same for the two indices, except for the directional measures which assume opposite values. To avoid repetition, only the specificity indicator was therefore used in the three sets of multinomial logistic regression analyses. In the first two sets (Models 1 and 2), *skill specificity* and *corporate age* were regressed separately (as the respective independent variable of each model) on *competitive strategy* (dependent variable), so as to test the individual explanatory power of both variables.[15] Model 3 then assesses the relative importance of *skill specificity* and *age* (independent variables) by regressing them jointly on *competitive strategy* (dependent variable). The multinomial logistic regression analysis carried out in Model 3 can thus be written as the following equations:

$$(1)\ \text{Odds}_{\text{RPI/LCP}} = \frac{\text{prob}_{\text{RPI}}}{\text{prob}_{\text{LCP}}} = e^{\beta_{10} + \beta_{11}\,\text{skill specificity} + \beta_{12}\,\text{corporate age}}$$

[15] Distinguishing between three discrete categories, the strategy variable assigns a value of '1' to any firm that pursues an RPI strategy, a value of '2' to any DQP pursuer, and a value of '3' to any LCP strategist.

$$(2)\ \text{Odds}_{\text{DQP/LCP}} = \frac{\text{prob}_{\text{DQP}}}{\text{prob}_{\text{LCP}}} = e^{\beta_{20} + \beta_{21}\ \text{skill specificity} + \beta_{22}\ \text{corporate age}}$$

Table 5.4 reports the results obtained.[16] They confirm the observations made on the basis of Table 5.3 and, hence, the propositions of hypotheses H1b, H2b, and H3b that particular skill profiles have a significant impact on RPI, DQP, and LCP strategies. To begin with RPI, Models 1 and 3 reveal that this strategy relies heavily on general skills. More precisely, Model 3 shows that – when controlled for corporate age – a 1 per cent decrease in the specificity or, respectively, a 1 per cent increase in the generality of skills held by a firm's workforce raises the likelihood that this firm pursues an RPI rather than a DQP strategy by 12.1 per cent. At the same time, it raises the probability that the firm pursues an RPI rather than an LCP strategy by 4.8 per cent (1 – 0.952 = 0.048). These results indicate support for hypothesis H1b, which states that general skills are required for RPI. By the same token, Models 1 and 3 show that DQP strategists substantially employ people with specific skills. Even when controlled for corporate age (see Model 3), a 1 per cent increase in the skill specificity of a firm's employees leads to an increase in the odds of this firm being a DQP rather than an RPI strategist by 12.1 per cent while the odds of the firm being a DQP rather than an LCP strategist increase by 6.3 per cent (1 – 0.937 = 0.063). These results also indicate support for hypothesis H2b, which states that employees with specific skills are at the basis of

**Table 5.4.** Importance of skill specificity and corporate age for RPI, DQP, and LCP strategies
(Results of multinomial logistic regression analyses: exponential *B*)

| **Model** | 1 | | | 2 | | | 3 | | |
|---|---|---|---|---|---|---|---|---|---|
| Comparing **to reference category** | DQP **RPI** | LCP **DQP** | RPI **LCP** | DQP **RPI** | LCP **DQP** | RPI **LCP** | DQP **RPI** | LCP **DQP** | RPI **LCP** |
| **Independent variables** | | | | | | | | | |
| Skill specifity | 1.126*** | .940*** | .945*** | | | | 1.121*** | .937*** | .952** |
| Corporate age | | | | 1.033*** | .996 | .972** | 1.008 | 1.003 | .989 |
| ***N*** | 68 | 69 | 68 | | | | | | |
| $R^2_{\text{Nagelkerke}}$ | .529 | .204 | .539 | | | | | | |

Significance levels: * <.10; ** <.05; *** <.01. Constant not reported in table.

[16] It is also interesting to note that multinomial logistic regression analyses with standard errors clustered by country lead to the same results as reported in Table 5.4. This, in turn, supports the finding that country-specific characteristics do not influence the employment policies of RPI, DQP, and LCP strategists.

DQP. It is finally noteworthy that the employment policy of LCP pursuers differs significantly from that of RPI and DQP strategists. Consequently, Model 3 shows that a 1 per cent decrease in the generality or, respectively, a 1 per cent increase in the specificity of the skills held by a workforce increases the probability that the employing firm pursues an LCP rather than an RPI strategy by 4.8 per cent (1 – 0.952 =0.048). Similarly, a 1 per cent decrease in the specificity or, respectively, a 1 per cent increase in the generality of the skills held by a workforce increases the likelihood that the employer is an LCP rather than a DQP strategist by 6.3 per cent (1 – 0.937 = 0.063). Taken together with the observations in Table 5.3, this finding indicates that employees of LCP pursuers hold neither specific nor general skills, which, in turn, supports hypothesis H3b.

The impact of different skill profiles for RPI, DQP, and LCP strategies is so strong that even the explanatory power of corporate age, the strongest rival explanatory variable, becomes statistically insignificant as soon as the two measures are regressed jointly in Model 3. Model 2, which only considers the individual impact of corporate age on competitive strategies, still provides empirical support for the hypothesis that young age facilitates RPI strategies (hypothesis H4a), whereas mature corporate age is conducive to DQP and LCP strategies (hypotheses H4b and H4c). For each additional year a firm exists, the odds of it pursuing a DQP rather than an RPI strategy increase by 3.3 per cent whereas the odds of a firm pursuing an LCP rather than an RPI strategy increase by 2.8 per cent (1 – 0.972 = 0.028). Given, however, that the explanatory power of corporate age becomes insignificant as soon as the skill variable is introduced as an additional predictor of competitive strategy in Model 3, it can be deduced that particular skill profiles constitute necessary input factors – and, possibly, more important input factors than corporate age.

In sum, the analyses of Section 5.2 have shown that the balance between the educational attainment of employees and their productivity means that particular education *levels* do not facilitate RPI, DQP, and LCP strategies. This is different for skill *profiles* in that general skills are required for RPI, while specific qualifications are necessary for DQP strategies. LCP strategies, in turn, are not affected by particular requirements for specific skill profiles as they can be pursued with a discretionary mixture of both skill types.

## 5.3. COMPETING DESPITE COMPARATIVE INSTITUTIONAL DISADVANTAGES: SECURING THE REQUIRED SKILL PROFILES IN DIFFERENT LABOUR-MARKET ECONOMIES

The importance of different skill profiles for RPI and DQP strategies raises one crucial question. If the competitiveness literature is right that rigid and flexible labour-market institutions offer comparative advantages for DQP and RPI strategies respectively because they motivate employees to acquire either specific or general skills,[17] how can firms compete in institutional environments that constitute comparative disadvantages? How can RPI strategists in rigid labour-market economies secure employees with general skills? And how do DQP pursuers in flexible labour markets motivate employees to acquire specific skills? Section 5.3 seeks to answer these questions. In doing so, Section 5.3.1 focuses on the comparative advantages and disadvantages resulting from national labour-market institutions for *RPI*, while Section 5.3.2 concentrates on the institutional advantages and disadvantages for *DQP*.

### 5.3.1. Hiring Employees with General Skills in Rigid Labour Markets

How do RPI strategists in flexible and, more importantly, in rigid labour markets secure employees with general qualifications? Interestingly, interviews with HR managers in the UK confirmed the argument of the competitiveness literature that the flexible labour-market institutions of this economy offer important comparative advantages for RPI strategists, as they motivate employees to acquire general qualifications.[18] More concretely, a decentralized bargaining system is an essential reason why the vocational training system is less well developed in the UK (Jon 2007) – with the result that adolescents find it easier to invest in general education. Furthermore, weak works councils and short notice periods promote the acquisition of general skills in that employees tend to change employment more often. As a result, average job tenure in the British RPI firms interviewed is rather low, namely 4.2 years.

Interestingly, though, average job tenure is not much higher in German and Italian RPI firms, namely 5.7 and 6 years respectively. And, as Table 5.3 has illustrated, RPI employees do hold general skills as well. How can RPI employers acquire a workforce with general qualifications in these countries given that they are often portrayed as ideal-typical examples of rigid labour-market economies? How do RPI firms compete in the face of comparative institutional disadvantages? In a nutshell, interviews with German and Italian HR managers indicate that RPI firms can circumvent national constraints by defecting from the typical labour-market institutions. When HR managers were asked whether a centralized wage-bargaining system was important to their wage-setting policy, they usually denied that this was the case.

[17] See note 2. [18] For proponents of this reasoning, see note 4.

In Germany, the broad majority of RPI strategists (namely 86 per cent of all RPI firms interviewed) are not *tarifgebunden* (i.e. adhering to the system of collective bargaining). Instead of paying their workforce according to salary levels determined in industry-wide collective agreements, German RPI strategists set wages on an individual basis with employees. In Italy, by contrast, all firms in an industry must pay their employees at least the salary determined in the *Contratto Collettivo Nazionale di Lavoro* (CCNL). However, the CCNL only determines the minimum remuneration that has to be disbursed. Employers can, and do, pay wages above the CCNL wage floor. Accordingly, the majority of Italian RPI pursuers (namely 57 per cent of all RPI firms interviewed) also negotiate wages on an individual basis with their employees instead of paying company-wide wage top-ups. It is further interesting to note that, in order to determine adequate salary levels, RPI strategists in both Germany (43 per cent) and Italy (71 per cent) draw substantially on the insights provided by industry-wide income surveys – as do RPI strategists in the UK (71 per cent). Overall, these insights suggest that a centralized wage-bargaining system does not prevent employers in rigid labour markets from setting wages according to their company's needs.

In a similar vein, the constraints resulting from labour-market institutions such as works councils, notice periods, and competition clauses are also more limited than one might expect from the competitiveness literature. As for competition clauses, interviews revealed that their use is generally more widespread in the UK than in Germany and Italy. In the two latter countries, legal notice periods are comparatively long and usually perceived as adequate when it comes to finding a suitable replacement for key employees. Since particular notice periods are not provided by British labour law, British firms often use competition clauses to ensure that they will have sufficient time to find a suitable replacement, should key employees wish to leave their firm. Given that competition clauses are generally less diffused in Germany and Italy, it may not be surprising to learn that German and Italian RPI strategists in particular hardly write these clauses into employment contracts. Furthermore, HR managers in Germany and Italy when interviewed did not perceive long notice *periods* to be an obstacle when wanting to lay off employees. If at all, it was the limited number of *reasons*, for which employees in Germany and Italy can lawfully be dismissed, that was sometimes perceived as constraining (Lanzenberger 2004; Sigillia 2005; see also Stöchler 2004). This is particularly true since German and Italian works councils have an important say in dismissal. Accordingly, they can make sure that these reasons are respected meticulously.

That said, it is particularly revealing that only a limited number of the German RPI strategists interviewed (14 per cent) actually had works councils in place, because communication between managers and subordinates in these often rather small firms is usually so well developed that employees had not asked for a works council to be installed. The majority of Italian RPI pursuers (71 per cent), in contrast, had installed works councils, usually because they had passed the threshold of employees above which they are required by law to put a works council in place. Interestingly, though, works councils in these firms were usually perceived as beneficial and an important means of communication between employers and employees (e.g. Lanzenberger 2004; Lumer 2004; Gullaner 2005; Sigillia 2005; Wessler 2005; Borelli 2006). And even in those rare instances where larger RPI strategists had (to have) works councils and wanted to dismiss employees for reasons not recognized by law,[19] works councils were hardly perceived as severe constraints. The reason for this is that, in such cases, it seems to be in the common interest of employers and employees to find a compromise, because lawsuits are costly, tedious, and potentially harmful to both the firm's and the employee's reputation. Depending on the individual relationship between managers and the respective works council, the latter was thus not necessarily seen as an obstacle but also as a beneficial mediator (Manci 2005; Schaffer 2006).

In sum, interviews with HR managers of German and Italian RPI strategists revealed that the interviewees perceive rigid labour-market institutions as less constraining than a reader might think when studying arguments on comparative institutional advantages propounded in the competitiveness literature in general, and the VoC debate in particular.[20] A centralized wage-bargaining system, competition clauses, and long notice periods do not force RPI employers to offer long job tenure. While it is true that limited possibilities for dismissal, in combination with strong works councils, militate *de jure* against short job tenure, they rarely oblige RPI strategists *de facto* to retain employees against the firm's will.

In addition, interviews also indicated that contributors to the competitiveness literature seem to underestimate the creativeness with which RPI pursuers in rigid labour markets circumvent national constraints and secure employees with general skills. On the one hand, RPI firms teach their employees general skills by offering on-the-job training courses, for example, in regulatory affairs, in relevant research areas, or in the field of corporate finance. On the other hand, given that German and Italian labour law makes the temporary employment of *workers* difficult, RPI strategists in these countries find a variety of

[19] That is, for reasons other than serious economic constraints or the wilful misconduct of an employee.

[20] See note 2.

ways to hire temporary *collaborators*. Most importantly, they cooperate closely with universities and public research institutes, by offering, among other things, PhD or post-doctoral positions to young academics, and commissioning research projects to university professors and their assistants. In doing so, RPI strategists gain highly qualified people with general skills to work on their research projects for a limited period of time.

In this respect, it is also interesting to note that project collaboration (*collaborazione a progetto*) can, by now, be considered institutionalized in Italy. Since 1973, the Italian government has launched a series of legislative decrees which grant tax relief to firms for employing so-called *collaboratori a progetto*, i.e. project collaborators (see DPR 597 1973). As each decree was valid only for a few years, it was systematically substituted by a subsequent decree with very similar content. The last substitution occurred in 2003 when the so-called Biagi law, *legge Biagi* (*legge delega 30/2003*), introduced the 'project employment contract', i.e. the *contratto di lavoro a progetto* (also called *co.co.pro*), thereby replacing the previous 'contract of coordinated and continuous collaboration', the *contratto di collaborazione coordinata e continuativa* (also called *co.co.co*). Interestingly, these *contratti* are atypical employment contracts as they allow firms to hire project collaborators who work on a company's (research) project for a maximum period of usually three years, during which the firm is granted fiscal advantages. Afterwards, firms are expected, but not obliged, to offer permanent employment contracts to collaborators (EIRO 2004*a*; see also EIRO 2005). But, since recruitment is not compulsory, Italian RPI firms often prefer to hire new collaborators instead of retaining the previous ones. In other words, radical product innovators use government subsidies as a means of securing general skills, rather than as an opportunity to endow future employees with specific qualifications. In doing so, the employment policies of Italian RPI strategists seem to differ from those of DQP pursuers in that the latter are more inclined to retain project collaborators at the end of the three-year period.[21]

[21] These insights suggest that the rigid German and Italian labour markets might even be advantageous to RPI strategists for the purpose of acquiring employees with general skills. In the UK, young academics are more easily absorbed by the labour market because their dismissal is less complicated. Compared to their British counterparts, German and, particularly, Italian graduates have more difficulty in finding a first job. On the one hand, this makes the number of young academics willing to gain initial work experience as (management) trainees, *collaboratori*, or assistants to university professors relatively high. Consequently, German and Italian RPI strategists can temporarily utilize highly skilled graduates by paying comparatively low remunerations. On the other hand, the large pool of recent graduates looking for a job can also stimulate government initiatives that subsidize firms for offering initial job experience.

Another, particularly noteworthy, way in which RPI strategists in Germany and Italy circumvent national rigidities and secure employees with general skills is perfectly in line with the findings of Chapter 3. RPI strategists hire key scientists and managers from abroad. In doing so, RPI strategists rely on international institutions, open labour markets, to 'import' the required labour skills. As revealed by a recent study of biotech firms based around Munich, such 'importation' has produced the unusual result that about half of those CEOs who led fifteen of the most established firms in the early years of the new millennium were recruited from foreign labour markets. This brings Jong (2006: 9) to conclude that '[r]ather than relying on German labor markets to recruit their CEOs, Munich-based therapeutic biotech firms overwhelmingly went abroad to attract their most senior managers'.

These findings suggest that RPI strategists in rigid labour markets circumvent the skill shortage of employees with general qualifications in two ways. First, they make use of international labour markets and hire key scientists from abroad. In line with Chapter 3, this indicates that *importation via international institutions* constitutes an alternative pathway to competitiveness. Second, RPI strategists circumvent national constraints by defecting from typical labour-market institutions so as to conclude atypical contracts with employees. *Improvisation on a contractual basis* thus constitutes another pathway to competitiveness.

### 5.3.2. Endowing Employees with Specific Skills in Flexible Labour Markets

Similar arguments result from the study of how DQP strategists secure employees with specific skills in the UK with its ideal-typical flexible labour market. To begin with, interviews with German and Italian HR managers largely support the claim of the competitiveness literature that rigid labour-market institutions constitute a comparative advantage to DQP. By adhering to the typical labour-market institutions of their economy, German and Italian DQP strategists can exploit their comparative advantages, as employees are motivated to acquire specific skills. Accordingly, interviews revealed that a broad majority (75 per cent) of the DQP pursuers interviewed in Germany were *tarifgebunden*, while the majority (60 per cent) of Italian DQP pursuers pay homogeneous wage top-ups to their workforce. Furthermore, works councils with strong authority over lay-offs, installed in 75 per cent of the German and 80 per cent of the Italian DQP firms, as well as legal notice periods and the occasional use of competition clauses tie employees to German and Italian DQP pursuers. This, in turn, motivates DQP employees to acquire specific skills and to work for 'their' firm for a long period of time. Consequently, average job tenure in German and Italian DQP strategists is 12.4 and 9.0 years respectively.

Interestingly, though, the average period during which employees work for British DQP firms is not much lower, namely 8.0 years. And, as Table 5.3 illustrates, DQP pursuers succeed in employing workers with specific skills. How is this possible? How can DQP pursuers in the UK compete despite the comparative disadvantages resulting from flexible labour-market institutions for their strategy? To answer this question, HR managers from British DQP strategists were asked about the importance of works councils, competition clauses, and notice periods as promoters of specific skills. Interestingly, it turned out that none of these institutions seems to play a significant role in tying employees to the company. Even though the use of competition clauses is more common in Britain than in Germany and Italy, they often serve as deterrents rather than strictly enforceable mechanisms. The reason for this is that, in the event of a lawsuit, judges tend to defend the position of the weaker party, namely the employee who wishes to change jobs. Hence, competition clauses do not necessarily insure employers of British DQP firms against the risk of poaching. They rather constitute a means of hindering key employees from leaving a firm on short notice (Jon 2005). Similarly, and in line with the argument of the competitiveness literature, weak works councils, short notice periods, and a variety of legally admitted causes of dismissal can expose employees of British DQP pursuers to the risk of lay-off.

Nevertheless, and contrary to the expectations of the competitiveness literature, DQP firms were found to endow their employees with specific skills in a variety of ways. First, they invest massively in training courses to advise employees on how their firm operates. Second, they offer attractive long-term career paths. To give an example, employees are offered the opportunity to participate in on-the-job training courses that prepare them for intra-firm promotion. About half of the DQP pursuers interviewed in the UK apply this measure. Some British DQP strategists also provide pension schemes which only become attractive over the long term (Tiny 2006). While these initiatives are generally not uncommon in the UK, they seem to be particularly widespread amongst DQP firms, which in this way make sure that long-term employment enables their workforce to gain an in-depth understanding of how the firm operates.

Finally, DQP firms in the UK also invest in vocational training of future employees. More precisely, they offer young people the opportunity to do an internship, or to undertake an industrial placement as a part of their degree. In doing so, it is the stated aim of DQP strategists to recruit high-performing trainees at the end of their educational programme (Bonn 2005; Jon 2005;

see also Tiny 2006).[22] Furthermore, British DQP firms encourage talented employees to enrol in higher education, for example, by embarking on an MSc in a field which is key to the company's activities, whereby the tuition fees for these programmes are usually covered by the firm. Obviously, employees are encouraged to obtain such degrees because the firm wishes to retain them upon completion of the programme. Before enrolling in higher education, DQP employees therefore sign a contract with their employers which stipulates that tuition fees have to be paid back if the employee in question leaves the company upon completion of the degree (Bakkering 2005; Bonn 2005; see also Murrian 2006; Tiny 2006). These findings lead to the same conclusion as in Section 5.3.1. British DQP pursuers often circumvent national institutions and conclude atypical contracts with their employees so as to motivate them to acquire specific qualifications. *Improvisation on a contractual basis* thus constitutes an alternative pathway to competitiveness.

Given the efforts of British DQP employers to endow employees with specific skills, and given the willingness of British DQP employees to acquire such skills, two final questions remain. First, why do DQP employers invest in specific training if a flexible labour market entails the risk of skilled employees being poached by competitors? When British HR managers were confronted with this question, they were amazed by its reasoning: Why should employees *leave* a firm which actively cares about their education? On the contrary, HR managers pointed out that the more a company invests in skills, the less likely the employees are to leave. The reason, simply, is that employees feel that their qualifications are appreciated, which, in turn, raises realistic hopes that the company will retain them and continue to invest in their careers (Jon 2005).

But why do employees of British DQP strategists invest in specific skills, given that they face the constant risk of overnight dismissal? Since interviews were carried out with HR managers, not with individual employees, only speculative answers can be offered here based on the overall insights gained in the course of this research project. As set out in the introduction to this chapter, the costs of further education in flexible labour-market economies are passed on to potential employees. This means that employees who do not want, or cannot afford, to enrol in further education are left with basic compulsory

[22] It is interesting to note that the British government was considering institutionalizing such training efforts at the time the interviews were carried out. In 2003, a pilot project was launched which mimics the German vocational training system in that trainees are educated in close collaboration with one firm. More precisely, firms offer the opportunity to undertake a one-year industrial placement as part of training courses that overall last three years. While it was still unclear when this research project ended, to what extent joint vocational training will be institutionalized, HR managers of British DQP strategists were very positive about this initiative (Jon 2005).

education levels. Compared to the opportunity of receiving specific on-the-job training, this option seems preferable to remaining unskilled. Even if employees were to lose their job, they are presumably better off if they have received specific training. Furthermore, the risk of dismissal seems to be less acute for DQP employees than for those of RPI strategists, because DQP is less risky. The danger of total failure is thus reduced. And considering that DQP strategists rely heavily on and invest in the skills of their workforce, the latter are unlikely to be dismissed overnight. It seems therefore rational for DQP employees to invest in specific skills – even if the company which provides such training is located in a flexible labour market.

This reasoning confirms the above findings that contributors to the competitiveness literature in general, and to the VoC debate in particular, overestimate the stringency of labour-market institutions.[23] Accordingly, the literature seems to overrate the risk of overnight dismissal related to the pursuit of a DQP strategy. The fact that DQP strategists in flexible labour markets *can* dismiss employees at short notice does not mean that they *must* do so. At the same time, the literature also seems to underestimate the opportunities related to teaching and acquiring specific skills in flexible labour-market economies.

## 5.4. CONCLUDING INTERPRETATION

What do these findings teach us about whether the comparative advantages of national institutions also offer a source of competitive advantage to RPI, DQP, and LCP strategists? Do firms need particular employee qualifications to pursue the same strategy? And, if so, do firms systematically use the labour-market institutions of their economy to secure the required skill types? Overall, Chapter 5 confirms the findings of Chapters 3 and 4 that RPI, DQP, and LCP strategists differ significantly from each other in the factor types they require. While RPI firms importantly rely on employees with general skill profiles, DQP strategists prefer employees with specific qualifications. LCP pursuers, in turn, do not require either of these skill profiles but rather use a mix of the two.

Interestingly, particular skill levels were not found to have a facilitative impact on competitive strategies, as a balance seems to exist between the educational attainment of workers, their productivity, and their wage levels. Low-skilled employees were therefore not found to be of competitive advantage to

[23] See, for example, Porter (1990: 126–30), Hollingsworth (2000: 626–30), Estevez-Abe et al. (2001), Hall and Soskice (2001*a*: 36–44), Lindbeck and Snower (2001*a*), Sinn (2005), and Casper (2007).

LCP. This finding should, however, be treated with a grain of salt as it results merely from studies of pharmaceutical firms. As set out in Chapter 4, the pharmaceutical industry is peculiar in its technological intensity on the one hand, and the strict requirements on the part of the legislators for quality and purity of pharmaceutical products on the other. This implies that not only incremental or radical innovation but even low-cost imitation of pharmaceuticals becomes a complex task. Consequently, the costs that can be saved from hiring inexpensive but low-skilled workers may be minor compared to the costs that arise when pharmaceutical purity standards are not met due to employee deviance. It could therefore be possible that low-skilled and inexpensive workers constitute a competitive advantage for LCP strategies in industries that are less technology intensive and less vulnerable to employee deviance.

These insights do not only lend support to suggestions of the competitiveness literature that similar types of an input factor are at the basis of the same competitive strategies; they also shed light on propositions of the RBV. To be clear, the latter has been developed since its emergence in the mid-1980s (Rumelt 1984; Wernerfelt 1984; Barney 1986, 1991; Dierickx and Cool 1989). However, the fundamental claim of RBV theory remains the same: valuable, rare, imperfectly imitable, and organizationally exploitable – in other words, unique – resources or capabilities are the key to corporate competitiveness (Barney and Clark 2007; Newbert 2007; see also Acedo et al. 2006). While RBV contributors tend to study the process through which unique capabilities can be built, their central claim seems to contradict the competitiveness literature's premise that the same competitive strategies rely on similar types of labour qualifications. The finding that firms can achieve competitive advantages not only through resource heterogeneity but also through factor homogeneity may thus complement RBV ideas.

The question is *how* firms can gain competitive advantages, even if they employ the same skill profiles for the same strategies? How do they avoid behaving like clones that merely imitate each other's behaviour? In brief, the above findings indicate that it is the *process* of factor acquisition which enables firms to gain competitive advantages. The comparative advantages offered by national labour-market institutions can thus constitute an important source of competitive advantage, because the pool of labour available with either specific or general skills is influenced by the shape of national institutions. While employees in flexible labour markets are encouraged to invest in general qualifications, workers in rigid labour markets are motivated to acquire specific skills. Consequently, RPI strategists in flexible labour markets find it comparatively easy to hire a workforce with the necessary general qualifications, as do DQP pursuers in rigid labour markets when seeking employees with specific skills. These findings support the idea of the competitiveness literature on comparative institutional advantages.

The central question which derives from these insights is how firms can pursue strategies that are not supported by national institutions. How can firms compete despite comparative institutional disadvantages? How can RPI strategists employ workers with general skills in rigid labour-market economies like Germany and Italy? And how do DQP pursuers in the UK convince employees to acquire specific skills despite the labour market's flexibility? The answer, in short, is that these firms circumvent national institutions and secure the required employee qualifications by relying on functionally equivalent institutions. Two such alternative institutional pathways to competitiveness have been identified. In line with Chapter 3, *importation via international institutions* has been found to constitute the first alternative, by means of which RPI strategists in rigid labour-market economies hire key scientists and managers from abroad. Instead of employing key personnel with the necessary qualifications via national labour markets, RPI pursuers simply hire from international labour markets. In the case of the biotech cluster around Munich, the pronounced use of this functional equivalent institution has led to the striking phenomenon that CEOs of the fifteen most established biotech firms were recruited from foreign labour markets at the start of the new millennium.

The second institutional alternative to securing the required labour qualifications instead of adhering to national institutions is, what I term here, *improvisation on a contractual basis*. By defecting from the economy's typical institutions – for example, by not installing works councils and by not adhering to national wage-bargaining agreements – RPI firms in Germany and Italy along with DQP strategists in the UK are able to conclude atypical contracts so as to secure the required skill types. Accordingly, DQP strategists in the UK tie employees to their firm by offering attractive long-term career opportunities. They invest massively in specific training, for example, in courses which prepare participants for intra-firm promotion, and they provide pension schemes that become profit-yielding only in the long term. They also participate actively in the training of young people, for example, by offering internships or industrial placements in order to retain the best performers upon completion of their degree. In a similar vein, RPI strategists in Germany and Italy hire project collaborators for a limited period of time, they offer young academics the opportunity to undertake a PhD or a postdoctoral qualification in collaboration with their firm, and they commission research projects to universities. Finally, they also provide on-the-job training courses which teach employees general skills. Given the nationwide labour-market organization, these measures constitute atypical forms of securing necessary qualifications in an improvisational way.

The creativity, not to say the verve, with which firms exploit comparative advantages and, even more importantly, circumvent the comparative disadvantages of national institutions indicates that corporate competitiveness results from entrepreneurial spirit rather than from the institutional constellations of political economies. Whether or not an RPI strategist in a rigid labour market can gain competitive advantages may, for example, depend on the individual wage top-ups it succeeds in negotiating with its workforce, or on the offers it can make to attract key personnel from abroad. In other words, it depends on the creativity of each entrepreneur whether or not her firm will acquire the necessary skill profiles and, thus, be competitive. This, in turn, indicates that Schumpeter's perception of firms as 'enterprises' is particularly helpful to understand how firms can compete even in the face of comparative institutional disadvantages. When studying how economies, sectors, or firms respond to changes 'in "condition"' (Schumpeter 1947: 150), Schumpeter illustrates that the 'creative responses' and, thus, the most persistent changes come from those firms that are run by entrepreneurs. Contrary to managers who merely head the administration of a firm, 'the defining characteristic [of entrepreneurs] is (. . .) the doing of new things or the doing of things that are already being done in a new way' (ibid.: 151). In line with Schumpeter's definition, this chapter has indicated that firms gain competitive advantages and, thus, international competitiveness because they are *not* administered by institution-taking managers, but because they are run by entrepreneurs who acquire all the necessary input factors in a creative way. Those contributions to the competitiveness literature which perceive firms as mere institution-takers therefore have a hard time explaining how firms compete in the face of increasing economic internationalization.[24]

This suggestion possibly brings institutional scholars to wonder whether institutions matter at all. If entrepreneurs succeed in their adopted strategies because they can cherry-pick the institutions through which they want to secure the necessary labour qualifications, can institutions constrain entrepreneurial behaviour at all? To be clear, the finding that entrepreneurs can choose the institutions they wish to draw on does not mean that these choices do not entail constraints. Any institution that enables also constrains. To give an example, if DQP strategists in rigid labour markets decide to adhere to the typical labour-market institutions, they are constrained by the commitments that result from this choice. They have to pay homogeneous wages to their employees and to determine the firm's employment policy in collaboration with its works council. But DQP strategists in flexible labour markets, too,

[24] See note 23.

which decide to tie employees to their firm by concluding atypical contracts, are constrained by the commitments they make. They have, for example, to elaborate, implement, and remunerate the pension schemes or intra-firm promotion programmes through which they offer long-term employment to key personnel. The finding that firms have a choice about the institutions they wish to use in order to make sure that employees have the necessary qualifications does, by no means, claim that the chosen institutions do not matter, that is, constrain.

# PART III

# Strategy Choice, Success, and Sustainability in Perspective

# 6

# Excursus: Success and Choice of Competitive Strategies

The analyses of the previous chapters are particularly telling in two respects. First, they have illustrated that firms do not choose their competitive strategies in line with national institutions facilitating the availability of necessary input factors. Pharmaceutical firms in Germany, Italy, and the UK were found to pursue strategies of radical product innovation (RPI), diversified quality production (DQP), and low-cost production (LCP) to a similar extent. Firms thus seem to choose their strategies independently of their institutional environment. Second, the previous chapters have illustrated how firms compete. More concretely, Chapters 3–5 have shown how firms secure those types of finance, component standards, and labour qualifications which they require for RPI, DQP, and LCP strategies respectively. In short, firms were found not only to exploit comparative institutional advantages but also to compete despite the comparative disadvantages of national institutions by importing scarce input factors from abroad and by acquiring missing factors through the conclusion of atypical contracts.

The finding *that* and *how* firms compete despite comparative institutional disadvantages, however, does not say anything about the *success* with which RPI, DQP, and LCP strategies are pursued in different institutional environments. It could be possible that firms choosing a non-conformist strategy are punished for their decision by failure in the long run. In other words, whenever firms neglect to exploit the advantage of pursuing the institutionally facilitated strategy, they are less competitive and sooner or later fail. And, while the previous findings indicate that institutional considerations are secondary for the strategy *choices* of entrepreneurs, they also leave the motivations of entrepreneurs when forming their strategy decisions unexplored. Seeking to address these open questions, this chapter examines the drivers of strategy success on the one hand and of strategy choice on the other.

To understand whether the success of competitive strategies is influenced by national institutions, accounting performance and changes in the legal status of firms are analysed in Section 6.1. In Section 6.2, reasons for strategy choice are identified through systematic comparisons of qualitative evidence obtained from interviewing CEOs and managers of pharmaceutical firms. Contrary to the previous chapters, these analyses are mostly of a diachronic nature, as they study change over time rather than the status quo. But even these diachronic analyses do not support the argument of the competitiveness literature that firms choose their strategies according to their institutional environment.[1] By contrast, empirical evidence suggests that entrepreneurs base their choice of competitive strategy on technological opportunities, i.e. on the inventions made by scientists and the facilities for developing these inventions into marketable products. To give an example, a group of university professors who have discovered a new chemical entity with promising potential for commercialization is more likely to set up a company that pursues an RPI or a DQP strategy than to engage in LCP. Similarly, a chemist with long-standing experience in the reverse engineering of pharmaceutical products will be more inclined to set up his own LCP firm instead of embarking on RPI or DQP strategies. Akin to explanations of strategy choice, empirical evidence does not support the argument of the literature on varieties of capitalism (VoC) that the success or sustainability of competitive strategies is determined by national institutions.[2] While possible explanations for the balance sheet performance of firms are too numerous to be systematically explored here, it can be speculated that the sustainability of the originally pursued strategy is influenced by the ease with which investors can acquire seed finance.

To illustrate these arguments, the remainder of this chapter is organized as follows. Section 6.1 enquires into strategy success by analysing whether firms perform less well and are less sustainable if they choose to pursue a competitive strategy that is not supported by national institutions. Section 6.2 proposes an alternative explanation for strategy choice by examining three sets of highly diverse firms which all agree in one central aspect: entrepreneurs chose or changed their firm's strategy on the basis of its technological opportunities. Section 6.3 summarizes and interprets the various findings.

## 6.1. STRATEGY SUCCESS

The question about the success of competitive strategies is of particular interest to the most recent strand of the competitiveness literature, namely

[1] For proponents of this argument, see in particular Estevez-Abe et al. (2001), Hall and Soskice (2001*a*: 36–44), Tate (2001: 442–55), Vitols (2001: 350–60), and Franzese and Mosher (2002); see also Heckscher (1919), Ohlin (1933), Porter (1990), Freeman (1992), Lindgaard Christensen (1992), Nelson (1993), Hollingsworth (2000: 626–30), Teubner (2001: 433–5), Casper and Matraves (2003), Casper and Whitley (2004), and Sinn (2005).

[2] For proponents of this argument, see Hall and Soskice (2001*a*: 17–21), Vitols (2001: 355–9), Hall and Gingerich (2004), and Casper (2007).

the VoC literature. Puzzled by the question of how a radically innovative biotech industry could develop in Germany since the mid-1990s, even though the rigid institutional environment of this economy does not support RPI strategies, contributors to the VoC literature propose the following explanation. Due to the massive investment assistance on the part of the German state in the late 1990s, entrepreneurs have started to pursue RPI strategies and established radically innovative biotech firms. Given, however, that national institutions in Germany do not support this strategy, these firms perform less well and are thus not sustainable in the long run (Vitols 2001: 355–9; Casper 2007: chapter 4).

To the credit of this argument, it must be said that the previous analyses have not considered how successful firms are in pursuing RPI, DQP, and LCP strategies in different institutional environments. To shed light on this question, Section 6.1 considers two different indicators of corporate success: accounting performance (Section 6.1.1) and change in legal status (Section 6.1.2). In other words, Section 6.1.1 addresses strategy success from a synchronic perspective by comparing various accounting ratios of RPI, DQP, and LCP pursuers in Germany, Italy, and the UK. Section 6.1.2 proceeds to diachronic analyses of strategy success, investigating the sustainability of the initially pursued strategy. It thus asks the question: Are firms more likely to merge, be acquired, or go bankrupt if they pursue strategies that are not supported by national institutions? The firm sample on which these analyses are grounded is the same as in Chapters 3–5. More precisely, this sample consists of the 102 pharmaceutical firms derived in Chapter 2 (Section 2.4),[3] augmented by the 28 generics and biotech companies identified in Chapter 3 (Section 3.2).[4] To countercheck the results obtained on the basis of this data-set, Section 6.1.2 explores an additional database including only British, German, and Italian biotech firms.

### 6.1.1. Synchronic Analyses of Strategy Success

Do firms perform less well if they pursue a strategy that is not supported by national institutions (see Hall and Soskice 2001*a*: 17–21; Hall and Gingerich 2004)? From a synchronic perspective, one way to answer this question is to

[3] Let us recall that a 'pharmaceutical firm' is used as an umbrella term for all firms that are active in the drug industry, including biotechnology, traditional pharmaceutical, and generics firms (see Section 1.2).

[4] A complete list of these 130 pharmaceutical firms is provided in the technical appendix (see Table A.1 for the British, Table A.2 for the German, and Table A.3 for the Italian firms included).

compare the accounting performance of the 130 aforementioned RPI, DQP, and LCP strategists. More precisely, it was compared how these firms perform in six accounting ratios which are among the most important indicators that analysts use to evaluate the financial conditions of a firm. They include: (*a*) *return on shareholders' funds*, a measure of corporate profitability indicating how much profit a firm has generated with the money that shareholders have invested; (*b*) *return on capital employed*, a ratio that reveals the profitability of a firm's capital investments; (*c*) *profit margin*, a ratio of profitability that indicates how much out of every dollar of sales a firm obtains in earnings; (*d*) *current ratio*, a liquidity ratio that measures a firm's ability to pay back its short-term liabilities (debt and payables) with its short-term assets (cash, inventory, and receivables); (*e*) *solvency ratio*, an indictor used to measure a firm's ability to meet long-term obligations; (*f*) *gearing*, an indicator that explains how a firm finances its operations either through outside lenders or through shareholders, whereby firms with a high gearing – i.e. with more long-term liabilities than shareholder equity – are considered speculative. As a rule of thumb, one can say that the higher the firms score on each of these indices, the better they perform – with the exception of their gearing, where the opposite applies.

All ratios were obtained from the AMADEUS database, which contains financial information on nine million public and private companies in thirty-eight European countries (Bureau van Dijk 2004). It was possible to obtain accounting ratios for 73 of the 130 pharmaceutical firms included in the overall sample. Before grouping these seventy-three firms according to their strategy and country, each accounting ratio was calculated for each firm as an average value of the past five years in order to correct for temporary peaks.

Table 6.1 presents the results. To find empirical support for the argument of VoC scholars that the success of competitive strategies is influenced by national institutions, Table 6.1 should reveal that RPI strategists perform particularly well in the UK, whereas DQP pursuers perform better than average in Germany, and LCP firms outperform their peers in Italy. Interestingly, though, this is not the case. For each of the six accounting ratios, British RPI strategists, German DQP pursuers, and Italian LCP firms are usually outperformed either by firms pursuing different strategies in the same country or by firms pursuing the same strategy in different countries – or even on both accounts. Crosstab analyses confirm the findings presented in Table 6.1. To run these analyses, it was calculated for each firm and each accounting ratio whether the respective RPI, DQP, or LCP strategist performed better or worse than the average seventy-three firms for which data could be obtained. Crosstab analyses

**Table 6.1.** Performance of RPI, DQP, and LCP strategists in six accounting ratios

| Group of firms | No. of cases | Return on share-holders' funds (%)[a] | Return on capital employed (%)[b] | Profit margin (%)[c] | Current ratio[d] | Solvency ratio (%)[e] | Gearing (%)[f] |
|---|---|---|---|---|---|---|---|
| **RPIs UK** | **11** | **−55.10** | **−58.13** | **−4.34** | **3.86** | **53.84** | **74.68** |
| DQPs UK | 12 | 49.37 | 59.30 | 5.63 | 3.41 | 52.22 | 106.43 |
| LCPs UK | 7 | −16.02 | −84.27 | −6.74 | 1.53 | 34.78 | 62.83 |
| RPIs Ger. | 5 | −34.07 | −14.89 | −16.72 | 7.89 | 66.77 | 36.01 |
| **DQPs Ger.** | **8** | **28.03** | **24.48** | **12.43** | **3.03** | **46.58** | **88.19** |
| LCPs Ger. | 3 | 169.49 | 42.22 | 12.95 | 1.31 | 25.29 | 856.68 |
| RPIs Italy | 8 | −8.03 | −7.30 | 2.36 | 3.19 | 43.34 | 196.84 |
| DQPs Italy | 13 | 20.77 | 18.50 | 10.33 | 1.50 | 40.37 | 78.32 |
| **LCPs Italy** | **6** | **48.39** | **62.35** | **9.06** | **1.28** | **17.47** | **466.02** |
| RPIs total | 24 | −35.03 | −31.78 | −4.92 | 4.48 | 53.03 | 112.07 |
| DQPs total | 33 | 32.93 | 34.02 | 9.13 | 2.56 | 46.18 | 91.02 |
| LCPs total | 16 | 42.92 | −0.32 | 2.88 | 1.40 | 26.51 | 362.87 |
| Total/Average | 73 | 12.78 | 5.57 | 4.13 | 2.94 | 44.12 | 159.77 |

[a] *Return on shareholders' funds* = profit or loss before tax/shareholders' equity.
[b] *Return on capital employed* = (profit or loss before tax + interest paid)/(shareholders' equity + non-current liabilities).
[c] *Profit margin* = profit or loss before tax/operating revenue.
[d] *Current ratio* = current assets/current liabilities.
[e] *Solvency ratio* = shareholders' funds/total assets.
[f] *Gearing* = (non-current liabilities + loans)/shareholders' equity.
*Source:* AMADEUS database, as sampled in December 2004 (Bureau van Dijk 2004).

of the respective *average performance indicators* with the firms' *countries* and *competitive strategies* unambiguously lead to the same results. If statistically significant deviations are observable at all, they are not in line with the predictions of the VoC contributors.[5] These results indicate that the success of competitive strategies is not influenced by the institutional environment within which firms operate.

Another noteworthy observation to be made on the basis of Table 6.1 is that RPI strategists perform overall rather poorly in all profitability ratios, including the return on shareholders' funds, return on capital employed, and

[5] Detailed results of the crosstab analyses performed can be provided by the author upon request.

the profit margin. This finding, in turn, indicates that RPI, DQP, and LCP strategies are characterized by a distinct investment–return profile, which is particularly evident in the case of radical product innovators. Given that it takes years before investment in research and development (R&D) of pharmaceutical products becomes profitable, newly established RPI strategists do not usually make a profit in the first years of their existence. This seems to explain why their profitability ratios are comparatively low. However, the possibility that competitive strategies differ in their risk–return profile also indicates that comparisons of accounting ratios between firms pursuing *different* strategies might be of limited help in understanding whether national institutions influence strategy success, because part of the variations among strategies in these indicators might stem from the differences in risk–return profiles rather than from differences in the institutional environment.

It is thus useful to cross-check the findings presented in Table 6.1 with indicators that eliminate the possible influences of different risk–return profiles. To this end, the AMADEUS database offers additional indicators that can be taken as synchronic measures of strategy success. In the so-called peer report of the database, a firm is ranked in comparison to its ten most direct competitors according to six economic items on the one hand and six accounting ratios on the other. While the accounting ratios are the same as those described in Table 6.1, the six economic items include: (*a*) the firm's *operating revenue* (in thousand US dollars); (*b*) its *profit or loss before tax* (in thousand US dollars); (*c*) the annual *cash flow* (in thousand US dollars); (*d*) the firm's *total assets* (in thousand US dollars); (*e*) its *shareholders' funds* (in thousand US dollars); and (*f*) its *number of employees*. Depending on how well a firm performs relative to its ten most direct competitors, it is thus assigned a score from 1 to 11, whereby higher scores indicate better performance.

Table 6.2 gives an overview of the peer performance of those seventy-three pharmaceutical firms for which data could be obtained from the AMADEUS database. For reasons of simplification, Table 6.2 does not report the scores of each of the twelve peer indicators separately. Instead, a firm's average position has been calculated for the six economic items on the one hand (column 3) and the six accounting ratios on the other (column 4). These two performance indicators of RPI, DQP, and LCP strategists in Germany, Italy, and the UK are reported on the left-hand side of Table 6.2. The right-hand side of Table 6.2 ranks the respective groups of firms according to their overall peer performance, which, in turn, was calculated by averaging out the scores obtained in economic items and accounting ratios. In order to correct for temporary peaks, each peer performance indicator was calculated as an average value of the past five years for which data were available.

Table 6.2 shows that RPI, DQP, and LCP strategists in Germany, Italy, and the UK achieve fairly similar positions on both the economic items index (col-

**Table 6.2.** Performance of RPI, DQP, and LCP strategists relative to their ten most direct competitors

| Group of firms | No. of cases | Ø peer performance in economic items[a] | Ø peer performance in accounting ratios[b] |
|---|---|---|---|
| **RPIs UK** | **11** | **5.73** | **5.26** |
| DQPs UK | 12 | 3.65 | 4.73 |
| LCPs UK | 7 | 4.87 | 4.42 |
| RPIs Ger. | 5 | 4.39 | 4.95 |
| **DQPs Ger.** | **8** | **4.56** | **5.83** |
| LCPs Ger. | 3 | 5.89 | 4.50 |
| RPIs Italy | 8 | 4.44 | 5.04 |
| DQPs Italy | 13 | 4.19 | 4.77 |
| **LCPs Italy** | **6** | **5.28** | **4.44** |
| RPIs total | 24 | 4.99 | 5.12 |
| DQPs total | 33 | 4.08 | 5.01 |
| LCPs total | 16 | 5.21 | 4.44 |
| Overall/ Average | 73 | 4.62 | 4.92 |

| Group of firms ranked by position obtained | No. of cases | Ø peer performance in eco. items and acc. ratios[c] |
|---|---|---|
| DQPs UK | 12 | 4.19 |
| DQPs Italy | 13 | 4.48 |
| LCPs UK | 7 | 4.64 |
| RPIs Ger. | 5 | 4.67 |
| RPIs Italy | 8 | 4.74 |
| **LCPs Italy** | **6** | **4.86** |
| **DQPs Ger.** | **8** | **5.19** |
| LCPs Ger. | 3 | 5.20 |
| **RPIs UK** | **11** | **5.50** |
| Overall/ Average | 73 | 4.77 |

[a] On a scale from 1 to 11, average of firms' ranking in *operating revenue, profit or loss before tax, cash flow, total assets, shareholders' funds,* and *number of employees.*

[b] On a scale from 1 to 11, average of firms' ranking in *return on shareholders' funds, return on capital employed, profit margin, current ratio, solvency ratio,* and *gearing.*

[c] On a scale from 1 to 11, average of peer performance in economic items and of peer performance in accounting ratios.

*Source:* AMADEUS database, as sampled in December 2004 (Bureau van Dijk 2004).

umn 3) and the accounting ratio measure (column 4). On a scale from 1 to 11, the average positions range from 3.65 (DQP pursuers in the UK) to 5.89 (LCP firms in Germany). In other words, all the pharmaceutical firms observed perform worse than at least three, but better than six of their most direct competitors – irrespective of the strategy they pursue and the country within which they are located. From the perspective of an entrepreneur, this result might be reassuring to the extent that the pursuit of any strategy seems to have about the same chances of success. From the VoC perspective, though, this result is troubling because it indicates that national institutions do not directly influence the success of corporate strategies. This idea is confirmed by the last three columns of Table 6.2, which rank the different groups of firms according to their overall peer performance. While one should keep in mind that differences between the individual positions are minor, it is striking to find British

RPI strategists, German DQP pursuers, and Italian LCP firms amongst those four groups of firms that perform least well. This finding, again, militates against the VoC idea that pharmaceutical firms perform less well if they pursue a strategy that is not supported by national institutions (see Hall and Soskice 2001*a*: 17–21; Hall and Gingerich 2004).

### 6.1.2. Diachronic Analyses of Strategy Success

It would be premature, however, to dismiss the VoC idea that national institutions influence strategy success purely on the basis of synchronic analyses, as it could be possible that firms perform equally well at a certain point in time. But, once corporate performance is considered over time, it may turn out that some strategies fail more often than others, depending on the institutional environment within which they are pursued. Section 6.1.2 thus takes up diachronic analyses of strategy success by enquiring into the frequency with which firms merge, are acquired, or go bankrupt. Are the initially pursued strategies more sustainable – that is, less susceptible to mergers, acquisitions, and bankruptcy – if they are supported by national institutions providing the required input factors (see Vitols 2001: 355–9; Casper 2007)? To answer this question, Section 6.1.2 first addresses the sustainability of competitive strategies on the basis of the previously employed PHID data-set comprising 130 pharmaceutical firms. It then counterchecks the findings obtained on the basis of an additional data-set comprising biotech firms only.

Does the PHID sample provide empirical support for the idea that competitive strategies are less sustainable unless firms pursue RPI strategies in the UK, DQP strategies in Germany, and LCP strategies in Italy? To answer this question, a retrospective check on each of the 130 pharmaceutical firms was carried out to see whether they have gone bankrupt, merged, been acquired, or kept their original legal status in the course of the last 20 years (i.e. between 1985 and 2006). Table 6.3 summarizes the results. Since mergers and acquisitions (M&As) do not necessarily constitute instances of corporate failure, whereas bankruptcy does, Table 6.3 makes the following distinction. Columns 2 to 5 list all instances of bankruptcy and M&As separately; these are then added up and reported in columns 6 and 7 as instances of change in legal status. Columns 8 and 9 report the remaining number and percentage of firms that did not experience a change in legal status. Taken together, all instances of status change and status stability lead to the overall number of firms surveyed, shown in columns 10 and 11.

**Table 6.3.** Changes in the legal status of RPI, DQP, and LCP strategies

| Group of firms | Bankruptcies | | M&As | | Legal status change | | Legal status stability | | Total | |
|---|---|---|---|---|---|---|---|---|---|---|
| | No. | % | No. | % | No. | % | No. | % | No. | % |
| **RPIs UK** | **1** | **5** | **6** | **32** | **7** | **37** | **12** | **63** | **19** | **100** |
| DQPs UK | 1 | 6 | 6 | 35 | 7 | 41 | 10 | 59 | 17 | 100 |
| LCPs UK | 2 | 20 | 3 | 30 | 5 | 50 | 5 | 50 | 10 | 100 |
| RPIs Germany | 0 | 0 | 2 | 13 | 2 | 13 | 14 | 87 | 16 | 100 |
| **DQPs Germany** | **1** | **6** | **2** | **12** | **3** | **18** | **14** | **82** | **17** | **100** |
| LCPs Germany | 0 | 0 | 5 | 42 | 5 | 42 | 7 | 58 | 12 | 100 |
| RPIs Italy | 1 | 7 | 2 | 13 | 3 | 20 | 12 | 80 | 15 | 100 |
| DQPs Italy | 1 | 7 | 0 | 0 | 1 | 7 | 13 | 93 | 14 | 100 |
| **LCPs Italy** | **1** | **10** | **3** | **30** | **4** | **40** | **6** | **60** | **10** | **100** |
| RPIs overall | 2 | 4 | 10 | 20 | 12 | 24 | 38 | 76 | 50 | 100 |
| DQPs overall | 3 | 6 | 8 | 17 | 11 | 23 | 37 | 77 | 48 | 100 |
| LCPs overall | 3 | 9 | 11 | 34 | 14 | 43 | 18 | 57 | 32 | 100 |
| Total/Average | 8 | 6 | 29 | 24 | 37 | 30 | 93 | 70 | 130 | 100 |

*Source:* PHID database, sampled in November 2004; changes occurred between 1985 and 2006.

Irrespective of whether M&As are perceived as instances of corporate success or failure, Table 6.3 indicates that firms go bankrupt, are acquired, or merge independently of the competitive strategy they pursue within a given institutional environment. For all instances of bankruptcy, it is particularly evident that national institutions providing required input factors do not influence the sustainability of competitive strategies. While bankruptcy is a rare event in general, the only instance observed for Germany concerns a firm which pursued a DQP strategy. In Italy, bankruptcy is – in relative terms – most widespread among LCP pursuers. Only RPI strategists in the UK show signs of strategy sustainability in line with the expectations of the VoC literature.

To assess statistically whether differences in the sustainability of competitive strategies vary significantly between countries, crosstab analyses were carried out. Detailed results are reported in Table A.4 of the technical appendix. As might have been expected on the basis of table 6.3., the association between a firm's *country*, its *strategy*, and the latter's *sustainability* (measured in terms of 'legal status change' and 'legal status stability') is not strong enough to produce statistically significant results. Synchronic analyses therefore cast doubt on the idea that national institutions influence strategy success, even when the latter is understood in terms of the sustainability of a firm's legal status.[6]

Since these analyses indicate that firms fail, change, or maintain their legal status irrespective of the country in which they pursue RPI, DQP, and LCP strategies, the question of an alternative explanation of strategy sustainability arises. While comparative data to perform regression analyses are not available, anecdotal evidence and one notable trend reflected in the data of Table 6.3 provide empirical support for the following counter-argument. The sustainability of *any* competitive strategy depends on the ease with which entrepreneurs can obtain seed capital for their business ventures. When managers whose firm was faced with bankruptcy, a merger, or acquisition were asked for the reasons for such instability, the respective interview partners often pointed to financial constraints (e.g. Frey 2004). The easier it had been to acquire seed capital in the beginning, the more likely the firm was to come under financial pressure at a later stage.

Table 6.3 argues in favour of this hypothesis as it shows British firms to be the most susceptible, and Italian firms the least susceptible, to legal status changes. More concretely, British firms prove the least stable, as 41 per cent of all companies studied have changed their legal status in the course of the last 20 years,[7] whereas status changes in Italy have occurred in only 20 per cent of all the firms reviewed.[8] With a 22 per cent rate of change in legal status, German companies are situated in-between, coming close to the Italian rate of status change.[9] Even though these figures are approximate due to the limited number of observations, strategy sustainability turns out to be in line with the availability of seed capital in the respective countries (see Leopold et al. 2003: 236–40). The comparative abundance of seed finance in the UK, which *inter alia* results from private pension and insurance systems (see Chapter 3), seems to make financiers less severe in their scrutiny before granting capital for new business ventures (Frey 2004). The opposite applies to Germany and, in particular, to Italy where 'institutional investors play a minor role (...) [because] pensions are provided by the state' (Aguilera 1998: 89; see also Breschi et al. 2003: 154; Pozzali 2004: 124–5).

[6] A more detailed crosstab analysis of the association between a firm's *country*, its *strategy*, and the latter's *sustainability* (measured in terms of 'bankruptcy', 'mergers and acquisitions' and 'legal status stability') can be provided by the author upon request. This analysis confirms the results of Table A.4 and therefore casts further doubt on the idea that national institutions influence the sustainability of competitive strategies.

[7] This figure was derived as follows from Table 6.3: (7 + 7 + 5)/(19 + 17 + 10) = 41%

[8] This figure was derived as follows from Table 6.3: (3 + 1 + 4)/(15 + 14 + 10) = 20%

[9] This figure was derived as follows from Table 6.3: (2 + 3 + 5)/(16 + 17 + 12) = 22%

These insights suggest that, in order to attract sponsors, business ideas have to be particularly promising in countries where seed finance is comparatively scarce (see Chapter 3); a factor which, in the long run, seems to make firms less susceptible to bankruptcy or M&As – irrespective of the competitive strategy they pursue. Importantly, this explanation goes beyond the institutional account proposed in the competitiveness literature in general and the VoC literature in particular, as the availability of seed capital is only partly influenced by national institutions, such as pension and insurance systems (see Chapter 3). In addition to institutional investors, private investors, banks, or – as will be illustrated below – the state can also offer seed capital. And the availability of these additional sources of finance is not affected by the shape of those national institutions that are of central concern in the competitiveness literature. Furthermore, and even more importantly, the present findings indicate that the availability of seed finance affects *all* strategies pursued within one economy to a similar extent – in addition to strategy-specific factors that impact on sustainability, such as different investment–return profiles. It is thus not only the sustainability of RPI strategies but also that of DQP and LCP strategies which is influenced by the ease with which seed finance can be acquired. This distinguishes the argument proposed here from that of the VoC literature, because the latter concentrates on exploring how the shape of national corporate governance systems determines the sustainability of RPI strategies (see, in particular, Vitols 2001; Casper and Matraves 2003; Casper 2007: chapter 4).

The above findings on strategy sustainability could be counterchecked – albeit only for firms pursuing an RPI strategy – on the basis the 'VentureXpert' database of Thomson Financial (2004). This database provides detailed information on a representative sample of firms in many Western economies which have received venture capital since the early 1980s (Bernard 2006). Because data can be sorted by country and industrial activity, it is possible to isolate those biotech firms that have obtained venture capital in the UK, Germany, and Italy. These firms can be assumed to pursue an RPI strategy for two reasons. First, Chapter 2 has shown that the majority of RPI strategists are biotech firms (see Tables 2.1–2.3). Second, in line with Chapter 3, several studies illustrate that institutional share capital in general, and venture capital in particular, constitute the most important source of finance for RPI pursuers (see Bottazzi and Da Rin 2002; Gompers and Lerner 2004: chapter 12; Kanniainen and Keuschnigg 2005). Firms that are active in the biotech industry *and* have received venture capital are thus very likely to pursue an RPI strategy.

While the sample obtained from VentureXpert for both Germany and the UK is representative, the one obtained for Italy must be completed. Since the

Italian biotech industry only started to take off around the turn of the millennium, many firms were not yet included in the VentureXpert data-set when the latter was sampled in October 2004. To make up for this shortcoming, the 'Italian Biotech Database' of *Venture Valuation* was consulted (Venture Valuation 2006). This database provides the most complete list of biotech firms which have received, or constitute attractive opportunities for, venture investment. In June 2006, it contained thirty-four firms. Like their British and German counterparts, these firms can be expected to pursue RPI strategies for the two previously mentioned reasons: they are active in the biotech industry and they are (potential) venture-capital recipients. Yet, unlike VentureXpert, the Italian Biotech Database does not provide systematic information on bankruptcy, M&As, and firms that have gone public. To reveal whether the firms in this database have a history of mergers or acquisitions and to discover possible additional instances of bankruptcy, interviews with experts of the Italian biotech industry (Barratti 2005; Vinci 2006) were carried out, and, various reports (Muffatto and Giardina 2003: 119; Chiesa 2004: 14–20; Fornasiero 2004) and the firms' web sites were consulted.

Table 6.4 provides an overview of the information obtained and illustrates the extent to which British, German, and Italian RPI strategists have changed their legal status since the mid-1980s. Whereas the upper section of Table 6.4 (lines 2 to 7) provides more detailed insight into corporate changes, the middle section (lines 9 to 11) regroups the respective events into successful, unsuccessful, and ambiguous cases. The lower section (lines 13 and 14) gives a summary of the initial events (lines 2 to 7) by distinguishing merely between legal status stability (line 13) and legal status change (line 14). It should be noted that this sample presumably conveys an overly optimistic impression of strategy sustainability because it only includes (potential) venture-capital recipients. Having been subject to the scrutiny of venture capitalists, these firms are more likely to be engaged in promising research projects than the average biotech firm in Germany, Italy, or the UK. However, this bias towards RPI stability is symmetric, so that actual failure can be assumed to be systematically higher in all three countries to the same extent.

The figures presented are particularly telling in two respects. First, they again cast doubt on the proposition of VoC contributors that RPI strategies are unsustainable in Germany (see Vitols 2001: 355–9; Casper 2007). Contrary to this claim, Table 6.4 shows that the aggregate figures of legal status sustainability are strikingly similar for British (90.5 per cent), German (93.5 per cent), and Italian (91.1 per cent) RPI strategists alike. The statistical robustness of this observation was tested through one crosstab analysis. Its complete

**Table 6.4.** Changes in the legal status of RPI strategists

| Radical product innovators | UK | | Germany | | Italy | |
|---|---|---|---|---|---|---|
| | No. | % | No. | % | No. | % |
| In registration | 1 | 0.8 | 0 | 0.0 | 0 | 0.0 |
| Active investment | 101 | 80.2 | 140 | 90.9 | 27 | 79.3 |
| Went public | 12 | 9.5 | 4 | 2.6 | 4 | 11.8 |
| Acquisition | 8 | 6.3 | 2 | 1.3 | 2 | 5.9 |
| Merger | 3 | 2.4 | 6 | 3.9 | 1 | 3.0 |
| Bankruptcy | 1 | 0.8 | 2 | 1.3 | 0 | 0.0 |
| Total | 126 | 100.0 | 154 | 100.0 | 34 | 100.0 |
| Successful RPIs[a] | 114 | 90.5 | 144 | 93.5 | 31 | 91.1 |
| Ambiguous RPIs[b] | 11 | 8.7 | 8 | 5.2 | 3 | 8.9 |
| Unsuccessful RPIs[c] | 1 | 0.8 | 2 | 1.3 | 0 | 0.0 |
| Total | 126 | 100.0 | 154 | 100.0 | 34 | 100.0 |
| Legal status stability[d] | 114 | 90.5 | 144 | 93.5 | 31 | 91.1 |
| Legal status change[e] | 12 | 9.5 | 10 | 6.5 | 3 | 8.9 |
| Total | 126 | 100.0 | 154 | 100.0 | 34 | 100.0 |

*Source:* VentureXpert, sampled in October 2004; changes occurred between mid-1980s and 2004.
Italian Biotech Database, sampled in June 2006; changes occurred between the mid-1990s and 2006.

*Notes:* a: Sum of biotech firms which were in the process of registration in 2004, which have remained unchanged since their establishment (active investment), or which went public between 1985 and 2004.

b: Sum of biotech firms which merged or were acquired between 1985 and 2004.

c: Biotech firms which went bankrupt between 1985 and 2004.

d: See 'a' above.

e: Sum of biotech firms which merged, were acquired, or went bankrupt between 1985 and 2004.

results are reported in Table A.5 of the technical appendix. In line with the previous analyses, this crosstab test assessed the associational strength between the *country* of RPI strategists and their *sustainability*, whereby strategy sustainability was measured in terms of 'legal status change' and 'legal status stability'.[10] The results obtained show that the scores are not statistically significant for either *Chi-square* or *Cramer's V*, with Cramer's V scoring low in addition. These indicators thus lend further statistical support to the observation that RPI strategies are about equally sustainable in Germany, Italy, and the UK.

[10] A further crosstab analysis of the associational strength between an RPI firm's *country* and its *strategy sustainability* (measured in terms of 'successful', 'ambiguous', and 'unsuccessful' instances) can be obtained from the author upon request. This analysis confirms the results of Table A.5 and thus casts additional doubt on the VoC idea that national institutions influence the sustainability of competitive strategies.

Also the second observation to be made on the basis of Table 6.4 is in line with the previous analyses of the PHID data-set, as Table 6.4 supports the idea that strategy sustainability is affected by easy access to seed capital. Yet, some background information needs to be provided to illustrate this point. To begin with, it is interesting to note that the VentureXpert database includes more German than British biotech firms, namely 154 against 126. What is more, RPI strategists are least successful in Germany, where 1.3 per cent of all observed firms failed, whereas they are most successful in Italy, where the failure rate is 0 per cent. While these figures may seem too similar to deserve closer attention, they point to a noteworthy difference in RPI sustainability in Germany, Italy, and the UK.

To comprehend this difference, it is necessary to review briefly how the German and Italian biotech industries emerged. In contrast to Italy, the beginnings of Germany's biotech industry were massively sponsored by the state. Aware that the biotech industry lagged behind other, mostly Anglo-Saxon, economies, the German government launched the 'BioRegio' project in 1995/6 and the 'BioProfile' initiative in 1999. Providing start-up capital and structural support to entrepreneurs, it was the explicit aim of these initiatives to boost the formation of biotech firms. Successful in this intention, a large number of biotech start-ups were founded in Germany in the late 1990s (Ernst & Young 2002: 92–8). This, in turn, explains the comparatively high number of German biotech companies included in the VentureXpert database. Yet public subsidies were only of a temporary nature. Furthermore, many newly established firms were university spin-offs with the result that their founders had little experience in (regulatory) issues concerning clinical development and product commercialization. These factors constituted major stumbling blocks to the prosperity of Germany's biotech industry because investment in general, and subsidies in particular, declined at the very moment that many start-ups sought to translate their discoveries into marketable products (Hofmann 2004*b*; Magenheim-Hörmann 2005). As a result, the German biotech industry went through a period of consolidation, which was most pronounced between 2003 and 2005. While some firms succeeded in merging or going public, others had to file for bankruptcy (Hofmann 2004*a*; 2005). Since consolidation was under way at the time the VentrueXpert database was sampled, the extent of this trend is not yet reflected in the data (see Ernst & Young 2006: chapter 1).

At first sight, it may be tempting to interpret the German experience in favour of the VoC argument that the pursuit of RPI strategies is unsustainable in Germany in the long run. However, the development of the Italian biotech industry provides counter-evidence which suggests the availability of seed capital to be the actual driver behind strategy stability. Since the Italian government did not provide any substantial (financial) support for the formation of a national biotech industry (Breschi et al. 2003: 145–6), the latter only began to take off in the early years of the new millennium. At that time, several international pharmaceutical firms decided to close their R&D facilities in Italy with the result that the scientists employed there risked losing their jobs. Faced with this situation, several scientists decided to try and set up their own business (Breschi et al. 2003: 150; Pozzali 2004: 122; Chiesa 2004: 9). However, seed capital was difficult to obtain as the Italian government did not provide (major) financial support, while national venture capitalists were virtually absent (see Chapter 3). Hence, only those firms with the most promising business ideas succeeded in bearing critical scrutiny from financiers, thereby attracting (venture) capital – mostly from abroad (see Breschi et al. 2003: 154; Pozzali 2004: 124–5). Unlike in Germany, the crystallization of the Italian biotech industry was therefore characterized by a process of 'Darwinian selection' (Vinci 2006). On the one hand, this explains why the number of Italian biotech firms was (still) very limited compared to Germany and the UK in 2005, when this research project ended. On the other hand, it also explains why Italian biotech firms have proven to be particularly stable. Since only the most attractive business ideas obtained seed finance, few firms had merged or been acquired, by the end of 2005, while no instances of bankruptcy were known (Muffatto and Giardina 2003: 119; Chiesa 2004: 14–20; Fornasiero 2004; Vinci 2006).

In sum, the previous analyses suggest that the sustainability of *specific* competitive strategies is not determined by the extent to which national institutions provide *specific* types of (financial) input factors. Instead, the stability of *any* competitive strategy rather seems to be influenced by the ease with which entrepreneurs can obtain seed capital. The more seed finance is available, the laxer the scrutiny of financiers, and the less stable is the financed strategy. As already mentioned above, this explanation goes beyond the institutional account of VoC contributors in that RPI, DQP, and LCP strategies alike are affected by the overall availability of seed capital – irrespective of whether the latter is provided by the state, banks, private, or institutional investors. An even more important discrepancy concerns the impact of capital affluence, in that VoC contributions indicate that easily available (venture) capital leads to superior RPI sustainability, whereas the previous analyses indicate the opposite: the easier seed capital can be accessed, the less sustainable are the pursued strategies.

## 6.2. STRATEGY CHOICE

Since Chapter 2 has shown that firms in different types of economies pursue RPI, DQP, and LCP strategies to the same extent, and since the previous analyses indicate that strategies are successful even if they are pursued in institutionally hostile environments, it can be ruled out that entrepreneurs base their strategy choice on institutional considerations. But what then drives an entrepreneur's choice of competitive strategy? Needless to say that the literature which addresses this question – in the field of strategic management alone – is huge, so that it would go beyond the scope of this research project to try and assess various strategy determinants systematically. However, the interviews carried out with CEOs and managers in the course of this project point to one particularly important explanation of strategy choice which, consequently, seems worthwhile elaborating here. To this end, it should be noted that *choice* and *change* of competitive strategies are synonymous events from an analytical point of view, as they are determined by the same cause. The use of one or the other term simply depends on a firm's stage of development. When a company is set up from scratch, it must choose the strategy it wishes to pursue. An established firm, by contrast, already pursues a strategy that it may wish to change at a certain point in time. Yet, the reasons why a newly founded firm chooses a particular strategy and an already established company changes its strategy are the same. In this section, instances of strategy choice and change are discussed to roughly the same extent.

In brief, qualitative evidence suggests that entrepreneurs base their choice of competitive strategy on technological opportunities, that is, on the inventions made by scientists and the facilities available for developing these inventions into marketable products. To illustrate this argument, three groups of particularly revealing cases are discussed below. The first group consists of three firms that resemble each other in all respects but three: the institutional environments in which they are situated, the technological opportunities available to them, and the strategies they pursue. The second group comprises four firms that are prototypical examples of German and Italian biotech firms. Differing in a variety of ways, their common feature consists in the extent to which technological opportunities have influenced the firms' strategy choices. Finally, the third group is made up of three companies which have changed their strategy at a particular point in time. Althrough the direction and moment of change as well as the firms' institutional environment differ, the most important driver of strategy change is the same in all three cases: technological opportunities.[11]

### 6.2.1. Similar Firms, Choice of Different Competitive Strategies

A particularly revealing example of how the choice of competitive strategy is influenced by technological opportunities is provided by three biotech firms

[11] The interviews on which Section 6.2 is based were carried out between March 2004 and March 2006. Changes after March 2006 are not considered.

which, for reasons of confidentiality, shall be called: *Chrome Ltd.*, *Chrome GmbH*, and *Chrome Srl.* These firms are strikingly similar in many respects. In addition to being active in the biotech industry, they are active in the same therapeutic area of vaccines against bacterial pathologies. Although they function independently in making their short- and medium-term decisions, all three firms are wholly owned by the same US corporation. Furthermore, they are similar in size, employing 750, 850, and 1,100 people respectively. All have a fully integrated value chain which includes an R&D department, production facilities, marketing and sales structures, and administrative support functions. However, the three companies differ in two crucial aspects. First, they are situated in three different institutional environments: *Chrome Ltd.* in the UK, *Chrome GmbH* in Germany, and *Chrome Srl.* in Italy. Furthermore, they differ in the competitive strategies they pursue. Whereas the German and British firms are engaged in development-oriented DQP strategies, the Italian company specializes in research-oriented RPI (Jon 2005; Maggi 2005; Weel 2005).

Because this strategic orientation runs counter to the expectations of the competitiveness literature, the HR managers of each company were asked about the reasons for their firm's strategy choice. Interestingly, the three interviewees agreed in their answer: the choice or change of competitive strategy was motivated by the technological opportunities of each firm; namely, the extent to which pharmaceutical inventions gave rise to hopes for the development of radically or, respectively, incrementally new products. When the US holding company bought the Italian affiliate in 1992, the latter had a long-standing history in pharmaceutical research due to its extensive R&D facilities and its links to internationally renowned research institutes. These technological capacities had not only produced radically new pharmaceuticals, but also raised hopes for further radical innovations. Accordingly, the Italian affiliate continued to pursue a research-focused RPI strategy after it had been acquired (Maggi 2005). This was different for both the German and the British affiliates. When the two firms were bought by the US holding company, their R&D facilities as well as their academic networks augured incremental rather than radical innovations. Therefore, the German biotech firm continued to pursue a development-focused DQP strategy (Weel 2005), whereas its British counterpart changed its strategy from an RPI to a DQP pursuer (Jon 2005).

### 6.2.2. Different Firms, Choice of Similar Competitive Strategies

Further evidence of firms choosing their strategies on the basis of technological opportunities is provided by the emergence of the German and Italian biotech industry in general, and by two German and two Italian biotech firms in particular. To preserve their confidentiality, the german firms shall be called *Melareen AG* and *Intrapharma AG*, the Italian firms *Belle SpA* and *Neverpharma SpA*. As pointed out in Section 3.2, the German and Italian biotech industry developed under very different circumstances. The firms cited here as ideal-typical cases are not only examples of Germany's and Italy's most successful biotech firms in the early years of the new millennium, they are also particularly representative examples of the following differences.

To begin with, the incentives to set up a biotech firm were diametrically opposed in Germany and Italy. Whereas structural and financial support from the government provided positive incentives for company formation in Germany, the opposite was true for Italy, where biotech firms were often founded as a response to downsizing measures by pharmaceutical companies. Furthermore, like many German biotech firms, *Melareen* and *Intrapharma* were spin-offs from academic institutions (Dom 2004; Schwer and Nes 2004), whereas *Belle* and *Neverpharma* grew out of existing pharmaceutical companies (Benta 2005; Sigillia 2005), as have almost all Italian biotech firms. Finally, company foundation took place at different points in time. Like many German biotech companies, the two German firms were founded in the mid and late 1990s, the two Italian firms, like most of their national counterparts, were set up around the turn of the millennium.

Despite these discrepancies, German and Italian biotech firms in general, and these four examples in particular, agreed in their choice of competitive strategy. Aiming at the commercial development of radical inventions made within the organization from which the firms in question emerged, all newly founded companies decided to pursue RPI strategies (Dom 2004; Schwer and Nes 2004; Benta 2005; Sigillia 2005). This decision was not affected by the extent to which national institutions provided the necessary input factors for RPI. Instead, the search for these factors came after the decision to establish an RPI firm.

### 6.2.3. Strategy Change Over Time

Three examples of strategy change complete the anecdotal evidence presented thus far. A German LCP strategist, renamed here as *Aetherpharma GmbH*, constitutes the first example. Until 2001, *Aetherpharma* was part of a larger pharmaceutical group, within which it pursued a DQP strategy. When the increasing need for innovative performance and flexibility led to the splitting of this group, *Aetherpharma* had to reconsider its strategic orientation. Following a prolonged period of reduced R&D efforts, *Aetherpharma*'s discovery record was bleak. Because its poor R&D performance dashed hopes for early inventions, *Aetherpharma* decided to change its competitive strategy from DQP to LCP (Sechoff 2005). This decision, in turn, demonstrates how technological opportunities and, more precisely, the prospect *not* to come up with marketable innovations influenced the firm's decision to change its strategy.

A similar example is provided by an Italian LCP strategist which, for reasons of confidentiality, is referred to here as *Glycerine SpA*. Until the early 1990s, *Glycerine* was a typical marketing specialist in that it imitated, produced, registered, and marketed the products of other pharmaceutical firms. While pursuing these activities, *Glycerine* happened to discover a recombinant protein, which raised hopes for the development of superior products and, hence, for incremental innovation. In an attempt to exploit this technological opportunity commercially, *Glycerine* opened a small research centre and changed from an LCP to a DQP strategy. But this change in general, and pharmaceutical development in particular, was not without problems. Although the R&D activities of *Glycerine* translated into several patents and international research collaborations, the firm became aware that it lacked both the financial means and the technological expertise to develop its discovery into a marketable product. Consequently, it decided to stop its R&D efforts and closed the research centre in the early twenty-first century (Maggio 2005). In other words, *Glycerine* changed from a DQP back to an LCP strategy – roughly ten years after its first strategy change. Like the experience of *Aetherpharma*, the change from LCP to DQP, and vice versa, was instigated by technological opportunities: namely, the firm's hope, then incapacity, to turn a pharmaceutical invention into a marketable product.

The final example of strategy change is again provided by an Italian firm, which is renamed here as *Allpharma SpA*. Unlike the two previous cases, *Allpharma* changes – and changes back – its competitive strategy from DQP to RPI rather than to LCP. In essence, this is possible because the firm's R&D activities take place at two levels. Having been among the first Italian firms to open their own R&D laboratories, the national research facilities of *Allpharma* constitute the basis for the firm's usual activities in incremental product innovation. Furthermore, *Allpharma* is one of the founding members of a European research alliance: an exclusive, private, and international research network established in 1989. Having the explicit aim of facilitating the 'joint research and development of innovative pharmaceutical products' (Rosa 2005), this research network occasionally serves as a platform for the development of *Allpharma*'s radical innovations. More concretely, *Allpharma* occasionally makes radical discoveries while pursuing its traditional DQP activities. Seizing these technological opportunities, the firm temporarily changes its strategy from DQP to RPI by relying extensively on its international research partners. Once the latter have helped to transform the radical invention into marketable patents, or even products, *Allpharma* changes back to incremental innovation and proceeds with product improvements (see Rosa 2005).

In sum, Section 6.2 shows technological opportunities to be of central concern to entrepreneurs when choosing their firm's strategy in two respects. First, the firms discussed here differ in all particulars but one: their strategy choice was driven by the expectation not to be inventive or, rather, to develop a radical or incremental invention into a marketable product. Second, all 'strategy changers' chose a new strategy that was technologically close to the former one. Firms switched from LCP to DQP strategies, and vice versa. They also changed back and forth from DQP to RPI strategies. However, not one firm switched from RPI to LCP – or the other way round. The decision to choose a new strategy that is close to the firm's former technological expertise underlines how important technological considerations are for the strategy choices of pharmaceutical companies.

## 6.3. CONCLUDING INTERPRETATION

What do these analyses teach us about the success and choice of competitive strategies pursued by pharmaceutical firms? Contrary to the central argument of the competitiveness literature,[12] entrepreneurs do not seem to make their choice of competitive strategies dependent on institutional considerations. They do not necessarily choose to pursue that strategy which is facilitated by national institutions providing specific input factors, but rather decide to engage in RPI, DQP, and LCP strategies irrespective of their institutional environment. Interestingly and contrary to the expectations of VoC scholars,[13] entrepreneurs are not punished for pursuing institutionally unsupported strategies, as neither the success nor the sustainability of competitive strategies seems to be dependent on national institutions providing the required input factors (Section 6.1). Although alternative explanations for strategic success measured in terms of balance sheet performance have not been explored here (see Section 6.1.1), the sustainability of competitive strategies seems to be influenced by the rigour with which financiers scrutinize a firm's business ideas before providing seed capital. The more severe financiers are in their

[12] See note 1. [13] See note 2.

scrutiny of business ideas before granting seed capital, the less do the receiving firms change their legal status over time (see Section 6.1.2).

Do these findings mean that national institutions do not matter at all for the sustainability of competitive strategies? Certainly, the finding that those institutions described in the competitiveness literature – most importantly national corporate governance systems and labour-market institutions – are not identifiable here as the main drivers of strategy sustainability does not mean that national institutions do not exert any influence. As illustrated previously, national pension and insurance systems can contribute to strategy sustainability to the extent that they facilitate, or hamper, the overall availability of finance for business ventures. Given however that firms can finance their business ventures from resources other than institutional share capital (see Chapter 3), the influence of national pension and insurance systems is limited. And, more importantly, the impact of these institutions takes the opposite form to the one suggested in the competitiveness literature. That is to say, national institutions which facilitate the availability of seed capital are here found to reduce, not improve, the sustainability of RPI, DQP, and LCP strategies.

As for the choice of competitive strategies, the scope of this research project does not make it possible to assess systematically how entrepreneurs form their decisions when choosing their firm's strategy. Qualitative evidence does, however, highlight the importance of technological opportunities as a major driver of strategy choice. More concretely, entrepreneurs have proven to opt for the pursuit of LCP strategies whenever the prospect of inventions is limited. But whenever the chances of developing an incremental or radical invention into a marketable product are reasonable, they rather decide to pursue RPI or DQP strategies (Section 6.2).

These insights challenge contributions to the competitiveness literature, which portray entrepreneurs as institution-takers.[14] By arguing that firms choose their strategy in line with those national institutions that provide the necessary types of finance and labour qualifications, the literature attributes important constraining capacities to the relevant financial and labour-market institutions. This idea is underlined by the reasoning that firms choosing to pursue institutionally unsupported strategies are less successful and thus, not sustainable over time (see Vitols 2001: 355–9; Casper 2007). The previous chapters have, however, illustrated how firms circumvent the constraints resulting from comparative institutional disadvantages. Given, furthermore, that individual technological opportunities seem to be more important than national institutions for entrepreneurs' strategy

[14] See in particular Porter (1990), Pavitt and Patel (1999), Hall and Soskice (2001*b*), Amable (2003), Hall and Gingerich (2004), and Hancké et al. (2007).

choices, the image of firms as constrained institution-takers should be revised. It is of little help to understand how firms choose and change their strategies, how they secure the required input factors, and how they can succeed even in disadvantageous institutional environments. In short, a perception of firms as institution-takers does not make it possible to explain how firms compete in the face of increasing pressure for competitiveness.

# 7

# Conclusion

This research has sought to reveal how economic internationalization affects the competitive behaviour of firms. How do firms compete in an increasingly international economy? Do they choose to specialize in those competitive strategies that are facilitated by the institutional environment of their economy? Do different strategies rely on specific types of finance, component standards, and employee skills, or can they be pursued by employing various types of these factors? Do national institutions influence firms' strategy choices, as they facilitate the availability of specific finance, standard, and skill types? Do firms seek to exploit these comparative institutional advantages? And do comparative disadvantages hinder firms from pursuing strategies that are not facilitated by national institutions?

The competitiveness literature has offered a particularly parsimonious framework to address these questions. Studying the competitive behaviour of more than 140 pharmaceutical firms in the UK, Germany, and Italy through this lens has made it possible to shed light on the above questions and, hence, to contribute to this literature. Furthermore, it has also resulted in various findings which provide insights into suggestions of the resource-based view (RBV) which underscore factor heterogeneity, into arguments of the institutional literature on how institutions matter, into suggestions of how national policymaking can promote corporate competitiveness, and into convergence and divergence theories of internationalization and its influence on entrepreneurial practices. The remainder of this chapter summarizes the various findings and relates them to these theoretical debates.

## 7.1. VARIETIES WITHIN CAPITALISM: ALTERNATIVE PATHWAYS TO COMPETITIVENESS

The analyses of pharmaceutical firms in Europe have clearly illustrated that when these firms decide how to compete, they are hardly concerned about their institutional environments. Instead of considering labour-market flexibility or the availability of particular financial resources, entrepreneurs choose their firm's strategy on the basis of technological opportunities, including the technological potential of the firm's inventions and its development facilities. Radical and incremental inventions, as well as opportunities for imitation, are thus at the basis of strategy choice. If the chances of turning these inventions or imitations into marketable products seem reasonably high, entrepreneurs decide to embark on strategies of radical product innovation (RPI), diversified quality production (DQP), or low-cost production (LCP) (see Chapter 6). Consequently, pharmaceutical firms in Germany, Italy, and the UK were found to pursue RPI, DQP, and LCP strategies alike and, even, to a very similar extent (Chapter 2).

This, in turn, casts doubt on the central claim of the competitiveness literature that firms choose their strategy in line with national institutions. To be clear, the four strands contributing to this literature focus on diverse opportunities and constraints that emanate from, or are channelled by, national institutions. While the originators of this literature consider how the availability of production factors influences corporate production decisions (Heckscher 1919; Ohlin 1933), its subsequent developers focus rather on the opportunities and threats that firms face in product markets (Porter 1980, 1985, 1990), on the shape of national innovation systems (Lundvall 1992*b*; Nelson 1993; Pavitt and Patel 1999), and on the design of national production regimes (Hall and Soskice 2001*b*; Amable 2003; Hancké et al. 2007) as determinants of corporate strategy decisions. Yet, all these research streams concur that the economy's institutional set-up offers important comparative advantages which bring firms to embark on the facilitated strategies. With increasing competitive pressure, firms are thus expected to gain competitiveness by exploiting these comparative institutional advantages and by specializing in the facilitated strategy (Chapter 1). Despite the persuasiveness of this reasoning, this book finds it to be the individual technological opportunities of firms (Chapter 6) rather than national institutions (Chapter 2) that are at the basis of corporate strategy choices.

Contrary to the macro-level assessment of competitive strategies on which the competitiveness literature grounds its arguments, the findings obtained here are based on micro-level studies of pharmaceutical firms. It should thus not pass unmentioned that the generalizability of the findings obtained here might be limited in two respects. First, the pharmaceutical industry is peculiar in its technology intensity on the one hand, and the strict legislative requirements for quality and purity of pharmaceutical products on the other. This implies that not only incremental or radical innovation but even low-cost imitation of pharmaceuticals becomes a complex task. Consequently, the costs that can be saved from outsourcing or offshoring parts of the value chain may be minor compared to the costs that arise when legislative requirements for purity of pharmaceutical products are not met. In less technology-intensive industries, the advantages offered by the institutional environment could therefore be more important for corporate strategy choices.

Second, the indicator employed here to identify a firm's strategy combines the technological novelty of a firm's products and its value chain focus. It is therefore more detailed than the measures employed by most competitiveness scholars, who often use macro-level indicators – such as revealed comparative advantages or relative patent registrations by industries – as a strategy proxy. Since the former measure captures more micro-level information than the latter, the patterns of strategy specialization found here are less pronounced than the patterns revealed in the competitiveness literature (Chapter 2).[1] Finding strong specialization patterns thus comes at the expense of reporting less micro-level variety. And yet, when the relative size of industries across economies is more important to an argument than the structural variety within these industries, it is of course useful to compare sectoral magnitude, and national institutions should not be discarded as explanations.

In sum, when studying industries other than pharmaceuticals and when analysing sectoral size across economies, one should neither overestimate the importance of technological opportunities nor underestimate the impact of national institutions as determinants of corporate choices. To explain how pharmaceutical firms cope with increasing pressures of competitiveness, though, the suggestion of the competitiveness literature that firms choose their strategy in line with national institutions is of limited help.

Given that this study finds pharmaceutical firms not to exploit comparative institutional advantages when choosing their strategy, how do they gain competitive advantages? How can they achieve a position of sustainable superior performance over their competitors? Adherents to the RBV have a clear-cut answer: firms achieve competitive advantages by building and exploiting idiosyncratic resources and capabilities. Even though manifold studies have sought to test and develop the RBV framework since its emergence in the mid-1980s (Rumelt 1984; Wernerfelt 1984; Barney 1986, 1991; Dierickx and Cool 1989), the fundamental claim of RBV theory is still the same. Valuable, rare, imperfectly imitable, and organizationally exploitable – in other words, unique – resources and capabilities are the key to corporate competitiveness (Barney and Clark 2007; Newbert 2007; see also Acedo et al. 2006). While RBV contributors tend to study the *process* through which unique capabilities can be built, their central claim seems to contradict the competitiveness

[1] For examples, see Dalum (1992), Fagerberg (1992), Chesnais (1993: 220–6), Keck (1993: 133–7), Walker (1993: 168–9), Pavitt and Patel (1999), Estevez-Abe et al. (2001: 174–6), Hall and Soskice (2001*a*: 36–44), and Hancké and Herrmann (2007); see also Porter (1990: 179–541), Amable (2003: 200–9), and Sinn (2005).

literature's premise that RPI, DQP, and LCP strategies each require a definite set of input factors.[2]

Interestingly, pharmaceutical firms in Europe have demonstrated strikingly homogeneous behaviour with regard to the factor types they use to pursue RPI, DQP, and LCP strategies. RPI strategists finance their activities mainly from institutional share capital, engage in competitive standardization, and employ a workforce with general skills. DQP pursuers, by contrast, make use of private share capital, competitive and coordinated standards, and a workforce with specific skill profiles. LCP firms are the least demanding in terms of input factors as they importantly finance their strategy from short-term liabilities, abstain from standardization, and do not require employees with particular skill profiles. In sum, firms pursuing the same strategy are characterized by a homogeneous factor structure rather than by an individualistic assembly of resources.

These findings do not only lend support to the argument of the competitiveness literature; they also differ from the RBV idea according to which firms need idiosyncratic resources and capabilities to gain competitive advantages. To be clear, RBV theory suggests that competitive advantage is gained by unique strategies supported by unique resources. The finding that firms pursuing similar strategies employ similar types of resources does not therefore directly refute the aforementioned premise. It is, however, interesting to note that firms can develop competitive advantages and, hence, achieve competitiveness not only through resource heterogeneity but also through factor homogeneity. The question is *how*. How can firms gain competitive advantages while employing similar factor types for the same strategies? How do they avoid behaving like lemmings, merely imitating each other's behaviour? The alternative pathways, which pharmaceutical firms choose in order to secure required input factors, indicate that it is the *process* of factor acquisition, rather than the nature of factor types, that enables companies to gain competitive advantages and cope with increasing pressures for competitiveness. In other words, the competitiveness-enhancing uniqueness of a resource does not stem from it being different, but from it being acquired in an original way.

The analyses of how firms secure necessary input factors have also lent support to the argument of the competitiveness literature on comparative institutional advantages.[3] National institutions have proven to be of advantage

[2] See, for example, Gelauff (1997: 346–56), Bronk (1998), Hollingsworth (2000: 626–30), Estevez-Abe et al. (2001: 146, 174–6), Hall and Soskice (2001*a*: 36–44), Lindbeck and Snower (2001*a*), Tate (2001: 445–6), Vitols (2001), Casper and Matraves (2003), and Casper and Whitley (2004); see also Ohlin (1933: 12, 68–75), Porter (1985), Freeman (1992), Lindgaard Christensen (1992), Patel and Pavitt (1994*a*: 89–92), Teubner (2001: 433–5), and Amable (2003).

[3] See in particular (Porter 1990), Pavitt and Patel (1999), Hall and Soskice (2001*b*), Amable (2003), Hall and Gingerich (2004), and Hancké et al. (2007).

whenever they promote the availability of factor types that are required for a given strategy. For example, private pension and insurance systems offer comparative advantages to RPI strategists by leading to an increased availability of institutional share capital. Flexible labour-market institutions are also of advantage to RPI pursuers, as they motivate employees to acquire rather general qualifications. A similar argument holds for countries with rigid labour-market institutions, which offer comparative advantages to DQP strategists insofar as employees are more inclined to acquire specific qualifications. Thus, while comparative institutional advantages do *not* bring firms to *choose* the institutionally facilitated strategy, they offer a source of competitive advantage by *providing easy access* to input factors that are required for the strategies which firms have chosen to pursue on the basis of their technological opportunities. In other words, firms can gain competitiveness from exploiting comparative institutional advantages.

This result, which broadly confirms the competitiveness literature's arguments, leads to the central puzzle addressed in this book. How can firms compete despite comparative institutional disadvantages? How can RPI strategists in public pension and insurance systems acquire the scarcely available institutional share capital here? How do they hire employees with general qualifications in countries with rigid labour markets? And how can DQP pursuers employ a workforce with specific skill profiles in economies with flexible labour markets? The answer given here is straightforward. Firms can circumvent national constraints and secure the required factors through functionally equivalent institutions. Two of these 'alternative pathways to competitiveness' have been identified in addition to factor provision through national institutions, namely *importation* via international institutions and *improvisation* on a contractual basis.

Whenever national institutions entail the necessary factors being in short supply, firms regularly take the second pathway to competitiveness and import the missing factors from abroad. RPI strategists in countries where pension and insurance schemes are administered by the state, for example, acquire institutional share capital from foreign economies. The development of Italy's biotech industry in the early years of the new millennium is particularly telling in this respect. Given that Italian venture capital was virtually non-existent at the time, entrepreneurs of these highly innovative firms turned to foreign venture capitalists and acquired finance from abroad (Chapter 3). Importation via international institutions also enables RPI pursuers in rigid labour markets to hire key personnel with the necessary general skill base from abroad. Here, the cluster of biotech firms around Munich offers an insightful example, in that about half of those CEOs who led fifteen of the most established firms in the early years of the new millennium were recruited from foreign labour markets (Chapter 5).

Critics of this argument may object that competitiveness via *international* institutions is better described as competitiveness via *foreign national* institutions, because firms import factors that are abundant as a result of the pension systems and labour-market institutions of other economies. Importantly, though, such factor transfer is only possible due to open financial and labour markets. Hence, it is international financial and labour-market institutions, rather than foreign national institutions that enable firms to secure input factors from abroad. A revealing example is provided by the European Union, where the free circulation of capital, goods, services, and people is guaranteed since the Single European Act of 1986. This seems to make it easier for RPI pursuers to hire EU rather than non-EU employees with general qualifications.

The second pathway that enables firms to compete despite the comparative disadvantages of national institutions is to acquire scarce factors *through improvisation on a contractual basis*. In so doing, firms circumvent national rigidities by defecting from the economy's 'typical' institutions: for example, by not installing works councils, or by not adhering to national wage-bargaining agreements. Such defection, then, enables firms to secure alternative factors in an improvisational way; usually by concluding atypical contracts. In deregulated economies, defection may not even be necessary to achieve this end, as national institutions that regulate economic interaction are by definition rare. Examples of factor provision through atypical contracts are numerous (see Chapter 5). To recall just a few, RPI strategists in rigid labour markets secure general employee skills through temporary contract work. Research projects are outsourced to university researchers; and both PhD students and recent graduates are employed as 'contract collaborators' for a limited time period, during which they work on specific projects. Similarly, DQP pursuers in flexible labour markets conclude employment contracts that can be considered atypical as they include incentives which tie employees to the company, so as to motivate the development of specific skills. Examples are pension and insurance schemes that become profitable only over the long term, opportunities for intra-firm promotion, and participation in sophisticated training programmes.

In sum, firms can gain competitive advantages and, thus, international competitiveness in three ways. First, they exploit comparative advantages offered by national institutions and make use of abundant factors. Second, they circumvent comparative institutional disadvantages and utilize open financial markets or labour markets in order to import factors from abroad. Third, they circumvent national rigidities and conclude atypical contracts which deliver scarce factors in an improvisational way.

One crucial insight follows from the above. Competitiveness is not an automatic result of specific institutional constellations; it arises from entrepreneurial creativity. As illustrated throughout this book, the characteristics which Schumpeter (1934, 1939, 1947) attributes to 'the entrepreneur', as opposed to 'the manager', are those that explain how firms compete: how they choose their competitive strategies, how they exploit comparative institutional advantages, and how they achieve competitiveness despite comparative disadvantages of national institutions – in brief, how firms build competitive advantages. Accordingly, the above findings indicate that competitive advantage initially depends on the skilfulness of entrepreneurs to weigh technological alternatives and to choose the most promising strategy, which may entail adjusting the previous strategy if more promising technological opportunities arise. The 'right' strategy is neither given from the outset nor likely to remain the same over time (Chapter 6). Once entrepreneurs have decided which strategy to pursue, competitive success depends on the process of factor provision and, thus, on the inventiveness with which entrepreneurs secure all the inputs required. Only if they succeed in exploiting comparative institutional advantages or in circumventing factor scarcity via importation or improvisation in a unique way will entrepreneurs be able to bring their firm to a position of sustainable competitive advantage. Those contributions to the competitiveness literature which perceive firms as mere institution-takers therefore have a hard time explaining how firms compete in the face of increasing economic internationalization.[4]

## 7.2. HOW INSTITUTIONS MATTER – AND HOW THEY DON'T

Whenever I present these findings at conferences or seminars, it is striking to see how institutional scholars among the audience are regularly concerned with the same question: Do institutions matter? If entrepreneurs can circumvent national institutions, why are they then constrained by international institutions, or by the institution of contracts? To answer the question of how institutions matter, it is first useful to reiterate *which* institutions have been investigated here. They include only those 'formalized rules that may be enforced by calling upon a third party' (Streeck and Thelen 2005*a*: 10), which solve collective action problems between economic actors so as to facilitate the provision of particular input factors. More concretely, these institutions are national corporate governance systems, systems of inter-firm collaboration, and labour-market institutions. To understand how firms

[4] See note 3.

compete despite comparative institutional disadvantages, it was further necessary to study the influence of pension and insurance systems, open financial markets, international labour markets, and contracts.

Importantly, though, legislation through which national governments can directly influence the competitive position of firms, such as fiscal law, patent legislation, subsidies, and health and safety regulation, have not been analysed here – deliberately so. Since it is the aim of this research project to test the hypotheses of the competitiveness literature on how firms adapt to economic internationalization, direct state influence has been controlled for. Consequently, only pharmaceutical firms within the (institutionally most different amongst the) legislatively harmonized EU member states have been investigated. Those seeking additional insights into whether and, if so, how the obtained findings are affected by studies of non-EU member states – be these India, China, or the US – cannot therefore be provided with systematic answers here. A speculative response is that legislative differences, for example, in the level of corporate taxes, in the protection of intellectual property rights, or in health and safety regulation, influence and – if favourable – stimulate corporate competitiveness. However, the crucial question linked to the idea of promoting competitiveness through governmental intervention is whether competitive advantages obtained from legislative generosity are sustainable in the long run. Additional research into whether legislative attempts to alleviate competitive pressures can promote *sustainable* competitive advantages is therefore highly desirable.

That said, how do the institutions investigated here matter? Do they constrain Schumpeterian entrepreneurs? The answer is straightforward: of course they do! The finding that entrepreneurs can *choose* the institutions they want to rely upon in order to secure required input factors does not necessarily mean that they do not have to commit to the obligations which result from this choice. Take for example the radical product innovators in Italy who, due to the scarcity of national venture capital at the start of the new millennium, had to secure institutional share capital from foreign investors. While international capital markets enabled Italian entrepreneurs to import finance from abroad (Chapter 3), cultural and geographical distance meant that entrepreneurs had to subject their business ideas to particularly severe scrutiny on the part of foreign investors (Chapter 6). This illustrates that institutions are both enabling and constraining, which holds true for national institutions, international institutions, and contracts alike. At the moment in which institutions enable entrepreneurs to secure required input factors, they also constrain them to adhere to the resulting commitments.

The above example illustrates a further aspect of how institutions matter. They can be a source of competitive advantage by exerting 'beneficial constraints' (see Streeck 1997). When Streeck coined this term in the mid-1990s, he illustrated how the necessity of *adapting* to the constraints of national institutions can lead to 'superior economic performance and competitiveness' (Streeck 2004: 426), in other words, to sustainable competitive advantages. The findings obtained here indicate that the necessity to *circumvent* constraints emanating from national institutions can be a source of competitive advantage as well. Take again the example of RPI strategists in Italy. When considering the additional efforts these firms had to make in order to acquire institutional share capital, one might be tempted to think that they would perform worse and, hence, fail in the long run. Interestingly, though, no signs of this have been observed until the completion of this research project in 2005. While it took quite a while for Italy's biotech industry to develop, those firms that succeeded in attracting foreign venture capital have demonstrated an amazing performance and resistance to mergers, acquisitions, and bankruptcy (Chapter 6). This indicates that entrepreneurs could transform the constraints related to importing finance from abroad into competitive advantages. In other words, the severe scrutiny on the part of foreign investors seems to have motivated Italian entrepreneurs to find particularly creative approaches to developing superior business ideas and to meeting the performance expectations of their financiers. National institutions thus matter as a possible source of 'beneficial constraints'.

A further aspect in which national institutions matter might be of particular interest to strategic management scholars in that institutions seem to influence corporate decisions on how to compete. From the perspective of strategic management, it may hardly be surprising that firms gain competitive advantages due to the creativity with which entrepreneurs pursue alternative pathways to competitiveness. Accordingly, one of the most recent studies of 'how we compete' (Berger 2005) finds that '[s]ucceeding in a world of global competition is a matter of choices, not a matter of searching for the one best way' (ibid.: 298). Despite the fundamental insight 'that there really are different ways of meeting the same economic challenges' (ibid.: 36), this – and some less recent – strategic management research offers only limited insights into the motivations of entrepreneurs to exploit institutional alternatives when acquiring necessary input factors. In the case of Berger's research, for example, it is left open in which circumstances entrepreneurs decide to compete: either by holding on to the fully integrated 'Fordist' model of production, by offshoring parts of the value chain, or by becoming part of a local cluster. The findings presented here do, however, indicate that such competitive decisions are not random. Depending on the shape of national institutions, firms find it easier to acquire the factors necessary for their strategy by relying on one rather than an alternative institutional pathway. RPI strategists in Germany, for example, hire key personnel from abroad rather than from the national labour market where managers tend to have a long-standing experience of working within the same firm. DQP pursuers in Britain, by contrast, prefer designing atypical contracts tying trainees to their company rather than hiring foreign key personnel. National institutions thus make some pathways to competitiveness preferable to others – depending on the strategy that is pursued within a given institutional environment.

This, in turn, points to yet another way in which institutions matter: they can provoke distinctive industry features. By this, I mean the peculiarities which national industries take on due to the way in which firms compete. In the case of Italy's biotech industry, the massive sponsoring by foreign investors and the sustained employment of contract collaborators (the so-called co.co. cos, later co.co.pros) are examples of such peculiarities. A further example is the high share of managers with foreign working experience leading biotech firms in the Munich cluster (Chapters 3 and 5).

Wherever national institutions contribute to the availability, or scarcity, of seed capital, they can also motivate distinct industry dynamics – albeit to a limited extent. As Chapter 6 has sought to argue, severe scrutiny of business plans on the part of seed capital providers promotes the sustainability of the pursued strategies. Accordingly, the scarcity of both venture capital and state subsidies in Italy around the turn of the millennium, which implied particularly severe scrutiny by venture capitalists, seems to explain why Italy's biotech firms, once they had succeeded in attracting finance, hardly experienced mergers or acquisitions. And not only radical innovators, but also incremental innovators and low-cost producers in Italy have manifested strategy sustainability more than the average – possibly due to the difficulties of obtaining capital for new business ideas. Conversely, easy access to seed capital seems to increase the likelihood that firms are acquired, merge, or even go bankrupt. The sustained availability of financing for new businesses in the UK, being partly a result of private pension and insurance systems, seems to be one reason for the increased strategy instability of British RPI, DQP, and LCP strategists. Importantly, though, the reasons why firms are acquired, merge, or suffer bankruptcy are numerous and go far beyond the availability of seed finance. Furthermore, seed capital is not only provided by institutional investors and in the form of subsidies; it is also made available by banks and private investors. National pension and insurance systems, facilitating the availability of institutional share capital, matter therefore only to a limited extent for strategy sustainability in general, and for the sustainability of RPI strategies in particular.

This, in turn, leads to one question of central concern to scholars, practitioners, and policymakers alike. Do national institutions matter for the success of competitive strategies? More concretely, if the sustainability of pursued strategies is taken as an indicator of their success, that is, of how firms evolve over time, do national pension and insurance systems influence strategy success, given that they influence the availability of institutional investment? The answer seems to be positive, which is particularly true of RPI strategists, as they finance their activities to a great extent from institutional share capital (Chapter 3). Importantly, though, the effect of these institutions is *the opposite* of the one predicted by contributors to the competitiveness literature (in particular Vitols 2001: 355–9; Casper 2007). That is to say, the *easier* RPI strategists can access institutional share capital, the *more likely* they are to merge, be acquired, or go bankrupt: in short, to fail from a dynamic point of view. Of course, this does not mean that RPI strategists are more successful, the more difficulties they have in obtaining venture capital. Neither does it mean that national pension and insurance schemes are of major concern for corporate decisions to merge, acquire, or file for bankruptcy. All it implies is that the institutionally facilitated *availability* of institutional share capital does not matter for long-term sustainability or *success* from a diachronic perspective.

That the institutionally facilitated availability of input factors does not matter for strategy success is confirmed by synchronic measures of corporate performance (Chapter 6). The comparison of various accounting ratios has clearly illustrated that the success of RPI, DQP, and LCP strategists is not attributable to national institutions providing the required input factors. While strategy success varies, these variations are usually greater between different strategies pursued within the same country, than for the same strategy pursued in different countries. This, in turn, indicates that RPI, DQP, and LCP strategies are characterized by a distinct investment–return profile, which is particularly obvious for radical product innovators. Given that it takes many years before investment in research and development of pharmaceutical products becomes profitable, newly established RPI strategists do not usually make a profit in the first years of their existence. That the institutional provision of input factors does not matter for static strategy success has also become evident from synchronic analyses which identify the competitive position of each firm relative to its major competitors. While RPI, DQP, and LCP strategists in Germany, Italy, and the UK overall achieve fairly similar scores, British RPI pursuers, German DQP firms, and Italian LCP strategists are part of those groups that perform least well. This indicates that the provision of input factors by national institutions does not explain, or 'matter' for, corporate success.

What do the above insights into how institutions matter, and how they do not, teach us about the contribution of national policies to corporate competitiveness? Can policymakers improve corporate performance at all? As noted earlier, instruments of direct policy intervention – such as patent legislation, pricing policies, health and safety regulation, subsidies, or fiscal legislation – have deliberately not been studied here. Since it is questionable whether direct state intervention can translate into lasting improvement of corporate competitiveness, this research has focused on institutions that solve collective action problems between firms and their most important business partners: financiers, suppliers, and employees. The question thus is: How should national policymakers design these institutions to improve corporate competitiveness? Is there an optimal way of shaping national pension and insurance systems, as well as labour-market institutions?

The first and maybe less comforting lesson to be learned from the above is that national policymakers *cannot* provide firms with an optimal institutional environment. Irrespective of whether pension and insurance systems are public or private, and irrespective of whether labour-market institutions are rigid or flexible, they only facilitate *one* competitive strategy, as they facilitate the availability of only *one* type of input factor. Given that pharmaceutical firms within the same economy pursue different strategies, factor-providing institutions cannot assume an optimal shape. They cannot provide radical product innovators and diversified quality producers with the required factors at the same time. The second, and perhaps comforting, conclusion to be drawn is that national policymakers *do not need* to provide firms with an optimal institutional environment. Given that competitive advantages do not result from the mere provision of input factors, but from entrepreneurial creativity in exploiting alternative institutional pathways, competitive advantages can be achieved as long as entrepreneurs have a choice: to rely either on national or on functionally equivalent institutions. Since national policymakers have to take a variety of socio-economic constraints into consideration when reforming pension and insurance systems, or labour-market institutions, it might be comforting that they do not need to make corporate interests their central concern in reform processes.

While this book has not studied how institutions evolve, the previous illustrations of how institutions matter, and how they do not, make it nevertheless possible to venture to draw some conclusions about the drivers of institutional development. Most importantly, it follows from the above that a functionalist explanation of how institutions develop seems to lack empirical support. This, in turn, militates against one fundamental argument of the most recent strand of the competitiveness literature: the varieties-of-capitalism (VoC) model. Going beyond the arguments of its precursors, the VoC literature perceives comparative institutional advantages to be not only a major source of competitive advantage, but also *the* main driving force behind institutional development. Accordingly, institutions in one realm of economic activity are said to assume a complementary shape to institutions in another realm. The reason for this, so the VoC scholars argue, is that institutional complementarities improve the outcome of one national production model, as they deliver all the necessary factors for one competitive strategy (Hall and Soskice 2001*a*: 17–36).

The functionalist logic underlying the VoC literature has often been criticized (Howell 2003; Allen 2004; Boyer 2005). The findings of this book give rise to similar doubts, as institutions do not seem to take shape out of the necessity of supporting a particular national production regime. On the one hand, competitive advantages have been found to arise from entrepreneurial creativity rather than from the institutional provision of input factors. This idea is supported by the insight that factor availability does not necessarily promote corporate success. On the other hand, entrepreneurs have been found to secure required factors through institutional pathways other than that of exploiting the comparative advantages of national institutions. These insights deprive the VoC reasoning of its rationale for why institutions take complementary forms. How can the necessity to support one national production system drive institutional development if entrepreneurs use functional equivalents with equal success? A historical account of institutional development seems thus more instructive for understanding how institutions evolve than the functionalist logic underlying the VoC reasoning.

This book has opened with the question of how firms adapt to the pressures of increasing international competition. Will increasing globalization lead to convergence or divergence of entrepreneurial practices? The book shall conclude with addressing this question. The findings of Katz and Darbishire (2000) on how employment systems evolve are highly instructive to this end, as 'converging divergence' also seems to be the outcome of the transformation process that economic internationalization has triggered in competitive approaches. Globalization as defined in the introduction to this book means that barriers to trade decrease, while business opportunities across borders increase. Given this increase in possible sources of competitive advantage, entrepreneurs can be expected 'to make use of their defining capacity, their *creativity*' (Streeck 2004: 428, original emphasis), and to exploit these new business opportunities: to relocate, to outsource and offshore, or simply to stay home and import required factors from abroad (see also Berger 2005). This, in turn, seems to trigger two simultaneous processes, which can be described as within-country divergence and between-country convergence of entrepreneurial practices. Within each economy, entrepreneurs increasingly deviate from the traditional production models which once motivated Albert (1993) and his successors (Hall and Soskice 2001*b*; Amable 2003; Hall and Gingerich 2004; Hancké et al. 2007) to describe competitive practices as nationally homogeneous production systems embedded in socio-economic institutions. At the same time, such within-country divergence entails that entrepreneurs in different economies converge in their competitive practices, as the number of approaches – be it the way in which input factors can be secured, be it the forms in which production can be organized (e.g. see Berger 2005) – seem to be limited. Given that economic internationalization increases the repertoire through which entrepreneurs can achieve competitive advantage, globalization and the related pressures for competitiveness thus seem to be at least as much an opportunity as a threat.

# References[1]

Acedo, F. J., Barroso, C., and Galan, J. L. (2006) The resource-based theory: Dissemination and main trends. *Strategic Management Journal*, 27, 621–36.

Aguilera, R. V. (1998) *Elites, corporations, and the wealth of nations: How do historical institutional settings shape intercorporate relations in Italian and Spanish capitalism?* Cambridge, MA, PhD thesis presented to the Department of Sociology, Harvard University.

Albert, M. (1993) *Capitalism vs. capitalism*. New York, Four Walls Eight Windows.

Allen, M. M. C. (2004) The varieties of capitalism paradigm: Not enough variety? *Socio-Economic Review*, 2, 87–108.

Aluse, D. (2005) Telephone Interview with D. Aluse (Qualitätssicherheit at German DQP Strategist). Darmstadt, 14th June 2005.

Amable, B. (2003) *The diversity of modern capitalism*. Oxford, Oxford University Press.

Andersen, E. S. (1992) Approaching national systems of innovation. In, B.-A. Lundvall (ed.) *National systems of innovation – Towards a theory of innovation and interactive learning*. London, Pinter Publishers.

Andrews, K. R. (1987) *The concept of corporate strategy*. Homewood, IL, Irwin.

Asoni, A. (2005) Telephone Interview with A. Asoni (HR Manager at Italian LCP Strategist). Milan, 18th November 2005.

Bakkering, S. (2005) Telephone Interview with S. Bakkering (HR Manager at British DQP Strategist). Worthing, 22nd December 2005.

Barney, J. B. (1986) Strategic factor markets: Expectations, luck, and business strategy. *Management Science*, 32, 1231–41.

—— (1991) Firm resources and sustained competitive advantage. *Journal of Management*, 17, 99–120.

—— and Clark, D. N. (2007) *Resource-based theory: Creating and sustaining competitive advantage*. Oxford, Oxford University Press.

Barratti, P. (2005) Interview with P. Barratti (Management Consultant and Expert of Italian Pharmaceutical and Biotechnology Industry). Milan, 14th February 2005.

Barro, R. J. and Sala-I-Martin, X. (1992) Convergence. *Journal of Political Economy*, 100, 223–51.

Bartlett, C. A. and Ghoshal, S. (1989) *Managing across borders: The transnational solution*. Boston, MA, Harvard Business School Press.

Baumann, A. and Voelzkow, H. (2004) Recombining governance modes: The media sector in Cologne. In C. Crouch, P. Le Galès, C. Trigilia, and H. Voelzkow (eds.)

[1] The names of the interviewees and their corporate affiliation have been changed to preserve their anonymity.

*Changing governance of local economies: Responses of European local production systems*. Oxford, Oxford University Press.

Baumol, W. J., Panzar, J. C., and Willig, R. D. (1982) *Contestable markets and the theory of industry structure*. New York, Harcourt.

Becker, G. S. (1975) *Human capital: A theoretical and empirical analysis, with special reference to education*. New York, National Bureau of Economic Research.

Benta, L. (2005) Interview with L. Benta (CEO of Italian RPI Strategist). Milan, 12th April 2005.

Berg, B. (2004) Interview with B. Berg (CEO of BB Consulting – Alternative Investments). Florence, 16th, 17th, and 18th March 2004.

Berger, S. (2005) *How we compete: What companies around the world are doing to make it in today's global economy*. New York, Doubleday.

—— and Dore, R. (eds.) (1996) *National diversity and global capitalism*. Ithaca, NY, Cornell University Press.

Bernard, D. (2006) E-mail on coverage of VentureXpert data, e-mail received on 23rd January 2006, Thomson Financial.

BfArM (2004) *Erläuterungen zu den Arzneibüchern*. Internet, accessed at: http://www.bfarm.de/de/Arzneimittel/azbuch/index.php on 20th September 2004, Bundesinstitut für Arzneimittel und Medizinprodukte.

Bhagwati, J. (2004) *In defense of globalization*. Oxford, Oxford University Press.

Biagiotti, A. and Burroni, L. (2004) Between cities and districts: Local software systems in Italy. In C. Crouch, P. Le Galès, C. Trigilia, and H. Voelzkow (eds.) *Changing governance of local economies: Responses of European local production systems*. Oxford, Oxford University Press.

Bonn, S. (2005) Telephone Interview with S. Bonn (HR Manager at British DQP Strategist). South England, 20th December 2005.

Bordo, M. D., Taylor, A. M., and Williamson, J. G. (2005) *Globalization in historical perspective*. Chicago, IL, The University of Chicago Press.

Borelli, S. (2006) Telephone Interview with S. Borelli (Head of HR Department at Italian RPI Strategist). Siena, 28th March 2006.

Börsch, A. (2007) Institutional variation and coordination patterns in CMEs: Swiss and German corporate governance in comparison. In B. Hancké, M. Rhodes, and M. Thatcher (eds.) *Beyond varieties of capitalism*. Oxford, Oxford University Press.

Bottazzi, G., Dosi, G., Lippi, M., Pammolli, F., and Riccaboni, M. (2001) Innovation and corporate growth in the evolution of the drug industry. *International Journal of Industrial Organization*, 19, 1161–87.

Bottazzi, L. and Da Rin, M. (2002) Venture capital in Europe and the financing of innovative companies. *Economic Policy*, 17, 229–69.

Boyer, R. (2005) Complementarity in regulation theory. *Socio-Economic Review*, 3, 366–71.

Breschi, S., Lissoni, F., and Orsenigo, L. (2003) Success and failure in the development of biotechnology clusters: The case of Lombardy. In G. Fuchs (ed.) *Biotechnology in comparative perspective*. London, Routledge.

Bresser, R. K. F. (2004) Ressourcenbasierter Ansatz. In G. Schreyögg and A. V. Werder (eds.) *Handwörterbuch Unternehmensführung und Organisation*. 4 edn. Stuttgart, Schäffel-Poeschel Verlag.

Bronk, R. (1998) EMU and corporate governance – Shareholder versus stakeholder model in post-EMU Europe. *Strategy paper for the Merrill Lynch/LSE debate on the appropriateness of the shareholder model for post-EMU Europe.* London, Merrill Lynch and Co.

Bureau Van Dijk (2004) *AMADEUS, a pan-European database of comparable financial information for 9 million public and private companies*, available at: http://www.bvdep.com/en/amadeus.html, sampled in December 2004.

Büthe, T. and Witte, J. M. (2004) *Product standards in transatlantic trade and investment: Domestic and international practices and institutions.* Johns Hopkins University, Washington DC, AICGS – American Institute for Contemporary German Studies.

Campbell, J. L. (2004) *Institutional change and globalization.* Princeton, Princeton University Press.

Casper, S. (2001) The legal framework for corporate governance: The influence of contract law on company strategies in Germany and the United States. In P. A. Hall and D. W. Soskice (eds.) *Varieties of capitalism – The institutional foundations of comparative advantage.* Oxford, Oxford University Press.

——(2007) *Creating Silicon Valley in Europe: Public policy towards new technology industries.* Oxford, Oxford University Press.

——and Matraves, C. (2003) Institutional frameworks and innovation in the German and UK pharmaceutical industry. *Research Policy*, 32, 1865–79.

——and Soskice, D. W. (2004) Sectoral systems of innovation and varieties of capitalism: explaining the development of high-technology entrepreneurship in Europe. In F. Malerba (ed.) *Sectoral systems of innovation.* Cambridge, Cambridge University Press.

——and Whitley, R. (2004) Managing competences in entrepreneurial technology firms: A comparative institutional analysis of Germany, Sweden, and the UK. *Research Policy*, 33, 89–106.

——Lehrer, M., and Soskice, D. W. (1999) Can high-technology industries prosper in Germany? Institutional frameworks and the evolution of the German software and biotechnology industries. *Industry and Innovation*, 6, 5–24.

Cerny, P. G. (ed.) (1993) *Finance and world politics: Markets, regimes and states in the post-hegemonic era*, Aldershot, Edward Elgar.

——(1994) Money and power: The American financial system from free banking to global competition. In G. Thompson (ed.) *Markets.* London, Open University.

Chesnais, F. (1993) The French national system of innovation. In R. R. Nelson (ed.) *National innovation systems: A comparative analysis.* Oxford, Oxford University Press.

Chiesa, V. (2004) *Il cluster biotecnologico lombardo.* Milano, Assobiotec (Federchimica).

Cocker, M. (2005) Telephone Interview with M. Cocker (Senior Manager, Global Compliance Management at British DQP Strategist), Cheshire, 6th January 2005.

Coin, C. (2005) Telephone Interview with C. Coin (CEO of German LCP Strategist), Berlin, 22nd March 2005.

Coleman, J. S. (1986) Social theory, social research, and a theory of action. *The American Journal of Sociology*, 91, 1309–35.

Coleman, J. S. (1990) *Foundations of social theory*, Cambridge, MA, The Belknap Press of Harvard University Press.

Collar, M. (2006) Telephone Interview with M. Collar (QA Technical Manager at British LCP Strategist), Hertfordshire, 26th January 2006.

Conner, K. R. (1991) A historical comparison of resource-based theory and five schools of thought within industrial organization economics: Do we have a new theory of the firm? *Journal of Management*, 17, 121–54.

Cooke, P., Uranga, M. G., and Etxebarria, G. (1997) Regional innovation systems: Institutional and organisational dimensions. *Research Policy*, 26, 475–91.

——————(1998) Regional systems of innovation: An evolutionary perspective. *Environment and Planning*, 30, 1563–84.

Cossentino, F., Pyke, F., and Sengenberger, W. (eds.) (1996) *Local and regional response to global pressure*. Geneva, International Institute for Labour Studies.

Cottidiani, F. (2006) Telephone Interview with F. Cottidiani (Amministratore Delegato at Italian LCP Strategist), Milan, 14th March 2006.

Crouch, C. (2005) *Capitalist diversity and change: Recombinant governance and institutional entrepreneurs*. Oxford, Oxford University Press.

——Le Galès, P., Trigilia, C., and Voelzkow, H. (eds.) (2001) *Local production systems in Europe: Rise or demise?* Oxford.

————————(eds.) (2004) *Changing governance of local economies: Responses of European local production systems*. Oxford, Oxford University Press.

Culpepper, P. D. (2001) Employers, public policy, and the politics of decentralized cooperation in Germany and France. In P. A. Hall and D. W. Soskice (eds.) *Varieties of capitalism – The institutional foundations of comparative advantage*. Oxford, Oxford University Press.

Dalum, B. (1992) Export specialisation, structural competitiveness and national systems of innovation. In B.-A. Lundvall (ed.) *National systems of innovation – Towards a theory of innovation and interactive learning*. London, Pinter Publishers.

De Vecchi, L. and Roussey, R. (2003) *Corporate governance in Italy – The board of auditors*. Rome, Consiglio Nazionale Dottori Commercialisti.

Deeg, R. (2005) Remaking Italian capitalism? The politics of corporate governance reform. *West European Politics*, 28, 521–48.

——(2006) Governance and the nation-state in a global era. In S. Lütz (ed.) *Governance in der politischen Ökonomie*. Wiesbaden, VS Verlag für Sozialwissenschaften.

Dierickx, I. and Cool, K. (1989) Asset stock accumulation and sustainability of competitive advantage. *Management Science*, 35, 1504–11.

Dom, H. (2004) Interview with H. Dom (Founder of German RPI Strategist and CEO of Association of German Biotechnology Companies), Munich, 7th December 2004.

Dore, R. (1986) *Flexible rigidities: Industrial policy and structural adjustment in the Japanese economy*. Stanford, CA, Stanford University Press.

DPR 597 (1973) *Decreto del Presidente della Repubblica; 29 settembre 1973, n. 597*. Roma, Il Presidente della Repubblica.

Drews, J. (1999) *In quest of tomorrow's medicines*. New York, Springer Verlag.

——(2000) Drug discovery: A historical perspective. *Science*, 287, 1960–4.

EIRO (2002) *Government seeks to expand and revitalise modern apprenticeships*, accessed at: http://www.eurofound.europa.eu/eiro/2002/10/feature/uk0210105f.html on 17th April 2007 European Industrial Relations Observatory.

——(2004*a*) *Emanata la circolare ministeriale che disciplina il lavoro para-subordinato*, accessed at: http://www.eurofound.europa.eu/eiro/2004/04/word/it0404303fit.doc on 17th April 2007 European Industrial Relations Observatory.

——(2004*b*) *Government announces reform of apprenticeship system*, accessed at: http://www.eurofound.europa.eu/eiro/2004/05/feature/uk0405105f.html on 17th April 2007 European Industrial Relations Observatory.

——(2005) *Atypical work spreads in Italy*, accessed at: http://www.eurofound.europa.eu/eiro/2005/04/word/it0504206fit.doc on 17th April 2007 European Industrial Relations Observatory.

EMEA (2006) *About the EMEA*, accessed at: http://www.emea.eu.int/htms/aboutus/emeaoverview.htm on 17th April 2007 European Medicines Agency.

EMIRE (2007) *National vocational qualifications (NVQs)*, accessed at: http://www.eurofound.europa.eu/emire/UNITED%20KINGDOM/NATIONALVOCATIONALQUALIFICATIONSNVQS-EN.html on 17th April 2007 European Foundation for the Improvement of Living and Working Conditions.

Ernst & Young (2002) *Neue Chancen: Deutscher Biotechnologie-Report 2002*. Mannheim, Ernst & Young Deutsche Allgemeine Treuhand AG.

——(2003) *Endurance – The European Biotechnology Report 2003: 10th Anniversary Edition*. London, Ernst & Young LLP.

——(2004) *Per Aspera ad Astra: Der steinige Weg zu den Sternen – Deutscher Biotechnologie-Report 2004*. Mannheim, Ernst & Young AG Wirtschaftsprüfungsgesellschaft.

——(2005) *Kräfte der Evolution – Deutscher Biotechnologie-Report 2005*. Mannheim, Ernst & Young AG Wirtschaftsprüfungsgesellschaft.

——(2006) *Zurück in die Zukunft: Deutscher Biotechnologie-Report 2006*. Mannheim, Ernst & Young AG Wirtschaftsprüfungsgesellschaft.

Estevez-Abe, M., Iversen, T. and Soskice, D. W. (2001) Social protection and the formation of skills: A reinterpretation of the welfare state. In P. A. Hall and D. W. Soskice (eds.) *Varieties of capitalism – The institutional foundations of comparative advantage*. Oxford, Oxford University Press.

Eudralex (2003) *The rules governing medicinal products in the European Union – Vol. 4: Good manufacturing practices*, available online at: http://pharmacos.eudra.org/F2/eudralex/vol-4/home.htm, European Commission; DG Enterprise and Industry.

Fagerberg, J. (1992) The home market hypothesis re-examined: The impact of domestic user-producer interaction on export specialisation. In B.-A. Lundvall (ed.) *National systems of innovation – Towards a theory of innovation and interactive learning*. London, Pinter Publishers.

Feige, E. L. and Watts, H. W. (1972) An investigation of the consequences of partial aggregation of micro-economic data. *Econometrica*, 40, 343–60.

Ferner, A. and Hyman, R. (1998) *Changing industrial relations in Europe*. Malden, MA, Blackwell Publishers.

Findlay, R. and O'Rourke, K. H. (2005) Commodity market integration, 1500–2000. In M. D. Bordo, A. M. Taylor and J. G. Williamson (eds.) *Globalization in historical perspective*. Chicago, IL, Chicago University Press.

Fiori, G., Tiscini, R., and Di Donato, F. (2004) Corporate governance, evoluzione normativa ed informazione esterna d'impresa. In D. M. Salvioni (ed.) *Corporate governance e sistemi di controllo della gestione aziendale*. Milan, FrancoAngeli.

Fornasiero, C. (2004) L'Italia rischia di non riuscire a prendere il treno biotech. *Doctor*, January 2004, 26–31.

Franzese, R. J. and Mosher, J. M. (2002) Comparative institutional and policy advantage – The scope for divergence within European economic integration. *European Union Politics*, 3, 177–203.

Freel, J. (2005) Telephone Interview with J. Freel (Human Resources Management at German LCP Strategist), Darmstadt, 15th March 2005.

Freeman, C. (1987) *Technology policy and economic performance: Lessons from Japan*. London, Pinter Publishers.

—— (1992) Formal scientific and technical institutions in the national system of innovation. In B.-A. Lundvall (ed.) *National systems of innovation – Towards a theory of innovation and interactive learning*. London, Pinter Publishers.

—— and Perez, C. (1988) Structural crises of adjustment: Business cycles and investment behaviour. In G. Dosi, C. Freeman, R. R. Nelson, G. Silverberg, and L. Soete (eds.) *Technical change and economic theory*. London, Pinter.

Frey, M. (2004) Telephone Interview with M. Frey (CEO of German Biotechnology Firm), Darmstadt, 23rd April 2004.

Friedner, M. (2005) Telephone Interview with M. Friedner (Qualitätssicherung at German LCP Strategist), Holzkirchen, 4th March 2005.

Gambardella, A., Orsenigo, L., and Pammolli, F. (2001) *Global competitiveness in pharmaceuticals: A European perspective*. Luxembourg, European Commission: Office for Official Publications of the European Communities.

Garda, G. (2005) Interview with G. Garda (Vice President of Italian DQP Strategist), Milan, 28th February 2005.

Gelauff, G. (1997) Corporate governance. In C. P. B. Netherlands Bureau For Economic Policy Analysis (ed.) *Challenging neighbours – rethinking German and Dutch economic institutions*. Berlin, Springer Verlag.

Gelsing, L. (1992) Innovation and the development of industrial networks. In B.-A. Lundvall (ed.) *National systems of innovation – Towards a theory of innovation and interactive learning*. London, Pinter Publishers.

Gerschenkron, A. (1962) *Economic backwardness in historical perspective*. Cambridge, MA, Belknap Press of Harvard University Press.

Ghoshal, S. (1987) Global strategy: An organising framework. *Strategic Management Journal*, 8, 425–40.

Gompers, P. and Lerner, J. (2004) *The venture capital cycle*, Cambridge, MA, MIT Press.

Gourevitch, P. (1986) *Politics in hard times: Comparative responses to international economic crises*, Ithaca, NY, Cornell University Press.

—— and Hawes, M. (2002) The politics of choice among national production systems. In R. Boyer (ed.) *L'année de la régulation*. Paris, Presses des Sciences Po.

Grant, R. M. (1998) *Contemporary strategy analysis*, Malden, MA, Blackwell Publishers.

Gries, J., Lindenau, M., Maaz, K., and Waleschkowski, U. (2005) *Bildungssysteme in Europa – Kurzdarstellungen*. Berlin, Institut für Sozialforschung, Informatik und Soziale Arbeit.

Grünecke, S. (2004) Interview with S. Grünecke (Qualitätssicherung at German DQP Strategist), Monheim, 30th March 2004.

Gullaner, R. (2005) Telephone Interview with R. Gullaner (CEO of German RPI Strategist), Esslingen, 24th November 2005.

Hall, P. A. and Gingerich, D. W. (2004) *Varieties of capitalism and institutional complementarities in the macroeconomy: An empirical analysis*. Cologne, Max-Planck-Institut für Gesellschaftsforschung, Discussion Paper 04/5.

—— and Soskice, D. W. (2001*a*) An introduction to varieties of capitalism. In P. A. Hall and D. W. Soskice (eds.) *Varieties of capitalism – The institutional foundations of comparative advantage*. Oxford, Oxford University Press.

—— —— (eds.) (2001*b*) *Varieties of capitalism – The institutional foundations of comparative advantage*, Oxford, Oxford University Press.

Hallerton, N. (2004) Interview with N. Hallerton (Advisor at British Consultancy on GMP and Regulatory Affairs), Brighton, 25th November 2004.

Hancké, B. and Herrmann, A. M. (2007) Wage bargaining and comparative advantage in EMU. In B. Hancké, M. Rhodes, and M. Thatcher (eds.) *Beyond varieties of capitalism*. Oxford, Oxford University Press.

—— Rhodes, M., and Thatcher, M. (eds.) (2007) *Beyond varieties of capitalism*. Oxford, Oxford University Press.

Heckscher, E. F. (1919) The effect of foreign trade on the distribution of income. In H. Flam and J. M. Flanders (eds.) *Heckscher-Ohlin trade theory*. Cambridge, MA, The MIT Press.

Herrigel, G. (1996) *Industrial constructions: The sources of German industrial power*. Cambridge, Cambridge University Press.

Hinze, S., Reiß, T., Dominguez-Lacasa, I., and Wörner, S. (2001) *Einfluss der Biotechnologie auf das Innovationssystem der pharmazeutischen Industrie*. Karlsruhe, Fraunhofer Institut für Systemtechnik.

Hofmann, S. (2004*a*) Biotechbranche fehlt Geld für die Konsolidierung. *Handelsblatt*, 8th October 2004, 12.

—— (2004*b*) Interesse an deutschen Biotechs wächst. *Handelsblatt*, 17th December 2004.

—— (2005) Biotechfirmen kämpfen um Kapital. *Handelsblatt*, 19th January 2005, 14.

Hollingsworth, R. J. (2000) Doing institutional analysis: Implications for the study of innovations. *Review of International Political Economy*, 7, 595–644.

—— and Boyer, R. (1997) *Contemporary capitalism: The embeddedness of institutions*. Cambridge, Cambridge University Press.

—— Schmitter, P. C., and Streeck, W. (eds.) (1994) *Governing capitalist economies*. Oxford, Oxford University Press.

Howell, C. (2003) Review: Varieties of capitalism: And then there was one? *Comparative Politics*, 36, 103–24.

Hu, Y.-S. (1992) Global and stateless corporations are national firms with international operations. *California Management Review*, 34, 107–26.

Iversen, T. and Soskice, D. W. (2001) An asset theory of social policy preferences. *American Political Science Review*, 95, 875–93.

Jenner, B. (2004) Telephone Interview with B. Jenner (Advisor at German Consultancy on GMP and Regulatory Affairs), Heidelberg, 20th September 2004.

Jon, A. (2004) Interview with A. Jon (Human Resources Advisor at British RPI Strategist), Slough Berkshire, 22nd October 2004.

Jon, S. (2005) Telephone Interview with S. Jon (Director, Employee Development of British DQP Strategist), Liverpool, 25th July 2005.

—— (2007) E-Mail by S. Jon (Director, Employee Development of British DQP Strategist) on National Vocational Qualifications and Vocational Apprenticeship Schemes in the British Pharamceutical and Biopharmaceutical Industry, e-mail received on 2nd May 2007.

Jong, S. (2006) *The development of Munich and Cambridge therapeutic biotech firms: A case study of institutional adaptation*. Florence, EUI Working Paper SPS No. 2006/10.

Kanniainen, V. and Keuschnigg, C. (2005) *Venture capital, entrepreneurship, and public policy*. Cambridge, MA, MIT Press.

Katz, H. C. and Darbishire, O. (2000) *Converging divergences – Worldwide changes in employment systems*. Ithaca, NY, Cornell University Press.

Keck, O. (1993) The national system for technical innovation in Germany. In R. R. Nelson (ed.) *National innovation systems: A comparative analysis*. Oxford, Oxford University Press.

Kenyon, T. and Vitols, S. (2004) *Corporate governance in Germany and the United States: Key challenges for the transatlantic business community*. Washington, American Institute for Contemporary German Studies; AICGS Policy Report.

Kerr, C., Dunlop, J. T., Harbison, F. H. M., and Charles A. (1973) *Industrialism and industrial man: The problems of labour and management in economic growth*. Harmondsworth, Penguin Books.

King, D. and Wood, S. (1999) The political economy of neoliberalism: Britain and the United States in the 1980s. In H. Kitschelt, P. Lange, G. Marks, and J. D. Stephens (eds.) *Continuity and change in contemporary capitalism*. Cambridge, Cambridge University Press.

Kitschelt, H., Lange, P., Marks, G., and Stephens, J. D. (eds.) (1999) *Continuity and change in contemporary capitalism*. Cambridge, Cambridge University Press.

Klein, B. (1996) Why hold-ups: The self-enforcing range of contractual relationships. *Economic Inquiry*, 34, 444–63.

Klepper, S. and Graddy, E. (1990) The evolution of new industries and the determinants of market structure. *RAND Journal of Economics*, 21, 27–44.

—— and Simons, K. L. (1997) Technological extinctions of industrial firms: An inquiry into their nature and causes. *Industrial and Corporate Change*, 6, 379–460.

Knyphausen-Aufseß, D. Z. (1997) Auf dem Weg zu einem ressourcenorientierten paradigma? Resource dependence-theorie der oranisation und resource-based view des strategischen managements im vergleich. In G. Ortmann, J. Sydow and K. Türk (eds.) *Theorien der organisation*. Opladen, Westdeutscher Verlag.

Kogut, B. (1985) Designing global strategies: Comparative and competitive value-added chains. *Sloan Management Review*, 26, 15–28.

Krugman, P. R. and Obstfeld, M. (2006) *International economics: Theory and policy*. Boston, MA, Addison Wesley.

Kurzer, P. (1993) *Business and banking: Political change and economic integration in Western Europe*. Ithaca, NY, Cornell University Press.

Lange, K. (2006) *Deutsche Biotech-Unternehmen und ihre Innovationsfähigkeit im internationalen Vergleich – Eine institutionentheoretische Analyse*. Groningen, Rijksuniversiteit.

Lanzenberger, M. (2004) Telephone Interview with M. Lanzenberger (Business Development Manager at German RPI Strategist), Bergisch Gladbach, 16th June 2004.

Lazonick, W. (1991) *Business organization and the myth of the market economy*. New York, Cambridge University Press.

Le Galès, P. and Voelzkow, H. (2001) Introduction: The governance of local economies. In C. Crouch, P. Le Galès, C. Trigilia, and H. Voelzkow (eds.) *Local production systems in Europe – Rise or demise?* Oxford, Oxford University Press.

Leopold, G., Frommann, H., and Kühr, T. (2003) *Private equity venture capital – Eigenkapital für innovative Unternehmen*. München, Verlag Franz Vahlen.

Levitt, T. (1965) Exploit the product life cycle. *Harvard Business Review*, November–December, 81–94.

Lindbeck, A. and Snower, D. J. (2001*a*) Centralized bargaining and reorganized work: Are they compatible? *European Economic Review*, 45, 1851–75.

—— —— (2001*b*) Insiders versus outsiders. *The Journal of Economic Perspectives*, 15, 165–88.

Lindgaard Christensen, J. (1992) The role of finance in national systems of innovation. In B.-A. Lundvall (ed.) *National systems of innovation – Towards a theory of innovation and interactive learning*. London, Pinter Publishers.

Lumer, K. (2004) Interview with K. Lumer (Senior Project Manager at German RPI Strategist), Köln, 30th March 2004.

Lundvall, B.-A. (1992*a*) Introduction. In B.-A. Lundvall (ed.) *National systems of innovation – Towards a theory of innovation and interactive learning*. London, Pinter Publishers.

—— (1992*b*) *National systems of innovation – Towards a theory of innovation and interactive learning*. London, Pinter Publishers.

—— (1992*c*) User-producer relationships, national systems of innovation and internationalisation. In B.-A. Lundvall (ed.) *National systems of innovation – Towards a theory of innovation and interactive learning*. London, Pinter Publishers.

—— and Maskell, P. (2000) Nation states and economic development: From national systems of production to national systems of knowledge creation and learning. In G. L. Clark, M. P. Feldman, and M. S. Gertler (eds.) *The Oxford handbook of economic geography*. Oxford, Oxford University Press.

Magenheim-Hörmann, T. (2005) Die großen Pharmabrüder sollen helfen: Biotech-Branche auf der Suche nach Finanzierungsgeldern – Experten empfehlen Börsengänge. *Stuttgarter Zeitung*, 12th April 2005.

Maggi, G. (2005) Interview with G. Maggi (Human Resources at Italian RPI Strategist), Florence: European University Institute, 4th August 2005.

Maggio, D. (2005) Telephone Interview with D. Maggio (Representative of Italian DQP Strategist), Anagni, 19th October 2005.

Malcomson, J. M. (1997) Contracts, hold-up, and labor markets. *Journal of Economic Literature*, 35, 1916–57.

Maler, A. (2004) Interview with A. Maler (Advisor at German Consultancy on GMP and Regulatory Affairs), Heidelberg, 13th September 2004.

Malerba, F. (1993) The national system of innovation: Italy. In R. R. Nelson (ed.) *National innovation systems: A comparative analysis*. Oxford, Oxford University Press.

Manci, A. (2005) Telephone Interview with A. Manci (Responsabile del Personale at Italian RPI Strategist), Pisa, 1st August 2005.

Marshall, A. (1920) *Principles of economics*. London, Macmillan.

Maurice, M., Sellier, F., and Silvestre, J.-J. (1986) *The social foundations of industrial power: A comparison of France and Germany*. Cambridge, MA, MIT Press.

Mayer, C. (1998) Financial systems and corporate governance: A review of the international evidence. *Journal of Institutional and Theoretical Economics*, 154, 144–65.

McKelvey, M. (2002) How do national systems of innovation differ?: A critical analysis of Porter, Freeman, Lundvall and Nelson. In G. M. Hodgson and E. Screpanti (eds.) *Rethinking economics*. Reprinted edn. Cheltenham, Edgar Elgar.

Meeus, M. and Oerlemans, L. (2005) National innovation systems. In S. Casper and F. van Waarden (eds.) *Innovation and institutions*. Cheltenham, Edward Elgar.

Muffatto, M. and Giardina, G. (2003) Innovazioni nei processi di ricerca in campo farmaceutico. *Economia & Management*, 6, 107–21.

Murrian, K. (2006) Telephone Interview with K. Murrian (Senior HR Projects and Change Management Director at British DQP Strategist), 6th April 2004.

Nelson, R. R. (1993) *National innovation systems: A comparative analysis*. Oxford, Oxford University Press.

Newbert, S. L. (2007) Empirical research on the resource-based view of the firm: An assessment and suggestions for future research. *Strategic Management Journal*, 28, 121–46.

Nohria, N. and Ghoshal, S. (1997) *The differentiated network: Organizing the multinational corporation for value creation*. San Francisco, Jossey-Bass Publishers.

Nokich, A. (2004) Interview with A. Nokich (Leiter Aus- und Weiterbildung at German RPI Strategist), Biberach, 6th April 2004.

Obstfeld, M. and Taylor, A. M. (2005) Globalization and capital markets. In M. D. Bordo, A. M. Taylor, and J. G. Williamson (eds.) *Globalization in historical perspective*. Chicago, IL, Chicago University Press.

OECD (1995) *Education at a glance: OECD indicators*. Paris, Centre for Educational Research and Innovation.

——(2007) *Glossary of statistical terms*. Internet.

Ohlin, B. (1924) The theory of trade. In H. Flam and J. M. Flanders (eds.) *Heckscher-Ohlin trade theory*. Cambridge, MA, The MIT Press.

——(1933) *Interregional and international trade*. Cambridge, MA, Harvard University Press.

Ohmae, K. (1999) *The borderless world: Power and strategy in the interlinked economy*. New York, HarperCollins.

Orsenigo, L., Pammolli, F., and Riccaboni, M. (2001) Technological change and network dynamics: Lessons from the pharmaceutical industry. *Research Policy*, 30, 485–508.

Owen-Smith, J., Riccaboni, M., Pammolli, F., and Powell, W. W. (2002) A comparison of U.S. and European university-industry relations in the life sciences. *Management Science*, 48, 24–43.

Pammolli, F., Magazzini, L., and Orsenigo, L. (2002) The intensity of competition after patent expiry in pharmaceuticals: A cross-country analysis. *Revue d'Économie Industrielle*, 99, 107–31.

Patel, P. K. and Pavitt, K. (1994*a*) National innovation systems: Why they are important, and how they might be measured and compared. *Economics of Innovation and New Technology*, 3, 77–95.

————(1994*b*) The nature and economic importance of national innovation systems. *STI Review*, 14, 9–32.

Pavitt, K. and Patel, P. K. (1999) Global corporations and national systems of innovation: Who dominates whom? In D. Archibugi, J. Howells, and J. Michie (eds.) *Innovation policy in a global economy*. Cambridge, Cambridge University Press.

Pellazzo, L. (2005) Telephone Interview with L. Pellazzo (Europe Quality Assurance Director at Italian DQP Strategist), Milan, 23rd June 2005.

Penrose, E. T. (1959) *The theory of the growth of the firm*. New York, Wiley.

Perrisson, H. (2006) Telephone Interview with H. Perrisson (Senior HR Officer at British LCP Strategist), Tyne and Wear, 5th January 2006.

Peteraf, M. A. (1993) The cornerstones of competitive advantage: A resource-based view. *Strategic Management Journal*, 14, 179–91.

Pfeffer, J. (1992) *Managing with power. Politics and influence in organizations*. Boston, MA, Harvard Business School Press.

——and Salancik, G. R. (1978) *The external control of organizations: A resource dependence perspective*. New York, Harper & Row.

Piore, M. J. and Sabel, C. F. (1984) *The second industrial divide*. New York, Basic Books.

Porter, M. E. (1980) *Competitive strategy – Techniques for analyzing industries and competitors*. London and New York, The Free Press.

——(1985) *Competitive advantage – Creating and sustaining superior performance*. New York, The Free Press.

——(1987) Changing patterns of international competition. In D. J. Teece (ed.) *The competitive challenge*. New York, Harper & Row.

——(1990) *The competitive advantage of nations*. London, Macmillan Press.

——(1998) Clusters and competition: New agendas for companies, governments, and institutions. In M. E. Porter (ed.) *On competition*. Boston, MA, Harvard Business School Press.

——(2000) Locations, clusters, and company strategy. In G. L. Clark, M. P. Feldman, and M. S. Gertler (eds.) *The Oxford handbook of economic geography*. Oxford, Oxford University Press.

——(ed.) (1986) *Competition in global industries*. Boston, MA, Harvard Business School Press.

Pozzali, A. (2004) La situazione italiana e lombarda nel settore biotecnologico. In D. Diamantini (ed.) *Il manager dell'innovazione*. Milano, Guerini.

Priem, R. L. and Butler, J. E. (2001) Is the resource-based 'view' a useful perspective for strategic management research? *The Academy of Management Review*, 26, 22–40.

Pyke, F. and Sengenberger, W. (eds.) (1992) *Industrial districts and local economic regeneration*, Geneva, International Institute for Labour Studies.

——Becattini, G., and Sengenberger, W. (eds.) (1990) *Industrial districts and inter-firm cooperation in Italy*. Geneva, International Institute for Labour Studies.

Rappaport, A. (1986) *Creating shareholder value*. New York, The Free Press.

Ricardo, D. (1821) *On the principles of political economy and taxation*. London, John Murray.

Rindner, B. (2005) Telephone Interview with B. Rindner (Batch Release/Deviation Management FSME at German DQP Strategist), Marburg, 12th August 2005.

Robinson, W. S. (1950) Ecological correlations and the behavior of individuals. *American Sociological Review*, 15, 351–7.

Rogerson, W. P. (1992) Contractual solutions to the hold-up problem. *Review of Economic Studies*, 777–94.

Rosa, L. (2005) Telephone Interview with L. Rosa (Human Resources Management at Italian RPI Strategist), Bologna, 17th October 2005.

Rumelt, R. P. (1984) Toward a strategic theory of the firm. In R. B. Lamb (ed.) *Competitive strategic management*. Englewood Cliffs, Prentice Hall.

——(1991) How much does industry matter? *Strategic Management Journal*, 12, 167–85.

Saxenian, A. (1994) *Regional advantage: Culture and competition in Silicon Valley and Route 128*. Cambridge, MA, Harvard University Press.

Schaffer, D. (2006) Telephone Interview with D. Schaffer (HR Management at German RPI Strategist), Frankfurt, 9th March 2006.

Scharpf, F. W. and Schmidt, V. A. (eds.) (2000) *Welfare and work in the open economy. Vol. II: Diverse responses to common challenges*. Oxford, Oxford University Press.

Schirm, S. A. (2006) *Globalisierung: Forschungsstand und Perspektiven*. Baden-Baden, Nomos.

Schmalensee, R. (1985) Do markets differ much? *American Economic Review*, 75, 341–51.

——and Willig, R. D. (1989) *Handbook of industrial organization. Part 2: Analysis of market behaviour*. Amsterdam, North Holland.

Schneck, O. (2007) *Lexikon der Betriebswirtschaft*, München, Deutscher Taschenbuch Verlag.

Scholz, A. (2003) Interview with A. Scholz (Consultant at Booz Allen Hamilton GmbH and Co-founder of German Biotechnology Company), Florence, 6th October 2003.

Schumpeter, J. A. (1934) *The theory of economic development: An inquiry into profits, capital, credit, interest, and the business cycle.* Cambridge, MA, Harvard University Press.

—— (1939) *Business cycles: A theoretical, historical, and statistical analysis of the capitalist process.* Philadelphia, PA, Porcupine Press.

—— (1947) The creative response in economic history. *The Journal of Economic History*, 2, 149–59.

Schwer, G. and Nes, M. (2004) Interview with G. Schwer and M. Nes (Vice President and CEO of German RPI Strategist), Munich, 6th December 2004.

Sechoff, S. (2005) Telephone Interview with S. Sechoff (Human Resources and Administration at German LCP Strategist), Dresden, 11th February 2005.

Shonfield, A. (1965) *Modern capitalism: The changing balance of public and private power.* London, Oxford University Press.

Sigillia, F. (2005) Interview with F. Sigillia (CEO of Italian RPI Strategist), Milan, 11th April 2005.

Sinn, H.-W. (2005) *Die Basar-Ökonomie; Deutschland: Exportweltmeister oder Schlusslicht?* Berlin, Econ Verlag.

Soskice, D. W. (1999) Divergent production regimes: Coordinated and uncoordinated market economies in the 1980s and 1990s. In H. Kitschelt, P. Lange, G. Marks, and J. D. Stephens (eds.) *Continuity and change in contemporary capitalism.* Cambridge, Cambridge University Press.

Steiner, S. (2004) Interview with S. Steiner (Qualitätssicherung at German DQP Strategist), Ulm, 7th April 2004.

Stiglitz, J. E. and Driffill, J. (2000) *Economics.* New York, W.W. Norton & Company.

Stöchler, B. (2004) Interview with B. Stöchler (Leiterin Personal- und Organisationsentwicklung at German DQP Strategist), Ulm, 7th April 2004.

Stolper, W. F. and Samuelson, P. A. (1941) Protection and real wages. *The Review of Economic Studies*, 9, 58–73.

Streeck, W. (1991) On the institutional conditions of diversified quality production. In E. Matzner and W. Streeck (eds.) *Beyond Keynesianism: The socio-economics of production and full employment.* Aldershot, Edward Elgar.

—— (1992) *Social institutions and economic performance.* London, Sage Publications.

—— (1997) Beneficial constraints: On the economic limits of rational voluntarism. In R. J. Hollingsworth and R. Boyer (eds.) *Contemporary capitalism: The embeddedness of institutions.* Cambridge, Cambridge University Press.

—— (2004) Educating capitalists: A rejoinder to Wright and Tsakalotos. *Socio-Economic Review*, 2, 425–38.

—— and Thelen, K. (2005*a*) Introduction: Institutional change in advanced political economies. In W. Streeck and K. Thelen (eds.) *Beyond continuity: Institutional change in advanced political economies.* Oxford, Oxford University Press.

—— —— (eds.) (2005*b*) *Beyond continuity: Institutional change in advanced political economies.* Oxford, Oxford University Press.

Tate, J. (2001) National varieties of standardization. In P. A. Hall and D. W. Soskice (eds.) *Varieties of capitalism – The institutional foundations of comparative advantage*. Oxford, Oxford University Press.

Teece, D. J. and Pisano, G. (1998) The dynamic capabilities of firms. In G. Dosi, D. J. Teece, and J. Chytry (eds.) Oxford, Oxford University Press.

———and Shuen, A. (1997) Dynamic capabilities and strategic management. *Strategic Management Journal*, 18, 509–33.

Teubner, G. (2001) Legal irritants: How unifying law ends up in new divergences. In P. A. Hall and D. W. Soskice (eds.) *Varieties of capitalism – The institutional foundations of comparative advantage*. Oxford, Oxford University Press.

Thomas III, L. G. (1994) Implicit industrial policy: The triumph of Britain and the failure of France in global pharmaceuticals. *Industrial and Corporate Change*, 3, 451–89.

——(2004) Are we all global now? Local vs. Foreign sources of corporate competence: The case of the Japanese pharmaceutical industry. *Strategic Management Journal*, 25, 865–86.

Thomson Financial (2004) *VentureXpert*, available at: http://www.venturexpert.com, sampled on 19th October 2004.

Tiny, S. (2006) Telephone Interview with S. Tiny (Human Resources Management at British DQP Strategist), 3rd February 2006.

Tom, S. (2005) Telephone Interview with S. Tom (Quality Assurance at British RPI Strategist), Wales, 17th Oct. 2005.

Underhill, G. R. D. (ed.) (1997) *The new world order in international finance*. Houndmills, Macmillan.

Utterback, J. M. (1994) *Mastering the dynamics of innovation – How companies can seize opportunities in the face of technological change*. Boston, MA, Havard Business School Press.

Venture Valuation (2006) *Italian biotech database*, available at: http://www.italianbiotech.com, sampled on 23rd January 2006.

Vinci, L. (2006) Interview with L. Vinci (Director of Association of Italian Biotechnology Companies), Milan, 16th January 2006.

Viner, J. (1937) *Studies in the theory of international trade*. New York, Harper and Brothers.

Vitols, S. (2001) Varieties of corporate governance: Comparing Germany and the UK. In P. A. Hall and D. W. Soskice (eds.) *Varieties of capitalism – The institutional foundations of comparative advantage*. Oxford, Oxford University Press.

Voelzkow, H., Elbing, S., and Schröder, M. (2007) *Jenseits nationaler Produktionsmodelle? Die Governance regionaler Wirtschaftscluster*. Marburg, Metropolis.

Walker, G. (2003) *Modern competitive strategy*. New York, McGraw-Hill.

Walker, W. (1993) National innovation systems: Britain. In R. R. Nelson (ed.) *National innovation systems: A comparative analysis*. Oxford, Oxford University Press.

Weel, S. (2005) Telephone Interviews with S. Weel (Head of Organizational Learning at German DQP Strategist), Marburg, 22nd July 2005 and 30th November 2005.

Wellam, P. (2006) Telephone Interview with P. Wellam (Human Resources Director at British LCP Strategist), Potters Bar, Hertfordshire, 4th January 2006.

Welteke, M. (1976) *Theorie und Praxis der Sozialen Marktwirtschaft: Einführung in die politische Ökonomie der BRD*. Frankfurt and New York, Campus Verlag.

Wernerfelt, B. (1984) A Resource-based view of the firm. *Strategic Management Journal*, 5, 171–80.

Wessler, A. (2005) Telephone Interview with A. Wessler (Human Resources Management at German RPI Strategist), Munich, 17th May 2005.

Whitley, R. (1999) *Divergent capitalisms: The social structuring and change of business systems*. Oxford, Oxford University Press.

Winer, R. (2005) Telephone Interview with R. Winer (HR Manager at German LCP Strategist), Fürstenfeldbruck, 3rd March 2005.

Wittner, P. (2003) *The European generics outlook: A country-by-country analysis of developing market opportunities and revenue defense strategies*. London, Datamonitor.

Yamamura, K. and Streeck, W. (eds.) (2003) *The end of diversity? Prospects for German and Japanese capitalism*. Ithaca, NY, Cornell University Press.

Yip, G. S. (2002) Global strategy in the twenty-first century. In M. Mazzucato (ed.) *Strategy for business*. London, Sage Publications.

Zysman, J. (1983) *Governments, markets, and growth: Financial systems and the politics of industrial change*. Ithaca, NY Cornell University Press.

# *Technical Appendix*

## 1. Criteria employed for sampling the PHID database

**Population: Composition of PHID Database (as of November 2004)**

**Unit of Analysis**
A research project which aims at the development of a pharmaceutical product that has reached at least the stage of preclinical development since 1980.

**Number of Units of Analysis**
Total of 6,751 pharmaceutical research projects, carried out by 3,522 firms and public research organizations.

**Overall Geographical Coverage**
Sixty-seven countries, whereby the nationality of a firm/public research organization is determined by the location of its headquarters.

**Representative Geographical Coverage**
Seven countries, namely France, Germany, Italy, Japan, Switzerland, USA, and UK.

**Characteristics of Units of Analysis, Relevant for Database Sampling (below)**
For each pharmaceutical project, the following characteristics can be identified:

- Which *firm* and/or *public research organization* (i.e. universities and research institutes) participate(s) in a pharmaceutical project?
- *At which stage* (preclinical R&D, clinical development phase I, clinical development phase II, clinical development phase III, pre-registration and registration, marketing) does a firm and/or a public research organization participate in a pharmaceutical project?
- *Which molecule* (*new chemical entity*, or *known chemical entity*) is at the basis of a pharmaceutical project?

**Sample: Criteria Used for Sampling the PHID Database**

**Type of Pharmaceutical Organization**
Only pharmaceutical projects carried out by firms are considered. Projects carried out by public research organizations (i.e. universities and research institutes) are excluded.

**Geographical Coverage**
All pharmaceutical projects carried out by firms with headquarters in the UK, Germany, or Italy.

**Identification of Competitive Strategies (for a complete discussion see Chapter 2)**
Firms are identified as radical product innovators, diversified quality producers, and low-cost producers according to the following criteria:

*Radical Product Innovators*

- Firms which carry/ied out themselves, or out-license/d, a pharmaceutical project based on a new chemical entity.

*Diversified Quality Producers*

- Firms which carry/ied out themselves, or out-license/d, a pharmaceutical project based on a known chemical entity.
- Firms which in-license/d a pharmaceutical project at any stage of clinical development.

*Low-Cost Producers*

- Firms which in-license/d a pharmaceutical project at the pre-registration, registration, or marketing phase.

**Sampling Bias: Firms Underrepresented in the Sample**

**(Generics) Firms Which Are Not Engaged in R&D Activities**
Given that the PHID database considers only firms which engage in pharmaceutical research projects (generics) firms abstaining from R&D activities are not included – unless they specialize in the registration or marketing of innovative pharmaceutical products.

**Biotechnology Firms in Germany and Italy**
Given that many German biotech firms were founded in the mid-1990s, whereas most Italian biotech firms were founded around the turn of the millennium, few German and almost no Italian biotech firms are included, because they had not yet brought a pharmaceutical project beyond the stage of preclinical development when the PHID database was sampled in November 2004.

## 2. Overall sample of pharmaceutical firms used as empirical basis of Chapters 3–6

**Table A.1.** RPI, DQP, and LCP strategists in the UK

| Company name | Technology focus | Firm age | Competitive strategy |
|---|---|---|---|
| Acambis | Biotech | 12 | RPI |
| Amarin | Biotech | 15 | RPI |
| Antisoma | Biotech | 16 | RPI |
| CRT (Cancer Res Tech) | Trad. pharma. | 41 | RPI |
| Celltech Group | Biotech | 24 | RPI |
| CeNeS | Biotech | 7 | RPI |
| Henderson Morley | Biotech | 8 | RPI |
| Imperial Cancer Res | Trad. pharma. | 102 | RPI |
| KS Biomedix | Biotech | n.a. | RPI |
| Onyvax | Biotech | 7 | RPI |
| Pharmagene | Biotech | 7 | RPI |
| PowderJect | Biotech | 11 | RPI |
| Protherics | Biotech | 5 | RPI |
| Scotia | Biotech | 20 | RPI |
| SkyePharma | Biotech | 8 | RPI |
| Xenova | Biotech | 17 | RPI |
| AstraZeneca | Trad. pharma. | 91 | RPI & DQP[a] |
| GlaxoSmithKline | Trad. pharma. | 174 | RPI & DQP[a] |
| Shire | Trad. pharma. | 18 | RPI & DQP[a] |
| Amersham Pharmacia Biotech | Trad. pharma. | n.a. | DQP |
| Axis Genetics | Biotech | n.a. | DQP |
| Bioglan | Biotech | 72 | DQP |
| Britannia | Trad. pharma. | 23 | DQP |
| British Biotech | Biotech | 18 | DQP |
| Cambridge Antibody Technology | Biotech | 14 | DQP |
| Crusade Laboratories | Biotech | 5 | DQP |
| DevCo | Trad. pharma. | 5 | DQP |
| Galen | Trad. pharma. | 36 | DQP |
| Napp | Trad. pharma. | 81 | DQP |
| Nycomed Amersham | Trad. pharma. | 130 | DQP |
| Oxford Glyco Sciences | Biotech | n.a. | DQP |
| Provalis | Biotech | 7 | DQP |
| Smith & Nephew | Trad. pharma. | 73 | DQP |
| Allergy Therapeutics | Trad. pharma. | 70 | LCP |
| Biopharm (UK) | Biotech | n.a. | LCP |
| Cambridge Laboratories | Trad. pharma. | 17 | LCP |
| CP Pharmaceuticals | Generics producer | 20 | LCP |
| Generics (UK) | Generics producer | 23 | LCP |
| Kent Pharmaceuticals | Generics producer | 18 | LCP |
| Sussex Pharmaceuticals | Generics producer | n.a. | LCP |
| Sterwin Medicines | Generics producer | 17 | LCP |
| Tillomed Laboratories | Generics producer | 13 | LCP |
| Virogen | Biotech | n.a. | LCP |

*Source*: Sample drawn from PHID database in November 2004, increased by six British generics producers (see Section 3.2).

*Notes*: a: RPI & DQP firms are counted as two cases each.

**Table A.2.** RPI, DQP, and LCP strategists in Germany

| Company name | Technology focus | Firm age | Competitive strategy |
|---|---|---|---|
| BASF | Trad. pharma. | 139 | RPI |
| Curacyte | Biotech | 5 | RPI |
| DeveloGen | Biotech | 7 | RPI |
| GPC Biotech | Biotech | 7 | RPI |
| Ingenium Pharmaceuticals | Biotech | 6 | RPI |
| Jerini Bio Tools | Biotech | 10 | RPI |
| MediGene | Biotech | 10 | RPI |
| Merz | Trad. pharma. | 96 | RPI |
| MorphoSys | Biotech | 12 | RPI |
| Scil Biomedicals | Biotech | 5 | RPI |
| Sirenade | Biotech | 2 | RPI |
| Wilex Biotechnology | Biotech | 7 | RPI |
| ASTA Medica | Trad. pharma. | 169 | RPI & DQP[a] |
| Bayer | Trad. pharma. | 141 | RPI & DQP[a] |
| Boehringer Ingelheim | Trad. pharma. | 119 | RPI & DQP[a] |
| Schering AG | Trad. pharma. | 133 | RPI & DQP[a] |
| Altana | Trad. pharma. | 27 | DQP |
| Degussa | Trad. pharma. | 5 | DQP |
| Falk | Trad. pharma. | 44 | DQP |
| GLE Medicon | Trad. pharma. | n.a. | DQP |
| Gruenenthal | Trad. pharma. | 58 | DQP |
| Jenapharm | Trad. pharma. | 54 | DQP |
| Madaus | Trad. pharma. | 85 | DQP |
| Medac | Biotech | 34 | DQP |
| Merck KGaA | Trad. pharma. | 336 | DQP |
| Merckle | Trad. pharma. | 59 | DQP |
| Paion | Biotech | 4 | DQP |
| Revotar | Biotech | 4 | DQP |
| Schwarz Pharma | Trad. pharma. | 58 | DQP |
| Aliud Pharma | Generics producer | 18 | LCP |
| Azupharm | Generics producer | 29 | LCP |
| Betapharm Arzneimittel | Generics producer | 11 | LCP |
| CT Arzneimittel | Generics producer | 82 | LCP |
| Hexal | Generics producer | 18 | LCP |
| Lichtenstein Pharmazeutica | Generics producer | 27 | LCP |
| Merck Dura | Generics producer | 9 | LCP |
| Plantorgan | Trad. pharma. | 30 | LCP |
| Ratiopharm | Generics producer | 30 | LCP |
| Schwabe | Trad. pharma. | 138 | LCP |
| Stada Arzneimittel | Generics producer | 109 | LCP |
| Strathmann | Trad. pharma. | 30 | LCP |

*Source*: Sample drawn from PHID database in November 2004, increased by nine German generics producers and three German biotech companies (see Section 3.2).

*Notes*: a: RPI & DQP firms are counted as two cases each.

**Table A.3.** RPI, DQP, and LCP strategists in Italy

| Company name | Technology focus | Firm age | Competitive strategy |
|---|---|---|---|
| Abiogen | Biotech | 7 | RPI |
| Alfa Wassermann | Trad. pharma. | 56 | RPI |
| Ausonia | n.a. | n.a. | RPI |
| BioXell | Biotech | 2 | RPI |
| Istituto di Ricerche Sigma Tau | Trad. pharma. | 19 | RPI |
| Medioloanum | Trad. pharma. | 32 | RPI |
| Newron Pharmaceuticals | Biotech | 5 | RPI |
| Novuspharma | Biotech | 6 | RPI |
| Poli | Trad. pharma. | 25 | RPI |
| Rotta Research | Biotech | 43 | RPI |
| Shar.dna | Biotech | 4 | RPI |
| Siena Biotech | Biotech | 4 | RPI |
| SPA | Trad. pharma. | 57 | RPI |
| Bracco | Trad. pharma. | 77 | RPI & DQP[a] |
| Menarini | Trad. pharma. | 118 | RPI & DQP[a] |
| Axxam | Biotech | 3 | DQP |
| Bruno | Trad. pharma. | n.a. | DQP |
| Chiesi | Trad. pharma. | 69 | DQP |
| Dompe | Trad. pharma. | 64 | DQP |
| Eurand | Trad. pharma. | 35 | DQP |
| Fidia | Trad. pharma. | 58 | DQP |
| Geymonat | Trad. pharma. | 76 | DQP |
| Italpharmaco | Trad. pharma. | 66 | DQP |
| Nikem Research | Biotech | n.a. | DQP |
| Primm | Biotech | 14 | DQP |
| Recordati | Trad. pharma. | 78 | DQP |
| Zambon | Trad. pharma. | 98 | DQP |
| Biotoscana | Biotech | n.a. | LCP |
| DOC Generici | Generics producer | 8 | LCP |
| Dorom | Generics producer | n.a. | LCP |
| Formenti | Trad. pharma. | 50 | LCP |
| Guidotti | Trad. pharma. | 90 | LCP |
| Lusopharmaco | Trad. pharma. | 53 | LCP |
| Mipharm | Trad. pharma. | 6 | LCP |
| Neopharmed | Trad. pharma. | n.a. | LCP |
| Rottapharm | Trad. pharma. | 43 | LCP |
| Segix | Trad. pharma. | 42 | LCP |

*Source*: Sample drawn from PHID database in November 2004, increased by two Italian generics producers and eight biotech companies (see Section 3.2).

*Notes*: a: RPI & DQP firms are counted as two cases each.

## 3. Further quantitative analyses

**Table A.4.** Results of crosstab analysis: 'Country' by 'competitive strategy' by 'strategy sustainability'

| **Country** | | | **Strategy sustainability** | **Legal status change** | **Legal status stability** | **Total** |
|---|---|---|---|---|---|---|
| **UK**[a] | Competitive strategy | RPI | *Count* | *7* | *12* | *19* |
| | | | Expected count | 7.8 | 11.2 | 19.0 |
| | | DQP | *Count* | *7* | *10* | *17* |
| | | | Expected count | 7.0 | 10.0 | 17.0 |
| | | LCP | *Count* | *5* | *5* | *10* |
| | | | Expected count | 4.1 | 5.9 | 10.0 |
| **Germany**[b] | Competitive strategy | RPI | *Count* | *2* | *14* | *16* |
| | | | Expected count | 3.6 | 12.4 | 16.0 |
| | | DQP | *Count* | *3* | *14* | *17* |
| | | | Expected count | 3.8 | 13.2 | 17.0 |
| | | LCP | *Count* | *5* | *7* | *12* |
| | | | Expected count | 2.7 | 9.3 | 12.0 |
| **Italy**[c] | Competitive strategy | RPI | *Count* | *3* | *12* | *15* |
| | | | Expected count | 3.1 | 11.9 | 15.0 |
| | | DQP | *Count* | *1* | *13* | *14* |
| | | | Expected count | 2.9 | 11.1 | 14.0 |
| | | LCP | *Count* | *4* | *6* | *10* |
| | | | Expected count | 2.1 | 7.9 | 10.0 |

[a] *Chi-square* = 0.468 (1 cell = 16.7% with expected count less than 5), $p > .10$; *Cramer's V* = 0.101, $p > .10$
[b] *Chi-square* = 3.706 (3 cells = 50.0% with expected count less than 5), $p > .10$; *Cramer's V* = 0.287, $p > .10$
[c] *Chi-square* = 3.866 (3 cells = 50.0% with expected count less than 5), $p > .10$; *Cramer's V* = 0.315, $p > .10$

**Table A.5.** Results of crosstab analysis: 'Country' by 'RPI sustainability'[a]

| | | | **RPI sustainability** | | **Total** |
|---|---|---|---|---|---|
| | | | Legal status stability | Legal status change | |
| **Country** | **UK** | *Count* | *114* | *12* | *126* |
| | | Expected count | 116.0 | 10.0 | 126.0 |
| | **Germany** | *Count* | *144* | *10* | *154* |
| | | Expected count | 141.7 | 12.3 | 154.0 |
| | **Italy** | *Count* | *31* | *3* | *34* |
| | | Expected count | 31.3 | 2.7 | 34.0 |
| **Total** | | Count | 289 | 25 | 314 |
| | | Expected count | 289.0 | 25.0 | 314.0 |

[a] *Chi-square* = 0.907 (1 cell = 16.7% with expected count less than 5), $p > .10$; *Cramer's V* = 0.054, $p > .10$

# Index

Graphs and tables are indexed in bold e.g. **g**, **t**.